Praise for Matt Bai's

ALL THE TRUTH IS OUT,
the basis for the film *The Front Runner*

"A miniclassic of political journalism that will restart the debate of 1987." —*The New York Times Book Review*

"Compelling. . . . Bai's superb book provokes many questions, and I gulped it down in a single sitting." —Ken Auletta, *The New Yorker*

"This book isn't just for politicos. It is a must read for anyone interested in contemporary politics and media."
—*The Christian Science Monitor*

"*All the Truth Is Out* offers a terrific portrait of how news gets made. . . . It's riveting, a slow-motion car crash . . . [with] shrewd observations on the miserable state of contemporary political journalism (and politicians). . . . The media, as Hart experienced, pick and choose raw material from an individual life and fashion an image that often bears only a slim resemblance to the human being behind it. What matters is not who someone really is or what he has done. What matters is the symbolic need he meets."
—*Salon*

"Fast-moving [and] vivid. . . . This book will tell you a lot about what politics asks of and takes out of people, and about the highly imperfect ways in which we now assess 'character' and 'substance' when choosing our leaders." —*The Atlantic*

"You think you know it all: Donna Rice, *Monkey Business*, Hart taunting the press. You don't. The combustible mix of new technology and politics was birthed in [the 1987] presidential campaign, and there was no turning back." —NPR

"A masterfully written account. . . . This first-rate work of political journalism will fan embers long thought to have gone out."
                              —*Publishers Weekly* (starred review)

"Bai shows that he is [Richard Ben] Cramer's worthy successor—his important cautionary tale will resonate with journalists and members of the media as well as with political players and readers of current history."   —*Library Journal* (starred review)

"In the tradition of his friend Richard Ben Cramer, Matt Bai astonishes us by delving deeply into a story and thus overturning our views about how the press should cover politics. This fascinating and deeply significant tale shows how the rules of American politics and journalism were upended for the worse by the frenzied coverage of Gary Hart's personal life. The soot still darkens our political process."   —Walter Isaacson, author of *Steve Jobs*

"What a tally of loss is to be found in this passionate and unsparing book about a turning point in modern America—an insider's account, brilliantly told by one of America's finest political journalists."   —Lawrence Wright, author of *The Looming Tower*

"Important and compassionate."   —Ted Koppel

"A volume of insight and wisdom, an uncommon page-turner about the turning points we don't recognize until we're too far beyond them to turn back."   —*Minneapolis Star Tribune*

MATT BAI
THE FRONT RUNNER

Matt Bai is the national political columnist for *Yahoo News*. For more than a decade he was a political correspondent for *The New York Times Magazine*, where he covered three presidential campaigns. He is the author of *The Argument: Inside the Battle to Remake Democratic Politics*, named a notable book by *The New York Times*. He lives in Bethesda, Maryland.

www.mattbai.com
@mattbai

ALSO BY MATT BAI

The Argument: Inside the Battle to Remake Democratic Politics

THE FRONT RUNNER

THE FRONT RUNNER

THE FRONT RUNNER

Originally published as *All The Truth Is Out*

MATT BAI

VINTAGE BOOKS
A Division of Penguin Random House LLC
New York

FIRST VINTAGE BOOKS MOVIE TIE-IN EDITION, OCTOBER 2018

Copyright © 2014 by Matt Bai

The Library of Congress has cataloged the Knopf edition of *All the Truth Is Out* as follows:
Bai, Matt.
All the truth is out : the week politics went tabloid / Matt Bai.—First edition.
pages cm
Includes index.
1. Hart, Gary, 1936—Public opinion.   2. Scandals—United States—History—20th century.   3. Presidential candidates—Press coverage—United States—History—20th century.   4. Press and politics—United States—History—20th century.   5. Mass media—Political aspects—United States—History—20th century.   6. Tabloid newspapers—United States—History—20th century.   7. Character—Political aspects—United States—History—20th century.   8. Public opinion—United States—History—20th century.   9. Legislators—United States—Biography.   10. United States. Congress. Senate—Biography.   I. Title.
E840.8.H285B35 2014   328.73'092—dc23   2014001033

Vintage Books MTI ISBN: 978-0-525-56613-7
Vintage Books Trade Paperback ISBN: 978-0-307-47468-1
eBook ISBN: 978-0-385-35312-0

Author photograph © Robyn Twomey
Book design by Maggie Hinders

www.vintagebooks.com

Printed in the United States of America
10 9 8 7 6 5 4 3 2 1

For Ellen

Gatsby turned out all right at the end; it is what preyed on Gatsby, what foul dust floated in the wake of his dreams that temporarily closed out my interest in the abortive sorrows and short-winded elations of men.

—F. SCOTT FITZGERALD

CONTENTS

WHAT IT TOOK

ONE OF THE FIRST PEOPLE I CALLED after I decided to write this book in 2009 was Richard Ben Cramer. This was not a call I made lightly. I had, by this time, been writing about politics for *The New York Times Magazine* for the better part of a decade, so I was not exactly a journalistic unknown. But Richard was in a different category altogether. He was one of the greatest nonfiction writers of this or any age, and his seminal, 1,047-page chronicle of the 1988 presidential campaign—*What It Takes: The Way to the White House*—was arguably the greatest and most ambitious work of political journalism in American history.

We had talked by phone in the past, and I had written about him once, but never before had I sought his counsel. I feared finding out that one of my literary heroes was just another dismissive egoist—the business is full of them—who didn't have time to dole out advice.

About thirty seconds into the conversation, Richard invited me to lunch at the old farmhouse he shared with his girlfriend (and later wife), Joan, on Maryland's idyllic Eastern Shore. Anytime I liked, he said, just pick a day, he wasn't doing much other than writing. The grace of that invitation wouldn't have surprised anyone who knew him.

The next week, I drove the ninety minutes down to Chestertown, where Richard treated me to a cheeseburger as we talked about the craft of journalism and the book I intended to write. I had come to believe that there was something misunderstood and significant in the story of Gary Hart, whose spectacular collapse Richard had followed in *What It Takes*. I thought the forces that led to Hart's undoing were more complicated and more consequential, looking back now, than anybody had really appreciated at the time. I had in mind a book not simply about a single, captivating episode in American politics, but also about the cultural transformation it portended.

I confessed that I had begun to doubt myself, however. Almost invariably, when I mentioned this idea to colleagues and friends in Washington, they reacted as if I might be teasing them—as if I had just said I was going to write my next book about bird migration or the Treaty of Westphalia. How could a discarded and discredited figure like Gary Hart possibly matter in the age of Obama? What did any of that have to do with the health care debate or the upcoming midterm elections? Maybe I should listen to the skeptics, I said to Richard. It seemed to me that there was a fine line between being visionary and being obstinate (Hart, more than anyone I could think of, illustrated this point), and most of us ended up on the wrong side of it most of the time.

Richard took all of this in, occasionally stroking his wispy beard or fiddling with his John Lennon–like glasses. And then he seemed to be in the grasp of a revelation, and he leaned back for a long moment and assessed me.

"You don't want my advice!" Richard said at last. "You want my permission!"

It was true. I did want his permission—not to drill more deeply into the rich seam he had first mined back in 1987, but rather to defy the conventions of my peers.

Richard told me to honor my instincts, that the last people on earth who could discern the deeper currents of our politics were the people who covered and practiced it on a daily basis, obsessing over every poll and campaign filing. (Richard answered email only sporadically, and he probably never read a tweet in his life.) He reminded me that most of the nation's journalism establishment had dismissed *What It Takes,* at the time it was published, as over-written and impossibly long, and the book had all but disappeared for many years before a new generation discovered it. Why in the world, Richard asked me, would I listen to *those* people?

You didn't write a memorable book, he said, by giving people the story they were clamoring to read. You had to tell them the story they needed to hear.

What It Takes is an astounding work—a contemporaneous biography of six different candidates, all portrayed from deep within their own psyches. Over the years, I have probably talked with a few dozen people who were subjects or sources in Richard's book, and not one has ever complained of a single inaccuracy. The question you hear most often, when the subject of the book comes up, is *how* Richard did it. How did he get so many politicians and so many of their aides to open up the way they did? How did he come to find himself in their rooms, and in their cars, and frequently even on their couches for the night?

To know Richard was to know part of the answer, at least. His mind was open, his curiosity genuine and boundless. I have known celebrated reporters who give entire seminars on the art of eliciting candor from their subjects—how to put someone at ease, how to structure the questions, where to put the digital recorder. Richard trafficked in none of this witchery. His only trick was his sincerity, a yearning to understand the vantage point of whomever he was talking to. He listened, which is the most underrated skill in journalism, and probably in life.

But had Richard come along ten or even five years after he did, it's doubtful that all the sincerity in the world could have yielded a book like *What It Takes.* Although this wasn't clear at the time, Richard undertook his life's defining project at precisely the moment when the rules of politics and political journalism were about to change; his book was, in a sense, a bridge between the last moment, when generations of politicians had trusted most journalists and had aspired to be understood, and the next, when they would retreat behind iron walls of bland rhetoric, heavily guarded by cynical consultants.

You could argue, with some merit, that Richard actually helped bring about this shift in the political ethos, or at least hastened it. *What It Takes* spawned legions of imitators who sought to penetrate the minds of candidates in exactly the same all-knowing way. But most often they mistook the point of Richard's work; where he was most interested in illuminating worldviews and reconstructing the experiences that shaped them, his disciples were increasingly obsessed with personalities and unflattering revelations, the portrayal of politicians as flawed celebrities. Where Richard built his work on mutual trust, the generation that came after him started with the opposite assumption. And the more these journalists tried to re-create the intimacy of *What It Takes,* the more unattainable their aspirations became.

After Richard died abruptly in early 2013, from the fast-spreading cancer he had essentially willed away for many months, two memorial services were held. At the small remembrance in Chestertown, the last eulogy was offered by Martin O'Malley, Maryland's governor, who had met Richard as a twenty-one-year-old operative and had stayed close to him ever after. (During O'Malley's first run for mayor of Baltimore, Richard would call him on his cell phone, barking out advice.) The featured speaker at the second service, at Columbia's Graduate School of Journalism in New York, was the sitting vice president, Joe Biden, whom Richard had profiled, heartbreakingly, in *What It Takes,* and whom he still called "Joey" twenty years later. Biden made the trip from Washington on a weekend, despite the fact that his presence would go unnoted by anyone outside the room.

It's almost inconceivable that any journalist of my generation could elicit such respect from leading politicians of the day, or could boast of true and lasting friendships with the people we write about. And most of my contemporaries would probably say that's as it should be. Those of us who gathered in Chestertown or New York weren't only saying goodbye to Richard. Whether we thought about it or not, we were also closing the door on the political era whose last days he managed to capture.

During the last year or two of his life, Richard enjoyed something of a resurgence among a new set of young, web-savvy journalists in Washington who admired him as I did and who made the pilgrimage east to meet the master. He loved their passion and enjoyed their company, but he found the new political journalism perplexing, with its incessant focus on granular data and emerging demographics, its emphasis on constantly predicting winners and losers. The last time I saw him, for a public event we did together in Chestertown a few months before his death, we spent a few hours at his house, talking over tea. Richard, who had long ago given up writing about politics for writing about baseball, was weak and much thinner than when I'd seen him last, but he asked me the same questions he had asked me before.

What had happened to old-fashioned political journalism? Richard wanted to know. Where was the sense of watching history reveal itself? Where, for Christ's sake, was the *humanity*?

Although he never had the chance to read it, this book is my best attempt to answer those questions, or at least to make more people consider them. It's a story of the moment when the worlds of public service and tabloid entertainment, which had been gradually orbiting closer to one another, finally collided, and of the man who found himself improbably trapped in that collision, and of the way that moment reverberated through the years and through the life of the nation.

While revisiting the tragic arc of Gary Hart's career, I found myself, inevitably, revisiting much of Richard's prose, too. The lines that stuck with me, and that were most quintessentially Richard's, actually didn't come from *What It Takes*. They appeared in another of Richard's staggeringly good books, *What Do You Think of Ted Williams Now?*

He wanted fame, and he wanted it with a pure, hot eagerness that would have been embarrassing in a smaller man. But he could not stand celebrity. This is a bitch of a line to draw in America's dust.

THE FRONT RUNNER

1

TROUBLESOME GULCH

TO GET TO THE TINY VILLAGE of Kittredge, Colorado, which for five days in 1987 became the unlikely center of the political solar system, you have to take the interstate about ten miles west of Denver and then follow Bear Creek Avenue as it winds its way up the mountain. Your average navigation device will get you pretty close, but Gary Hart, despite having once been an evangelist for the digital age, doesn't really believe in such wizardry, so he insisted I follow him from downtown. This was a clear July day in 2009, with the heat visibly baking the city sidewalk. He poked his head into my driver's side window like a nervous father, genuine concern in his gray-blue eyes as he ran through the list of turns we would soon be taking and which I couldn't possibly have remembered. Then he jumped into his red Ford Escape—a hybrid, of course—and started toward the entrance to I-70.

I followed him for twenty minutes or so, until just before we hit Bear Creek Canyon, near a row of touristy restaurants and gift shops. There he unexpectedly alit, leaving the Escape idling in the middle of the road with the door wide open, and approached my window. "Did I show you Red Rocks last time you were up here?" he asked. I mentally winced, remembering my last trip out here to interview him, almost seven years earlier, and the painful story that had come of it. Hart now professed not to remember that incident in our relationship, and I came to see that this was his most common defense mechanism; when he wished not to revisit something in his life, he often affected a kind of fogginess about it, as if it existed only in his mind and could somehow be expunged. I said no, I hadn't seen Red Rocks, and he assured me it was worth a look.

And so we headed for Red Rocks Park and brought our cars to a stop in a deserted gravel lot, maybe a hundred yards from the breathtaking copper cliffs and boulders—the kind of thing one can find only in the American West or the Arabian desert—into which Franklin Roosevelt's WPA had ingeniously carved what is now a famous American amphitheater. The rocks were brilliantly lit in the midday sun, which burned our uncovered heads as we trudged up a steep incline toward the amphitheater's entrance.

I found myself breathing heavily in the mile-high air, but I was more aware of Hart, who labored audibly despite his legendary ruggedness. Wouldn't it be his luck to collapse in the company of a journalist, a member of the fraternity he had resented all these years? The most famous picture from Hart's first presidential campaign, where he came from nowhere in 1984 to stalemate Walter Mondale and overturn the aging Democratic establishment in the process, was the one from New Hampshire in which the flannel-clad candidate had just managed to hurl an ax through a log from a distance of forty feet. (At least Hart remembered it as being forty feet. No one was going to quibble with him now.) Hart had been youthful even in middle age, his chestnut hair evocatively Kennedyesque, his smile magnetic and knowing.

Glancing sidelong at the seventy-two-year-old Hart now, though, I saw that he had developed a paunch and was slightly stooped, his arms swinging crookedly at his sides. He wore black pants and a black Nike polo shirt, from which tufts of chest hair sprouted near the unbuttoned collar. His famous mane, still intact but now white and unruly, framed a sunburned, square-jawed face. From a short distance, you could easily have mistaken this older Hart for Charlton Heston.

"When I announced for president in 1987, we did it right up there," Hart said, pointing toward a rock formation at the top of the hill. He had a strange mannerism, which some of his longtime acolytes still liked to ape good-naturedly, in which he would raise his bushy eyebrows several times in quick succession before making some wry observation. *Flicker flicker flicker,* the eyebrows went. "Those reporters looked like they were going to drop," he said in his Kansas-bred twang.

I tried to imagine the podium set against the red rocks and blue sky, the crush of cameras and the palpable sense of history. Hart's aides had wanted him to do something more conventional, with a ballroom and streamers and all of that, but he had insisted on standing alone against the mountainous backdrop, near the amphitheater he had called "a symbol of what a benevolent government can do." Pledging to run a campaign of ideas, he had added, in words that later seemed ominous: "Since we are running for the highest and most important office in the land, all of us must try to hold ourselves to the very highest possible standards of integrity and ethics, and soundness of judgment and ideas, of policies, of imagination, and vision for the future."

Standing amid that outcropping, Hart had been as close to a lock for the nomination—and likely the presidency—as any challenger of the modern era. According to Gallup, the leading polling firm of the day, Hart had a double-digit lead over the rest of the potential Democratic field; the second and third most popular choices, Chrysler chairman Lee Iacocca and New York governor Mario Cuomo, weren't even running. In a preview of the general election against the presumed Republican nominee, Vice President George H. W. Bush, Hart was polling over 50 percent among registered voters and beating Bush by thirteen points, with only 11 percent saying they were undecided.

In its annual survey the previous year, Gallup placed Hart fourteenth on the list of the most admired men in America, a few places ahead of Bill Cosby, Tip O'Neill and Clint Eastwood, and within striking distance of Ted Kennedy and the Bishop Desmond Tutu. He would have been hard to stop.

"Must have been a hell of a backdrop," I said. Hart said nothing further, and after an awkward moment, I let it drop.

We took a quick tour of the amphitheater, and then Hart led me back onto the road. Here the mountain pass serpentined for miles as it climbed to seven thousand feet above sea level, with nothing but rock facings and fir trees for long stretches of the ride. I flipped on the radio in my rented four-wheeler and hit the "seek" button until I landed on the public radio station one can almost always find in such places, nestled near the low end of the dial. The American media at that moment was obsessed with the case of Mark Sanford, South Carolina's governor and a guy who had been considered a likely Republican presidential candidate until his life had recently unraveled on national television. Sanford, who had been quite the moralizer during the scandal over Bill Clinton's affair with an intern years earlier, had apparently been carrying on his own long extramarital affair with an Argentinian woman, which came to light when he disappeared from the state for several days, apparently because he had fallen deeply in love and lost all sense of time or self-preservation.

Now, on *Planet Money*, a reporter was talking to a behavioral economist named Tim Harford, an Oxford professor who had apparently decided it was worth his time to apply his skills to the phenomenon of adultery. According to Harford, illicit relationships were the function of a simple cost-benefit equation; people stayed in them when the benefits outweighed the costs, and got out of them when the reverse was true. After Harford went on about this theory at some length, the interviewer, in the studiously understated tone of public radio reporters everywhere, asked him a question. Why, if this business about costs and benefits were true, didn't politicians ever seem to learn from their mistakes? Why cheat on your wife when you know that the cost to your career ambitions would very likely be catastrophic?

Politicians screwed up his modeling, Harford admitted. Clearly there were mysterious human factors at play, beyond our scientific reach.

There was, of course, something surreal about hearing this conversation while simultaneously maintaining a respectful distance behind Gary Hart's red Escape. As anyone alive during the 1980s knew, Hart, the first serious presidential contender of the 1960s generation, had been taken down and eternally humiliated by a scandal of his own making, an alleged affair with a beautiful blonde whose name, Donna Rice, had entered the cultural lexicon, along with the boat beside which they had been photographed together—*Monkey Business*. This was Hart's enduring legacy, the inevitable first line in his front-page obituary, no matter what else he did thereafter, even if he cured cancer or found the unified string theory or went completely bonkers and tried to hijack an airplane midflight.

When they talked about him now in Washington, Hart was invariably described as a brilliant and serious man, perhaps the most visionary political mind of his generation, an old-school statesman of the kind Washington had lost its capacity to produce. A top Democratic strategist in town had once described Hart to me as "the most important politician of his generation who didn't become president." But such descriptions were generally punctuated by a smirk or a sad shake of the head. Hardly a modern scandal passed, whether it involved a politician or athlete or entertainer, that didn't evoke inevitable comparisons to Hart among reflective commentators. In popular culture, Gary Hart would forever be that archetypal antihero of presidential politics: the iconic adulterer.

I felt a stab of anxiety now as I stared at the outline of his head, just visible above his car's cushioned headrest. Hart was exactly the kind of guy who would listen to NPR while traveling back and forth to Denver several times a week; he might not even know that other stations existed. I imagined him now, listening to Professor Harford hold forth with great gravitas on the folly of promiscuous politicians. Perhaps Hart felt tempted to simply yank the wheel to his left and plunge into the steep ravine below, to make sure once and for all that he would never again have to endure the musings of those who professed to know what made a man fit to serve. Or maybe Hart had long ago resigned himself to such discussions and was grateful simply to have escaped, in this instance, the almost automatic allusion to his once promising career.

. . .

Soon the expanse of scrub and rock on either side of the canyon road gave way to a village with a five-and-dime, a feed store, an animal hospital, and a nursery, and then Hart turned right onto Troublesome Gulch Road. Old cabins with penned animals sat alongside newish, seven-bedroom monstrosities along the gravel drive, and our tires kicked up plumes of dust as we made our way to the place where the road ended at a wood gate, immediately in front of us. Other than the sign that greeted us—PRIVATE ROAD KEEP OFF— the only hint that anyone of note lived here was the security keypad that Hart now bypassed using some device inside the Escape, so that the gate swung open and he waved for me to follow.

We rumbled past the old, 1,200-square-foot cabin where Hart and his wife, Lee, used to live, the sparse kind you normally think of when you hear about bygone politicians and their log cabins. That's where the Harts found themselves barricaded for days in 1987, hiding behind covered windows while choppers circled overhead. Further up the road sat the grander cabin the Harts built almost immediately after his forced retirement. The campaign supporter who had promised to secure a loan for the full 167 acres disappeared after the scandal. It was Warren Beatty, Hart's close friend from his days on the McGovern campaign and one of the few to stick with him, who lent them the money, which Hart quickly repaid.

The cabin was a two-level, two-bedroom affair fashioned from one hundred tons of beetle-killed Rocky Mountain pine. Four rambunctious dogs, including one the size of a love seat and another that was missing an eye, jumped and splayed around Lee as she greeted us in the kitchen. "Mrs. Hart," as her husband unfailingly referred to her (or sometimes "the widow Hart," if he was feeling sardonic), explained to me that their son, John, kept collecting the dogs from shelters. "Apache, down!" Hart shouted in annoyance as the largest one tried to knock me backward. "C'mon, Patch!" Then to Lee, with exasperation: "Babe, get the dog."

Lee was a year older than Hart and still pretty in a timeless, prairie sort of way. The Harts met at Bethany, a small Nazarene college in Oklahoma, where Lee was something of a celebrity, her father having been a church elder and past president of the college (and where Hart very narrowly lost his first political race, for student body president, because he had allegedly been present at a gathering where an open can of beer had been spotted—an allegation he would deny, persuasively, for the rest of his days). Together they had made an unthinkable journey from those days of small-town Bible groups to the halls of Yale, where Hart started at the Divinity School and went on to study law, and ultimately to the Capitol, swept forward by the social upheaval of the age and Hart's emergence as a political celebrity and then a senator and presidential candidate. They had nearly lost each other in the historical current. But all of that seemed distant now, as Hart and his wife of fifty years wrestled the dogs outside and bustled about the kitchen preparing a lunch of chicken over greens, grandparents given to habitual patter and comforting routine.

We strolled out onto the front deck, the three of us, and listened to the birds chirping and the stillness beneath. Hart pointed across the meadow to where the rushing creek had recently swelled and washed away a layer of soil, leaving roots perilously exposed beneath towering pines. This was how Troublesome Gulch got its name, he explained. A small fox approached and sat back on its hind legs, peering up at us expectantly. Lee rose and went inside to retrieve a piece of raw chicken, then tossed it like a horseshoe out onto the grass, where the grateful fox snapped it up and did a little dance. The couple looked out at the fox admiringly, Hart making a show of mild disapproval at this daily perversion of nature, but clearly pleased by the spectacle nonetheless.

It was right about then that we heard an awful *thwunk,* and Lee Hart gasped. She ran to the window. What had happened was this: in anticipation of my arrival, Lee had lifted the automatic shades on the towering glass windows that spanned the width of the living room, from floor to ceiling. In case we decided to talk indoors, on the couches next to the replica of Thomas Jefferson's bookstand in Monticello, she had wanted me to be able to take in the view of the meadow and the creek and the old wooden footbridge beyond. But without its shade to blunt the midday glare, the darkened glass wall now reflected the distant trees as faithfully as a mirror, and a small bird had mistaken that reflected image for the real thing and hurled himself into it kamikaze-style. The thing lay there now on the deck, motionless as a dishrag.

"Oh, no!" Lee said, something cracking inside her. "Oh, no!" she said again. She knelt down, cooing through the onset of tears. The fox turned its head sidelong. The creek burbled on indifferently. I felt powerless and somehow responsible, utterly untrained for such an event. I imagined the Harts might see this as an omen of my return, and maybe it was.

Hart never flinched. He rushed over and lifted the bird in his cupped hands. He walked toward the edge of the deck and gently stroked the feathers, as Lee looked on from one side and I the other. His long torso hovered over the patient and obscured our view as he softly set the bird down on the railing. "He's breathing," Hart assured his wife in a soothing, protective tone. Lee finally exhaled, deeply, and retreated a few steps. "He'll be fine," Hart said firmly.

And I believed it, too, until Hart shot me a furtive, conspiratorial look and shook his head quickly, as if to say: Not a chance in hell.

How I came to return to Troublesome Gulch on that day in 2009, visiting with some washed-up politician at the moment when just about every other political writer in America was absorbed by the ascension of our first African American president, is a story of failure and the hope for redemption, I guess. Not just Hart's, but mine, too.

The whole thing began a few weeks before Christmas in 2002, when, as a new writer for *The New York Times Magazine,* I came across a short newspaper item about how Hart was considering a quixotic comeback bid for the presidency. Like everyone else, I knew Hart only from the memory of scandal—in my case, from reading *Newsweek* in my college dorm room in 1987—and what motivated such a man to want to rekindle this memory in his advancing years, to want to relive in some way the defining ordeal of his life, struck me as the kind of mystery at the intersection of politics and psychology I found most intriguing. The idea of interviewing Hart after all these years struck my editors and friends as kind of spooky and fun, like attending a séance in the French Quarter.

I met Hart at the Denver headquarters of the global law firm Coudert Brothers, which, as it happened, consisted of a single non-descript office—Hart's—and a waiting room, in the corner of which stood a sad little Christmas tree. Hart sat in a swiveling office chair next to his computer and invited me to take a seat a few feet away. He explained, alluding to the modest surroundings, that Coudert Brothers had informed him it intended to close its Denver office—or, in other words, that it no longer needed Hart's services as an international lawyer, specializing in executing deals in the former Soviet Union. He would soon need to find another professional home. Hart spoke lightly of this conundrum, laughing easily at himself, as if the circumstances of his career had reached a level of absurdity even he couldn't fail to find amusing. Whatever arrogance he had once possessed, a famous incapacity for suffering those less intellectually inclined than himself, had been replaced in his advancing years by a sense of goodhearted resignation, which had the effect of making him immediately and immensely likable.

Two things struck me very clearly during that first meeting with Hart. The first, and more surprising, was that he was probably the flat-out smartest politician I had ever met, and I had met quite a few. Not smart in the Newt Gingrich sense, meaning that he had memorized a small library of philosophical and literary texts and could quote them back to you—although Hart had this going for him, too. Nor smart in the Bill Clinton sense, meaning that he could juggle a Sunday crossword puzzle while simultaneously dissecting a point of policy and committing to memory the names of ten strangers in the room, which was a kind of freakishness. Hart didn't care that much for people's approval. No, Hart's gift was to connect politics and culture and theology and history and technology seamlessly and all at once—to draw from all available data points (extemporaneously, it seemed) a larger picture of where *everything* was headed.

Richard Ben Cramer, who profiled Hart in *What It Takes,* had a name for these periodic revelations; he called them "Hart-facts," because once Hart offered them up, they became self-evident, as if it would have been impossible for anyone to have overlooked them in the first place. Hart himself would tell me, "I have only one talent. I can see farther ahead than other people. And I can put pieces together in constructive ways, both to avoid disaster and to capitalize on change."

During that first day in Denver, Hart explained, by way of a brief history of the Middle East, why a war in Iraq, if in fact that's what George W. Bush was planning, would ultimately be a catastrophe. We might win a quick military victory, he said, but it would become difficult to extricate ourselves, and it would create more terrorists than it would root out. (Decades before, he had insisted that America's reliance on oil would lead us, inevitably, into a series of desert wars.) He also mused that growing inequality and the recklessness of the markets might well plunge us, sooner or later, into another depression or something very close. By the end of the decade, both of these offhand riffs, which could have been dismissed in the moment as the rants of a gloomy old man, would prove stunningly accurate.

The second thing I quickly realized was that Hart had no real intention of running for president again, even if he wasn't yet ready to admit that to himself. The idea had come from some students Hart met during a yearlong sojourn at Oxford. That Hart wouldn't quite slam the door on the notion was a measure of how much he wanted something else that had nothing to do with the presidency: to be reclaimed. Hart longed to be back in the mix for high-profile assignments or maybe even a cabinet post. He wanted to be the elder statesman he had always imagined he would someday become. If openly mulling a return to the campaign trail was the only way to get someone like me to write about his political ideas, rather than a fifteen-year-old marital infidelity, then so be it.

"I made a mistake," Hart told me, which seemed to me as close to admitting an affair with Donna Rice as he had ever come. "I think there are very few people in the world who don't know that. I've apologized." It was "a single incident fifteen years ago," Hart said, and because of it he had been denied the opportunity to serve his country ever since. "I think I've paid my dues," he said.

"I think all I want is some degree of fairness," Hart said quietly.

"I'm not even asking for forgiveness, but fairness." He shook his head in enduring disbelief. "Perspective," he said, then repeated the word quietly to himself. "Perspective."

Hart didn't say any of this happily, or even willingly. I did what a reporter is supposed to do. I pushed him on it. I waited the better part of my thirty-hour visit until I felt he was sufficiently comfortable talking to me, and then I bored in on the past, poked at the scar tissue, hoping for . . . what? A catharsis, maybe. An admission that justice had been done all those years ago, that the truth had won out, as I had been taught to believe it always does. That somehow my role models in journalism—men who had covered that campaign and gone on to become, in some cases, my editors and senior colleagues—had through their tenacity spared the nation something worse than what we ultimately got.

Hart might have been excused for throwing me out of his office, but instead he patiently pleaded with me to move on. He had invited me to visit for the same reason that he was hopeful of a reentry into political life—because he thought the past might finally be the past, of interest to no one at last. "This whole business of '87 is flypaper to me," he told me, throwing up his hands. "It's so frustrating. It's like being in a time warp. I want to get unstuck."

The three-thousand-word piece I wrote about Hart did nothing to unstick him, although it was about what he should have expected. I revisited the scandal, talked about his tortured journey in the intervening years, cast doubt on his sincerity about the prospect of running again. I repeated the truism (half true at best, as I later came to understand) that Hart had blithely challenged reporters to follow him around back in 1987, and I arrived at the same psychoanalytical conclusion on which a lot of Hart's contemporaries had settled back then—that Hart had to have harbored some self-destructive impulse to begin with, because otherwise he wouldn't have risked his lifelong ambitions on some model and then dared his interrogators to prove it.

I mused on why it was that Hart had become a relic from another time—"the political version of a Members Only jacket" is how I put it—and concluded that Hart mostly had himself to blame. If he was stuck in flypaper while others mired in lesser scandals had managed to escape, it was mostly because he refused to do the things you had to do if you wanted to rehabilitate yourself in the modern society—write an apologetic memoir, shed a tear on *Oprah,* plot out a publicly orchestrated comeback on the cover of *People.*

Hart detested the piece, of course, and shortly thereafter he publicly dropped any notion of a presidential campaign. I called him a few times afterward and even asked to have a drink on one of his occasional trips to Washington. I liked him, and it seemed to me his perspective on events would be different from the usual Washington wisdom. Hart was cordial but unavailable, and I stopped pestering him.

Once, just before the Iowa caucuses in 2004, after he had endorsed his friend John Kerry, Hart and I ended up standing next to each other in a huge barn somewhere near Ames, where Kerry was holding a rally. I thought Hart recognized me when I turned to him, but he said little and seemed to look right through me as we shook hands. He wasn't invited onstage with some of Kerry's other endorsers, and no one else there seemed to take note of him. We stood awkwardly and in silence throughout much of the rally, our backs pressed up against the wood beams of the barn wall, until I wandered off to say hello to some reporters I knew, and Hart slipped out into the cold, alone.

That was the second presidential campaign I had covered, and by then I was beginning to surmise that something critical was missing from our coverage of political candidates—mainly, the candidates themselves. Like a lot of my younger colleagues who'd passed on Wall Street jobs or law degrees so they could go off to small, middling newspapers and pursue elusive careers in journalism, my ambition had been forged by reading (and rereading) influential books: *The Making of the President 1960, Fear and Loathing: On the Campaign Trail '72,* and *What It Takes.* What made political journalism so alluring, and so important, was the idea that you actually got to know the minds of the public servants you were writing about. You were supposed to share beers at the hotel bar and late-night confidences aboard the chartered plane. You were supposed to understand not just the candidates' policy papers or their strategies for winning, but also what made them good and worthy of trust, or what didn't.

There was the danger of getting too close, perhaps, in the way that a young Ben Bradlee ignored—willfully or otherwise—the dubious associations of his friend John Kennedy, or in the way that Richard Harwood, a reporter for *The Washington Post,* decided to remove himself from Robert Kennedy's 1968 campaign because he had grown to like the candidate too much. (Kennedy was killed before Harwood had the chance to follow through.) But such was the challenge that came with sitting in history's orchestra seats, charged with the sacred task of transmitting all that immediacy to the people crammed into the balcony and watching at home.

By the time my contemporaries and I got there, though, presidential politics—indeed, all of politics—was really nothing like that. With rare exceptions, our cautious candidates were like smiling holograms programmed to speak and smile but not to interact, so that it sometimes seemed you could run your hand right through them. They left the drinking and private dinners to the handlers who were expert in such things, whose job it was to help reporters by "reconstructing" the scenes of the day with self-serving narratives (*"And then I heard the senator say, 'Don't tell me what the polls say! I care about what's right!'* "). Candidates in the age of Oprah "shared" more than ever before, but what they shared of themselves—boxers rather than briefs, allusions to youthful drug use—was trivial and often rehearsed, as authentic as a piece of plastic fruit, and about as illuminating.

Our candidates shared the same planes as their attendant reporters, but unlike their predecessors in the books of our youth, they literally hid behind curtains that divided their cabin from ours. Occasionally, prompted by press aides, they wandered back to have an impromptu, off-the-record conversation, which they conducted with all the fluency and abandon of a North Korean prisoner offering his televised confession. They issued gauzy position papers and used perfunctory interviews to recite their talking points, but they almost never engaged in informal, candid conversations about what they believed and how they had come to believe it. Their existences were guided by a single imperative, which was to say nothing unscripted and expose nothing complex.

Defensively, almost unconsciously, we tried to obscure this new reality from our readers and viewers. Reporters of my generation (some of us more than others) showed up on cable TV all day long and spoke wryly and knowingly of what the politicians thought, in tones that suggested we had just come from a private dinner or a late-night bull session, that we enjoyed the same insight as our role models. As time went on, some Americans who paid close attention to the news began to suspect that we were holding out on them, that our studied detachment was masking deeper convictions about our subjects, things we really knew about the candidates but were afraid to say because we might lose our precious access or jeopardize "cozy relationships," or because it might violate the outmoded tenets of objectivity. The truth was harder to admit: most of the time, we had no real access, and we really didn't know anything about the candidates personally you couldn't have learned from browsing their websites or watching speeches on YouTube. And absent any genuine familiarity or argument of ideas, our glib prognostications sounded cynical and bland. There existed an unbridgeable divide—our own kind of troublesome gulch—between our candidates and our media.

There were lots of reasons that our politics had grown so dispiriting and so destructive over the years. They ranged from the growing dominance of political consultants to the decline of the industrial engine that once drove the American economy. And there were plenty of people, including a lot of campaign operatives, who argued that the shrinking influence of the professional class of political journalists was a good thing, that new technologies had broken the monopoly once held by a handful of self-appointed guardians of the public good, that candidates could now go around the media and speak, unfiltered, to the American voter. But when candidates no longer dared to speak unguardedly, or to explain the evolution of their thinking, or to say anything that might contradict anything else they'd ever said, they lost the ability to grapple with nuanced or controversial topics; essentially, they gave up trying to win the larger debate in the country, choosing to focus solely on the tactics of the next election, instead. New digital tools may have enabled them to reach voters directly, without a middleman, but all those voters were getting were the same old platitudes and scripted evasions, issued in a tweet or a video instead of a press release.

There was no single moment when all of this had suddenly come to pass. But as I chronicled one candidate's campaign after another, grasping for some moment of authenticity or illumination, it was clear to me that something in the political culture had been badly broken in the years since Cramer had written *What It Takes*. And slowly, almost imperceptibly, Hart began to creep back into my thoughts.

It started as a stray reflection here and there, the brief connection of synapses as I drove across Iowa under an inky black sky, or as I sat in some god-awful roadside New Hampshire hotel, staring out at the snow-covered interstate at dawn. It grew into a doubt more pressing—a sense of something important that I had left unfinished or unexplored. I noticed how often Hart's name came up now in the articles about John Edwards or about Tiger Woods, as if his was the most important or immoral one-night stand in the history of one-night stands, the standard of public humiliation against which all others had to be measured. Perspective, I could hear Hart saying. Perspective.

I began to notice how the issues he had first brought to the debate in the early 1980s, like energy independence and Islamic terrorism, were the same ones we were debating now, because so little had been achieved in all the time since. When a friend sent me a link to a sale on eBay, in which some collector was selling the issue of *People* from 1987 with Donna Rice sprawled across the cover in a bathing suit, I paid fifteen bucks for the plastic-wrapped magazine. I had no real reason to buy it, except that I suddenly felt compelled to take it out of circulation. I figured I was sparing the man one more indignity.

It wasn't guilt, exactly, this feeling that had led me back to Hart's cabin almost seven years after my first visit, like an archaeologist searching for shards of a lost political age. What I had written about Hart back then, a story I had now reread so often that I knew it almost by heart, hadn't been wrong, at least not in any technical sense. But I had now come to believe there was something deeper I had missed, a connection between Hart's defining moment and the era I inhabited. And I felt pulled to retrace that connection in order to understand how our politicians became so paralyzed and our media so reviled. It was worth figuring out what had really happened at Troublesome Gulch, and why, and how it had led the rest of us here.

For two decades after his abrupt exit from politics, Hart said almost nothing revealing about the incident that had precipitated it. (In a 240-page memoir published in 2010, titled *The Thunder and the Sunshine,* he dispensed with the entire scandal in a few lines, noting, "The circumstances are too well known, and to some degree, still too painful, to require repetition.") This was, in part, because people stopped asking. After a few months, the TV producers and reporters had moved on to other scandals, and the lecture agents were only calling, sporadically, to see if Hart might want to do some kind of crass confession tour. Eventually the gravel road through Troublesome Gulch, like the ancient city of Petra, became lost to political explorers, too remote for anyone to care.

It was also because Hart thought—foolishly, as it turned out—that the rest of the world would move on faster if he didn't keep reminding us of what had happened. Sitting in his cabin, far removed from affairs of state and having established himself as a prolific author and a specialist in international law, Hart would occasionally persuade himself that no one really thought about any of this anymore, that he might at last be remembered for his brilliance. Away from Washington, he could go months, even years, without feeling the prurient stares of strangers or the judgment of old friends. Then someone like me would come along, or some other politician or celebrity would be caught in an adulterous affair, and *Monkey Business* would surface again, tawdry and unsinkable. Even into his seventies, he could not outlast it.

But more than any of this, Hart stayed quiet because he held fast to the central conviction that had guided him, disastrously, through his existential career crisis in 1987—that what happened or didn't happen with Donna Rice or any other woman was nobody's goddamn business but his and his wife's, and about as relevant to his qualifications for higher office as a birthmark or a missing tooth. For more than twenty years, despite the instant opportunity for public redemption it would have afforded him, Hart would not admit to the affair or shed any light on the events that had led to his disgrace— not to interviewers, and not to the friends and former aides who were more reluctant to broach the subject. He believed the entire question, even now, to be an incursion into his zone of privacy, a triviality that it was his duty, as a public figure, not to legitimize.

Once, over drinks, one of Hart's close aides from the period told me that Rice, like Hart, had steadfastly denied, even in private, having consummated an affair. I asked him whether he was actually suggesting that Hart, despite his reputation for promiscuity at the time, hadn't slept with the woman who would forever be linked to his ruined ambitions. The former aide looked around the bar and leaned closer to me, his voice dropping to a whisper. "I fear not," he said, looking genuinely pained.

If this was so, then the historical irony was hard to fathom. Because the story of Hart and the blonde didn't just prove to be Hart's undoing; it was the story that changed all the rules, a sudden detonation whose smoke and soot would shadow American politics for decades to come. Somehow, political and personal lives had collided overnight to create what was, in hindsight, the first modern political scandal, with all the attendant satellite trucks and saturation coverage and hourly turns in the narrative that Kafka himself could not have dreamed up. The unrelenting assault that Hart and family and their closest advisors had encountered during those five days would become an almost predictable rhythm of political life at the dawn of the twenty-first century, and it would spawn an entire industry of experts who knew—or claimed to know—how to navigate it. But it was Hart, the standout prodigy of a new generation, who opened the door.

All these years later, Hart confided, he mostly remembered snippets from that week, painful and disjointed scenes that surfaced only when he allowed them to. Like the moment in New Hampshire when, nearly toppled by the scrum and blinded by flashbulbs, he saw a small boy, maybe four or five, about to be run over by the human crush of cameramen and photographers. Panicked and furious, Hart spotted Ira Wyman, the venerable *Newsweek* photographer, crouched in front of him. Ira, an amiable, decent man and esteemed photojournalist, had long been with Hart and his wife, through all the days on planes and nights in hotel bars. "Help me," Hart remembered croaking, in a kind of woozy desperation. He grabbed for Ira's camera strap. "Ira, help me."

Flash, came the response from the ground near his knees, as Ira evaded Hart's grasp. *Flash flash flash.*

"It was a nightmare," Hart told me flatly one night as we sat in his upstairs study. "We were in some kind of Oz land. For years and years after, people would stop me in airports and say, 'You should have stayed in the race.' I mean, they had no idea." He paused, shook his head. "They had *no idea.*"

In his own mind, he had not been driven out of presidential politics, as most everyone else saw it, but rather had walked away disgustedly. He thought of himself as Gary Cooper in that last scene of *High Noon,* throwing his badge in the dirt, thinking, If this is how it has to be, then find someone else. (Hart preferred not to think about his failed and embarrassing attempt to reenter the race late in 1987, which he would ever after regret.) This had, after all, been the animating theme of the statement he made at the end of that week of scandal, when he came down from the cabin and officially withdrew—a speech that probably should have been remembered, like Eisenhower's oration on the military-industrial complex, as one of the most prescient warnings in modern American politics, but that, like so much else about the moment, had been almost entirely buried in the public consciousness. Even Hart, perhaps falling back on his usual coping mechanism, claimed barely to remember it.

"I'm not a beaten man—I'm an angry and defiant man," Hart had declared then, to raucous cheers that he felt the need to quiet. "I said that I bend but I don't break, and believe me I'm not broken." Red-cheeked and gripping the lectern, he went on:

> In public life, some things may be interesting, but that doesn't necessarily mean they're important. . . . We're all going to have to seriously question the system for selecting our national leaders that reduces the press of this nation to hunters and presidential candidates to being hunted, that has reporters in bushes, false and inaccurate stories printed, photographers peeking in our windows, swarms of helicopters hovering over our roofs, and my very strong wife close to tears because she can't even get into her own house at night without being harassed. And then after all that, ponderous pundits wonder in mock seriousness why some of the best people in this country choose not to run for higher office. Now, I want those talented people who supported me to insist that this system be changed. Too much of it is just a mockery. And if it continues to destroy people's integrity and honor, then that system will eventually destroy itself. Politics in this country, take it from me, is on the verge of becoming another form of athletic competition or a sporting match. We'd all better do something to make this system work, or we're all going to be soon rephrasing Jefferson to say, "I tremble for my country when I think we may, in fact, get the kind of leaders we deserve."

Indeed, what had it gotten us, this violent compression of politics and celebrity and moral policing? You could argue, I guess, that it brought us closer somehow to our politicians, by making their flaws and failings harder to obscure. You could argue, and many have, that we deserved the information necessary to elect politicians who could be moral, trustworthy stewards of our children's future, and so on. There was a word that encapsulated all of this, a concept that, more than any issue or ideology, came to dominate our campaigns long after Hart had retreated to Troublesome Gulch. That word was *character*. It wasn't just about sex, as it was in Hart's case, but also about whether you uttered a line you wished you could take back or made an investment you probably shouldn't have, about whether you'd ever gotten stoned or written something idiotic in a school paper. Nothing mattered more in a politician than his essential character, and no shred of private behavior, no moment of weakness or questionable judgment, was too insignificant to illuminate it.

It would be facile to dismiss this new focus on character as being entirely trivial or misrepresentative. In a few cases, unfortunately, it was anything but. Consider the example of John Edwards. In June 2007, as the former North Carolina senator and vice presidential nominee was preparing to run a second time for the presidency, I wrote a highly detailed, eight-thousand-word cover story for *The New York Times Magazine* about his agenda, weighing with great seriousness his signature plan to combat poverty and inequality. I traveled with him to the devastated Ninth Ward in New Orleans, and I consulted a faculty's worth of antipoverty experts on his proposals. At the time (and for a long while after), I congratulated myself on having taken the most substantive look at Edwards's depth and rationale as a candidate, even while pundits continued to ignore his policies in favor of commenting on his floppy hair and his fundraising prowess and his wife's battle with cancer. This was the kind of long-form examination that voters and candidates complained was lacking from political coverage.

Four months after my cover piece was published, the *National Enquirer* ran the first in a series of stories alleging that Edwards had fathered a "love child" with a filmmaker who was following him around. Edwards denied the story repeatedly, and the rest of the media mostly ignored it—until the following August, when the *Enquirer* caught him visiting his lover and his new baby daughter in a Beverly Hills hotel. After that, Edwards went on *Nightline*—much as Gary Hart had, under different circumstances, twenty-one years earlier—to admit that the child was his. By this time, he was no longer a presidential candidate, having withdrawn after getting drubbed by Hillary Clinton and Barack Obama in the early primaries six months earlier. But had things gone a little differently in Iowa or New Hampshire, it was not inconceivable that Edwards could have been the nominee by the time the full measure of his deceit became clear. He was, in any event, a likely pick for attorney general or some other cabinet post.

The revelation about Edwards's personal behavior struck me as highly relevant to his fitness for office, though not simply because he had been sleazy and dishonest. (Edwards would not have been the first president, or even the second, to have secretly fathered a child out of wedlock.) As I had written in the magazine, most of Edwards's "new ideas" for combating inequality, his main rationale for running, were in fact leftover proposals from the last century, and they were grounded in the underlying assumption that simply giving poor people more money would eradicate poverty—an assumption that ignored an emerging consensus about the importance of families and communities in that equation. About the only major plank of Edwards's platform that even hinted at this broader social problem in impoverished communities was his insistence that absentee dads take responsibility for their children. And so here was Edwards, whose agenda included this ardent call for "responsible fatherhood," refusing to publicly acknowledge his own child.

I could think of no condition under which I would have felt obliged to stake out the Beverly Hilton, waiting to confirm that John Edwards (or anyone else) was visiting his paramour and his illegitimate child. But at the same time, I found it impossible to argue that what the *National Enquirer* had done constituted any less of a service to the voters than my own exhaustive reporting on Edwards; if anything, the opposite was true. How could it matter whether Edwards had the right ideas about poverty if he could so readily jettison his convictions for his own self-interest? In this particular instance, it seemed pointless to wrestle with the intellectual questions I had posed without also considering the question of Edwards's dubious character.

And yet, while there were these isolated cases where the character of a politician clearly informed everything else about his candidacy, never before in our political life had the concept of character been so narrowly defined. American history is rife with examples of people who were crappy husbands or shady dealers but great stewards of the state, just as we've had thoroughly decent men who couldn't summon the executive skills to run a bake sale. Hart's humiliation had been the first in a seemingly endless parade of exaggerated scandals and public floggings, the harbinger of an age when the threat of instant destruction would mute any thoughtful debate, and when even the perception of some personal imperfection could obliterate, or at least eclipse, whatever else had accumulated in the public record. And all this transpired while a series of more genuine tests of character for a nation and its leaders—challenges posed by industrial collapse, the digital revolution, energy crises, and stateless terrorism—went unmet, with tragic consequences.

It was hard to say whether the man sitting in front of me in his study, made wiser and softer now by age and ill fortune, would have been the good president so many Americans at the time had believed he would be, let alone a great one. But it was hard, too, not to feel some sense of loss as I listened to him describe the plan he had carried with him during that doomed campaign. How he would send an emissary to Moscow after the election to begin secretly negotiating an immediate end to the arms race. How he planned to then invite Mikhail Gorbachev, with whom he had bonded on a mission abroad, when both men had been young and ambitious and pushing up against the hardened ideologies of their elders ("They call me the Russian Gary Hart," Gorbachev had informed him), to join him at his swearing-in, making him the first Soviet premier to witness democracy's proudest moment. How he and Gorbachev could have used that moment, with the world watching, to sign a historic agreement to drastically scale back their nuclear arsenals. How years later, after a warm embrace and plenty of drinks with his old friend during a trip to Russia, Gorbachev had said yes, of course he would have accepted this proposal in an instant. Quite possibly the Cold War would have ended right there, in one dramatic gesture, rather than gradually winding down as the "new world order" slipped away.

Who knew what might have been possible in the afterglow of such a thing? And who knew how many other bold and creative ideas had been sacrificed to these years of human wreckage, when so many less conventional, less timid thinkers had drifted away from politics, ceding government to the dogmatic and dully predictable? Sitting in Hart's study all these years later, it would have been easy to feel sorry for him, and sometimes I did. But I felt sorrier for the rest of us.

At one point, I asked Hart whether he ever felt a sense of relief at having not actually become president. He shook his head emphatically.

"It was a huge disappointment," Hart said. "A huge disappointment."

Lee had entered the study and was refilling our water glasses, and she overheard him.

"That's why he accepts every invitation where someone wants him to speak," she told me, interrupting him. "Every time he can make any kind of a contribution, he does it, because he thinks he's salving his conscience. Or salving his place after death or something." She appeared to try to stop herself from continuing, but couldn't quite do it. "I don't know," she said. "It's been very difficult."

"Is that why I give speeches?" Hart said, in an accusatory tone.

"No, no," Lee answered quickly. "But you do things when you're tired to the bone that you shouldn't be doing."

"Why not?" Hart asked.

"But people keep asking him," she said, turning again to me. "I mean, they're all good things."

"I'm flattered, babe," Hart said testily. It was not the only time I would see the two of them do this—work through years of unspoken tension under the pretext of answering my questions. I asked Hart what it was he might have to feel guilty about. It seemed we were veering close to the boundary beyond which he had always refused to travel.

"I don't feel guilty," Hart snapped. "She's accusing me of salving my conscience."

"No, I don't mean your conscience," Lee stammered.

"You said it wrong, babe."

"I said it wrong."

I asked Lee what she had meant to say.

"What *did* you mean?" Hart asked, his tone a warning.

"Gary feels guilty," Lee said finally. "Because he feels like he could have been a very good president."

"I wouldn't call it guilt," Hart said.

"No. Well."

"It's not guilt, babe," he protested. "It's a sense of obligation."

"Yeah, okay," Lee said, sounding relieved. "That's better. Perfect."

"You don't have to be president to care about what you care about," Hart said.

"It's what he could have done for this country," Lee said, "that I think bothers him to this very day."

"Well, at the very least, George W. Bush wouldn't have been president," Hart said ruefully. This sounded a little narcissistic, but it was, in fact, a hard premise to refute. Had Hart bested George H. W. Bush in 1988, as he was well on his way to doing, it's difficult to imagine that Bush's aimless eldest son would have somehow ascended from nowhere to become governor of Texas and then president within twelve years' time.

"And we wouldn't have invaded Iraq," Hart went on. "And a lot of people would be alive who are dead." A brief silence surrounded us. Hart sighed loudly, as if literally deflating.

"You have to live with that, you know?"

2

TILTING TOWARD CULTURE DEATH

THE HART EPISODE is almost universally remembered, on the rare occasion that anyone bothers to remember it at all, as the tale of classic hubris I mentioned earlier. A Kennedy-like figure on a fast track to the presidency defies the media to find anything nonexemplary in his personal life, even as he carries on an affair with a woman half his age and poses for pictures with her, and naturally he gets caught and humiliated. *How could he not have known this would happen? Was he actually* trying *to get caught?* During the years after Hart entered my consciousness, I found myself moved to mention my fascination with him to scores of people, and almost invariably I heard some version of the same dismissive response from anyone who was alive at the time, to the point where I could almost finish the sentences for them. *How could such a smart guy have been that stupid?*

Of course, you could reasonably have asked that same question of the three most important political figures of Hart's lifetime, all Democratic presidents remembered as towering successes. Franklin Roosevelt, John Kennedy, and Lyndon Johnson had all been adulterers, before and during their presidencies, and we can safely assume they had plenty of company. In his 1978 memoir, Theodore White, the most prolific and influential chronicler of presidential politics in the last half of the twentieth century, made John Kennedy and most of the other candidates he'd known sound like the Rolling Stones gathering up groupies on a North American tour.

"What was later written about Kennedy and women bothered White but little," he wrote. "He knew that Kennedy loved his wife—but that Kennedy, the politician, exuded that musk odor of power which acts as an aphrodisiac to many women. White was reasonably sure that only three presidential candidates he had ever met had denied themselves the pleasures invited by that aphrodisiac—Harry Truman, George Romney and Jimmy Carter. He was reasonably sure that all the others he had met had, at one time or another, on the campaign trail, accepted casual partners." (Yes, White wrote his memoir in the reportorial third-person voice, and he used terms like "musk odor." It was a different time.)

Just after the Hart scandal broke in 1987, *The New York Times*'s R. W. "Johnny" Apple, the preeminent political writer of his day, wrote a piece in which he tried to explain how disconnected the moment was from what had come before. Apple described what was probably a fairly typical experience for reporters covering the Kennedy White House:

> In early 1963, for example, a fledgling reporter for this newspaper was assigned to patrol the lobby of the Carlyle Hotel while President Kennedy was visiting New York City. The reporter's job was to observe the comings and goings of politicians, but what he saw was the comings and going of a prominent actress, so that was what he reported to his editor. "No story there," said the editor, and the matter was dropped.

It was this very understanding between politicians and chroniclers—that just because something was sleazy didn't make it a story—that emboldened presidents and presidential candidates to keep reporters close when it came to the more weighty business of governing. There was little reason to fear being ambushed on the personal front while trying to make oneself accessible on the political front. In a 2012 letter to *The New Yorker*, Hal Wingo, who was a

Life correspondent in the early 1960s, recalled spending New Year's Eve 1963 with the newly inaugurated Lyndon Johnson and a group of other reporters. Johnson put his hand on Wingo's knee and said, "One more thing, boys. You may see me coming in and out of a few women's bedrooms while I am in the White House, but just remember, that is none of your business." They remembered, and they complied.

No one should pretend that character wasn't always a part of politics, of course, and there were times when private lives became genuine political issues. When Nelson Rockefeller, New York's governor and a Republican presidential hopeful, divorced his wife of thirty-one years in 1962, and then married a former staff member, "Happy," who was eighteen years his junior and the mother of four small children, the story became inseparable from Rocky's political prospects. You couldn't do a credible job of covering the Republican schism in those years without delving at least somewhat into Rockefeller's private life. When a lit-up Teddy Kennedy drove off a bridge in Chappaquiddick, off Martha's Vineyard, in 1969, killing twenty-eight-year-old Mary Jo Kopechne, Kennedy's private recklessness became a relevant and enduring political story; no politician, let alone a newspaper editor, would seriously have argued otherwise. When Thomas Eagleton, shortly after joining George McGovern on the Democratic ticket in 1972, was revealed to have undergone shock treatment for depression, his temperament became a legitimate news story, along with the fact that he had neglected to mention it.

But reporters didn't go looking for a politician's private transgressions; they covered such things only when they rose to the level of political relevance. And even when personal lives did explode into public scandal in those days, it didn't necessarily overwhelm everything else there was to know about a man. Whether a politician took bribes, whether he stood on conscience or took direction from powerful backers, whether he lied to voters or had the courage to tell hard truths, whether he stood up to power or whether he bothered showing up for votes—all of this had been, for at least a hundred years, more critical to a politician's public standing than his marital fidelity or his drinking habits or his doctor's records. Scandalous behavior mattered, but so did the larger context.

In fact, for most of the twentieth century, while a private scandal might complicate your ambitions for the moment, it wasn't necessarily the kind of thing that permanently derailed a promising political career. Consider the case of the three scandalized politicians I just mentioned. Rockefeller failed in his presidential bid in 1964—in large part because of the uproar over his marital situation—and again in 1968, when he dithered long enough to allow Richard Nixon's resurgence. But by 1974, in the wake of Watergate and Nixon's resignation, when the country desperately needed the reassurance of trusted leadership, Rocky's personal controversy had faded to the point where Gerald Ford thought him worthy of the vice presidency. He might well have been a leading candidate for the presidency again had Ford stepped aside in 1976.

Eagleton would always be best known for hiding his electroshock therapy, and any hope he had of holding national office evaporated after his disastrous, eighteen-day stint as McGovern's running mate in 1972. But that humiliation hardly finished him as a viable and serious politician of the era. He went on to win two more Senate elections before retiring as something of an elder statesman in 1986; his name adorns the federal courthouse in St. Louis.

And then there's Ted Kennedy, whose career not only survived the haunted waters off Chappaquiddick, but which had only just begun its historic ascent. By 1980, Kennedy felt sufficiently rehabilitated in the public mind not only to run for president, but to challenge the sitting president of his own party. In fact, Kennedy entered the race with a significant advantage in the polls, and while Chappaquiddick surfaced repeatedly, it was an intellectual failure that cast the most doubt on his prospects—mainly that he couldn't articulate, in an interview with the newsman Roger Mudd, why he actually wanted the job that his brother once held. When he died in 2009, having served in the Senate for four decades after Chappaquiddick, Kennedy was celebrated as one of the most consequential political figures of the century, his passion and conviction lauded even by those who disagreed with him. Remarkably, somehow, he had come to embody the idea of character, at least in the public arena.

From the start, though, Hart's downfall was of an entirely different genre than any of these other scandals, which had afforded their protagonists some room for redemption—not simply a modern variation on a timeless theme, but a new kind of political narrative altogether. What befell Hart in that spring of 1987 was swift, spiraling, and irreversible, as instantly ruinous and blackening as the fiercest hurricane. It washed away any sense of proportion or doubt. It blew away decades of precedent in a matter of hours.

In the strangeness of that moment, as *Time*'s Walter Shapiro described it, Hart would find himself at the center of "the most harrowing public ordeal ever endured by a modern presidential candidate." The old rules going back to FDR and before were suddenly upended. This time, the reporters would go searching for evidence of Hart's indiscretion, staking out his Washington townhouse like something out of *Starsky and Hutch*. And the evidence they would uncover, however tawdry and circumstantial, would manage, with staggering speed, to eclipse every other aspect of Hart's otherwise unblemished career. What no one could fully explain, at the time, was why.

Often, as a society, we assign credit or blame for tectonic shifts in the political culture to whichever politician becomes the first to expose or capitalize on them, rather than recognizing that the reverse is true—that political careers are made and lost by underlying forces that have little to do with individual politicians. We tend to think of the "Great Communicator" Ronald Reagan, for instance, as the man who masterfully reinvented the presidency for the television age, expertly manipulating public opinion with sound bites and imagery, when in fact television had been transforming the presidency for twenty years before Reagan ever got to Washington, which is why a movie actor could get himself elected in the first place. We credit Barack Obama with having broken down the whites-only barrier to the Oval Office, when in fact icons of popular culture had been trampling racial boundaries for years before Obama came along, so that much of the country was entranced by a candidate who might do the same thing in politics. (Obama's candidacy, based on little by way of experience or substance, might well have been less resonant or realistic had he been white.)

The dominance of broadcast television made Reagan possible, just as changed racial attitudes made the Obama presidency plausible, and not the other way around. As the cliché says, if these men hadn't already existed as near perfect reflections of what was already churning in the larger culture, we would have had to invent them.

And so it is, in a less heroic way, with Gary Hart. We marvel at his stupidity because we blame him, in a sense, for having brought on all this triviality and personal destruction, for having literally invited the media to poke around in his personal business, and by extension everyone else's. Before Hart there was almost none of this incessant "character" business in our presidential campaigns, which must mean he was the first leading candidate dumb enough to get caught, and after that there was no escaping the issue. But what you can see now, some twenty-five years on, is that a series of powerful, external forces in the society were colliding by the late 1980s, and this was creating a dangerous vortex on the edge of our politics. Hart didn't create that vortex. He was, rather, the first to wander into its path.

The organizing principle of politics itself was changing in 1987. The country was about to witness its first presidential campaign in forty years that didn't revolve in large part around the global stalemate between East and West. Glasnost and perestroika in Moscow were beginning to thaw the Cold War, and while that would ultimately lead to some disjointed talk of a "peace dividend" and whatever else came next, it was also bound to leave a sizable vacuum in the national political debate. If an election wasn't going to be about peace-through-strength versus disarmament, about how to deal with the perennial threat of Communist domination, then it was going to have to be about something else.

Inevitably, that something was going to include a new kind of discussion about "character." The concept had been gaining currency at least since 1972, when the political scientist James David Barber first published his influential textbook, *The Presidential Character*, in which he tried to place the presidents on a graph depicting two highly subjective axes: "positive-negative" and "active-passive." (Barber put John Kennedy, incidentally, in the most exalted category of "positive-active," rumors of his affairs notwithstanding.) By the time the third edition of Barber's book was published in 1985, the conversation about character in politics had taken on more immediacy.

The nation was still feeling the residual effects of Watergate, which thirteen years earlier had led to the first resignation of a sitting president. Richard Nixon's fall had been shocking, not least because it was more personal than it was political, the result of instability and pettiness rather than pure ideology. And for this reason Watergate, along with the deception over what was really happening in Vietnam, had injected into presidential politics a new focus on personal morality. Jimmy Carter had come from nowhere to occupy the White House mostly on the strength of his religiosity and rectitude, the promise to always be candid and upright. His failed presidency had given way to Reagan, who relied on an emerging army of religious zealots, "culture warriors" bent on restoring American values of godliness. After Nixon, Americans wanted a president they could not only trust with the nuclear codes, but whom they could trust as a friend or a father figure, too. Judging from history as Teddy White and others had witnessed it, this was no small ambition.

Social mores were changing, too. For most of the twentieth century, adultery as a practice—at least for men—had been rarely discussed but widely accepted. Kennedy and Johnson had governed during the era *Mad Men* would later portray, when the powerful man's meaningless tryst with a secretary was no less common than the three-martini lunch. (Kennedy, it would later be said, had no problem with his friends and aides cheating on their wives, provided they never got confused about the order of things and decided to break up their marriages.) Of course Johnny Apple's editor would tell him there was no story in the president taking strange women into his hotel room; like smoking, adultery in the early 1960s was considered more of a minor vice than a moral crime.

Twenty years later, however, social forces on both the left and right, unleashed by the tumult of the 1960s, were rising up to contest this view. Feminism and the "women's lib" movement had transformed expectations for a woman's role in a marriage, just as the civil rights movement had changed prevailing attitudes toward African Americans. As America continued to debate the Equal Rights Amendment for women well into the 1980s, younger liberals—the same permissive generation that had ushered in the sexual revolution and free love and all of that—were suddenly apt to see adultery as a kind of political betrayal, and one that needed to be exposed. And in this, at least, they had common cause with the new breed of conservative culture warriors, who saw their main brief as reversing America's moral decline wherever they found it.

In the past, perhaps, a politician's record on gender equality or moral issues—whether he supported the ERA or prayer in school or whatever—had been the only metric by which activists in either party took his measure. But everywhere you looked in American politics now, the tolerance for this long-standing dissonance between public principles and private behavior was wearing thin. For the sixties generation, as the feminists liked to say, the personal *was* the political, and it was fast becoming impossible to separate the two. "This is the last time a candidate will be able to treat women as bimbos," is how the famous feminist Betty Friedan put it after Hart's withdrawal. (If only she'd known.)

Perhaps most salient, though, the nation's media was changing in profound ways. When giants like White came up through the newspaper business in the postwar years, the surest path to success was to gain the trust of politicians and infiltrate their world. Proximity to power, and the information and insight once derived from having it, was the currency of the trade. And success, in the age of print dominance, meant having a secure job with decent pay and significant prestige in your city; national celebrity was for Hollywood starlets, not reporters.

By the 1980s, however, Watergate and television had combined to awaken an entirely new kind of career ambition. If you were an aspiring journalist born in the 1950s, when the baby boom was in full swing, then you entered the business at almost exactly the moment when *The Washington Post*'s Bob Woodward and Carl Bernstein—portrayed by Robert Redford and Dustin Hoffman in the cinematic version of the two journalists' first book, *All the President's Men*—were becoming not just the most celebrated reporters of their day, but very likely the wealthiest and most famous journalists in American history (with the possible exception of Walter Cronkite). And what made Woodward and Bernstein so iconic wasn't proximity, but scandal. They had actually managed to take down a mendacious American president, and in doing so they had come to symbolize the hope and heroism of a new generation.

It would be hard to overstate the impact this had, especially on younger reporters. If you were one of the new breed of middle-class, Ivy League–educated boomers who had decided to change the world through journalism, then there was simply no one you could want to become other than Woodward and Bernstein—which is to say, there was no greater calling than to expose the lies of a politician, no matter how inconsequential those lies might be or in how dark a place they might be lurking.

For decades after the break-in at the Watergate complex, virtually every political scandal of note would be instantly packaged using the same evocative suffix that had made heroes of Woodward and Bernstein, even though generations of Americans couldn't have told you what its actual origin was; the media trumpeted the arrival of "Contragate" and "Troopergate" and "Monicagate." In a sense, the Hart fiasco, coming thirteen years after Nixon's resignation, marked the inescapable end point of all the post-Watergate idolatry in the media, and the logical next phase in our political coverage. It marked the start of an era when reporters would vie endlessly to re-create the drama and glory of the industry's most mythologized moment, no matter how petty or insignificant the excuse.

And even if you couldn't be Woodward or Bernstein, exactly, you might still have a shot at getting relatively rich and famous, thanks to the evolving ethos of TV news. Ted Turner launched CNN in 1980, and within two years the network began airing what would become its signature program: *Crossfire*. The initial hosts of this televised debate were the liberal journalist Tom Braden and the conservative Pat Buchanan (who would interrupt his tenure, between 1985 and 1987, to serve as Reagan's communications director). But the evolving cast mattered less than the conceit, which in many ways gave rise to the modern scourge of unending Washington punditry, with glib debate as a cheap replacement for actual news; within a few years, even the staid network Sunday shows that had been around for decades would come to resemble *Crossfire* in their penchant for partisan clashes and valueless prognostication. (Any thought that CNN, in hindsight, might regret what it had wrought on the political culture was banished in 2013, when the network decided to bring back the show, with Newt Gingrich on the right and Stephanie Cutter, a sharp-tongued Democratic aide, on the left.)

The same year that *Crossfire* premiered, a local Washington station started syndicating a weekend show called *The McLaughlin Group*, on which the host, the former Nixon advisor John McLaughlin, fired off abrupt questions at a panel of print journalists who were supposed to opine on all things political, like clairvoyants at a carnival show. The show would become enough of a pop culture sensation that by 1990 *Saturday Night Live* would be spoofing it regularly, with Dana Carvey doing a dead-on impersonation of the way McLaughlin bullied his guests to weigh in on every imaginable topic. *Issue number three: life after death! Some pundits say it doesn't exist! Theologians disagree! Is there an afterlife?*

The boomer brand of newspaperman, cocky and overeducated compared to his predecessors, coveted a cameo on *Crossfire* or a seat on McLaughlin's stage, which conferred a new kind of instant celebrity—at least among your colleagues. Shows like these ratcheted up the pressure on reporters to separate themselves from the pack by whatever means they could. And such venues contributed mightily to a shallower conversation about politicians generally, since, increasingly as the years went on, puffed-up panelists were just as likely to speculate on the personalities of candidates—more likely, in fact—as they were on the ideas and issues that were ostensibly under discussion.

And CNN's existence itself had only been made viable by two relatively recent and revolutionary innovations: the replacement of film with modern videotape, and the proliferation of mobile satellite dishes that could bring news to you instantly, from anywhere. Until the late 1970s, the only way a network could "go live" from the scene of breaking news was to get the telephone company to install expensive audio and video lines—a process that took weeks to complete. You could manage that for an inauguration or an Olympics or some other planned event, but if you wanted to report today's unscheduled news from some remote location, then you needed to hand the film to some guy on a motorcycle . . . who would speed it to a studio . . . where it would be developed, synced with sound, and fed into a Telecine machine that converted film into video . . . and ultimately couriered or transmitted on permanent lines back to editors in New York, or maybe edited in some local studio—by which time the deadline for the evening news might well have passed.

But then came the advent of what was known in the business as "ENG"—electronic news gathering—which relied on lighter and more portable videotape cameras, freeing networks from the shackles of film. And now that videotape could be transmitted, almost miraculously, from a new generation of mobile satellites. The first satellite dishes, unwieldy and temperamental, arrived strapped to the roofs of bulky trucks (with their own onboard generators) in the early 1980s. In 1986, CNN began issuing its correspondents "flyaway dishes" that could fold up and move around the world, which were destined to become the industry standard. The 1988 campaign would be the first where the three networks and this new, twenty-four-hour cable channel would be able to easily bring you updates and interviews from any location relevant to a breaking story.

When Joe Trippi, then a young aide on the Hart campaign, arrived in the remote reaches of Troublesome Gulch to rescue Lee Hart on the first full day of the scandal, he was stunned to find a row of dishes lined up on the gravel drive like an invading army at the gate. Within a few years, this would be a familiar sight even to Americans who had nothing to do with making or covering the news, but in 1987 it seemed as if aliens had landed from Mars. "Holy shit," Trippi remembered thinking. "They *move* now."

As Trippi and his colleagues on the campaign were about to learn, videotape and satellite technology had tremendous implications not just for the transmission of news—that is, how it literally got on air, and how fast—but also for the industry's notion of what constituted it. Before the mid-eighties, which stories got on the air, and how prominently they were featured, depended almost entirely on their objective news value—that is, on how relevant they were to the public interest. But now that calculation had a lot more to do with immediacy; suddenly a story could be captivating without being especially important. After all, how could you lead with economic data when a little girl was lost in some God-forsaken well, and your correspondent was live on the scene?

What might have been a minor story in years past could now explode into a national event, within hours, provided it had the element of human drama necessary to keep viewers planted in their seats. Even as Hart prepared to announce his campaign at Red Rock, for instance, the media had become thoroughly obsessed with two sensational stories. The first concerned Fawn Hall, who worked as a secretary for Colonel Oliver North, the star of the Iran-contra hearings, and who had smuggled documents out of the White House in her boots and the back of her skirt. (The facts of the Iran-contra scandal itself, having to do with illegal arms sales to Iran in order to secretly finance an insurgency in Nicaragua, made for less compelling TV and weren't as widely known.) The second story had to do with the disgrace and supposed extortion of Jim Bakker, a television evangelist accused of rape and adultery, and with his wife, Tammy Faye, whose blubbering, mascara-streaked face transfixed the nation for days.

It was an omen of things to come.

. . .

You could argue that all of this hinted at something corrosive not just in American media at the time, but in the culture as a whole. In 1985, the New York University professor Neil Postman published his treatise on the television age, *Amusing Ourselves to Death,* which stands even now as a stunning work of social criticism. Postman's central thesis is worth revisiting. He declared that George Orwell's fear for humanity, as depicted in *1984,* had not come to pass; obviously, Americans in 1984 did not labor under the repression of an authoritarian, mind-controlling regime, nor did anything like that seem imminent. But Postman posited that by the mid-1980s we were well on our way, instead, to realizing Aldous Huxley's disturbing vision in *Brave New World*—that of a citizenry lulled into docility and self-destruction by a never-ending parade of mindless entertainment.

Expanding on the theories of the sixties philosopher Marshall McLuhan, Postman explained that the dominant media in any given society didn't just convey news and ideas neutrally, but in fact defined the very concepts of news and ideas in its time. During what Postman called the Age of Exposition, which saw America through its birth and lasted well into the twentieth century, all of our metaphors and frames of reference had come from the printed word. When political candidates debated issues, for instance, as Abraham Lincoln and Stephen Douglas famously did in 1858, they debated in what were essentially entire paragraphs and essays, because this was the only way they knew to receive and impart information. But that era had now given way to the Age of Show Business, in which television was the undisputed king of media. (At the time of Postman's writing, at the dawn of cable and before the Internet, some ninety million Americans were said to watch TV every night.) And in a television-dominated society, Postman theorized, news and politics had to be entertaining in order for anyone to really pay attention.

"Entertainment is the supra-ideology of all discourse on television," Postman wrote. The mere fact that TV news shows called themselves "shows" at all, Postman pointed out, hinted at the way they were transforming the expository culture of journalism. He went on:

No matter what is depicted or from what point of view, the over-arching presumption is that it is there for our amusement and pleasure. That is why even on news shows which provide us daily with fragments of tragedy and barbarism, we are urged by the newscasters to "join them tomorrow." What for? One would think that several minutes of murder and mayhem would suffice as material for a month of sleepless nights. We accept the news-casters' invitation because we know that the "news" is not to be taken seriously, that it is all in fun, so to say. Everything about a news show tells us this—the good looks and amiability of the cast, their pleasant banter, the exciting music that opens and closes the show, the vivid film footage, the attractive commercials—all these and more suggest that what we have just seen is no cause for weep-ing. A news show, to put it plainly, is a format for entertainment, not for education, reflection or catharsis.

Postman noted the list of political figures who had now achieved the status of TV celebrity. Senator Sam Ervin, the hero of the Water-gate hearings, was doing ads for American Express. Gerald Ford and Henry Kissinger were popping up on *Dynasty*. George McGov-ern was hosting *Saturday Night Live,* and New York mayor Ed Koch (also an *SNL* host) was actually playing a fight manager in a made-for-TV movie. "Would anyone be surprised if Gary Hart turned up on *Hill Street Blues*?" Postman wondered. (Actually, Hart's star turn came the year after Postman's book, on an episode of the sitcom *Cheers.*) The problem with all of this, he believed, was that Ameri-cans were bound to lose hold of the distinction between those who were supposed to be doing the country's serious business, on one hand, and those who were supposed to make them laugh or cry or buy mouthwash, on the other. Soon policymakers would be nothing more than characters in a national soap opera.

"When a population becomes distracted by trivia," Postman warned, "when cultural life is redefined as a perpetual round of entertainments, when serious public conversation becomes a form of baby-talk, when, in short, a people become an audience and their public business a vaudeville act, then a nation finds itself at risk; culture-death is a clear possibility."

There isn't much about Postman's attack on the show business society that isn't accepted as plain fact today. But in the 1980s, when most Americans still trusted their evening news anchor and their congressman to explain and grapple with serious issues, his argument was provocative and, viewed now through the prism of time, visionary. In fact, in many ways, the 1988 campaign—occurring just as political consulting was becoming a millionaire-making industry, and just before Americans and their media had really gotten savvy about what these consultants were trying to do—marked the nadir of televised politics. When it was over, Americans would remember only three things about the eventual Democratic nominee, Michael Dukakis: the silly image of him riding around in a tank with an ill-fitting helmet; his flat answer when asked about the hypothetical rape of his wife; and the racially charged ad that claimed he had let a convicted killer, Willie Horton, go free on furlough. Each was an enduring image made specifically for television, the stuff of cheap drama or sitcom farce, and none had very much to do with governing the country. (It probably isn't incidental that just over 50 percent of Americans bothered to show up at the polls on Election Day—the lowest voting rate in a presidential election in more than sixty years.)

All of these disparate, emerging forces in the society—a vacuum in the political debate, changing ideas about morality, a new generational ethos and new technologies in the media, the tabloidization of every aspect of American life—were coming together by the spring of 1987. The vortex was spinning madly and gaining speed. If Gary Hart hadn't been the first to get sucked into it, someone else— Bill Clinton, surely—would have found himself there before long.

And yet, it *was* Hart who was about to lead the way into the modern age of political destruction, consigning himself to disgrace and infamy in the process. And this was more than a mere accident of history. If anyone had been designed to attract the vortex, to pull all of its currents together in a single violent tempest, it was Hart. On the issues of the day, Hart could see around corners with more clarity than any political figure of his time, or for some time after. But when it came to this shift in the way the society vetted its leaders, he remained disastrously, even willfully clueless.

To his younger supporters, Hart was emblematic of the generational shift that was reshaping America—and not a moment too soon. The rebellious teens of the sixties were just now moving into middle age, with all the angst and self-absorption that had characterized their youth. (The second most popular sitcom in America, after *The Cosby Show,* was *Family Ties,* in which two former hippies struggled with their Reagan-loving teenage son, played by Michael J. Fox.) They had, in many ways, remade the popular culture already, creating an entirely new template for social justice through movies and TV, literature and music; Cosby himself was a transformational figure, drawing a huge number of white Americans into the story of the emerging black middle class. But when it came to political leadership, the Man still wasn't getting out of the way. By the dawn of 1987, President Reagan was seventy-five (and finally starting to look it), and his main Democratic foil, House speaker Tip O'Neill, was seventy-four. Reagan's likely successor among Republicans, George H. W. Bush, was a comparatively sprightly sixty-two. Someone had to kick open the door to Washington and let the sixties generation come rushing through. And even before his thrilling run in 1984, Hart had been first in line.

After all, wherever politics—and Democratic politics specifically—had been headed in the two tumultuous decades before 1987, Hart had managed to lead the way. In 1969, when Hart was an unknown Denver lawyer with some ideas about reforming the electoral system, George McGovern picked him to serve on the commission that would institute the primary system for choosing Democratic nominees—an innovation that transformed presidential politics almost immediately by taking power from the old urban bosses and handing it to a new generation of activists, including women and African Americans. A few years later, McGovern, seeking to take

Gary Hart, at right, as Senator George McGovern's campaign manager in the 1972 presidential election: thirty-five and a celebrity CREDIT: KEITH WESSEL

advantage of the new primary system, tapped Hart to assemble and run his improbable, antiwar presidential campaign. McGovern overturned the party establishment on his way to the nomination (and a crushing defeat in the general election), and Hart became famous as the young, brilliant operative in cowboy boots, straddling the motorcycle of his new pal, Hunter S. Thompson.

Hart got himself elected to the Senate just two years later, making him, at thirty-eight, its second youngest member. (Joe Biden, who got there in 1972, was six years younger.) Some older colleagues expected the glamorous ex-strategist to fashion himself as a left-wing revolutionary. But Hart was from the burgeoning West, where the party's Eastern orthodoxies were always viewed with some contempt, and he was, by nature, too inquisitive to follow the crowd. Instead, he made a name for himself by leading the emerging movement to modernize the Cold War military. (Among those who shared his passion was a young Georgia congressman by the name of Newt Gingrich, who joined Hart's new "military reform caucus.") Hart's foray into advances in modern weaponry led him, inevitably, to start thinking about the silicon chip and what it would mean for industry and education, too. Years later, Hart would remember an eye-opening lunch near Stanford with a couple of scruffy entrepreneurs named Steve Jobs and Steve Wozniak, who had recently set up a company called Apple in Jobs's garage.

By the early eighties, having been reelected despite the Reagan tide that wiped out nine of his Democratic colleagues (including McGovern), Hart was the front man for a small group of younger, mostly Western lawmakers whom the media dubbed the "Atari Democrats." Their main preoccupation—which few politicians of the time understood, much less talked about—was how to transition the country and its military from the industrial economy to the computer-based world of the twenty-first century. This was dangerous ground for a Democrat in the 1980s, when industrial states and labor unions still threw around immense political power. Whenever anyone would ask Hart about whether his challenge to the status quo made him a liberal or a centrist, he would answer by drawing a simple graph on the back of a napkin or whatever else might be handy, sketching out a horizontal axis for notions of left and right, and then a vertical axis that represented the past and the future. Hart always placed himself in the upper left quadrant—progressive, yes, but tilting strongly toward a new set of policies to match up with new realities.

This is precisely how Hart positioned himself in 1984, when his underfunded and undermanned campaign erupted in New Hampshire and swept the West—as the young, forward-thinking alternative to his party's aging liberal establishment. "Not since the Beatles had stormed onto the stage of the *Ed Sullivan Show* twenty years before had any new face so quickly captivated the popular culture," *The Washington Post*'s Paul Taylor later wrote of the 1984 campaign.

"Indeed, the velocity of Hart's rise in the polls was unprecedented in American political history." Except that Hart's youthful image belied what was, in retrospect, a critical distinction between the candidate and a lot of those who were assumed to be his contemporaries—the activists, operatives, and reporters who represented the vanguard of the boomers. The baby boom had technically commenced in 1946. Hart, on the other hand, had been born a full decade earlier, in 1936. And those particular ten years happened to make a very big difference, temperamentally and philosophically, in the life of an American.

Those ten years meant that Hart's essential worldview and personality were shaped more by his upbringing in the post-Depression Dust Bowl than by the beatniks or the social movements that later rocked Southern cities and college campuses. (Hart read about civil rights while doing his graduate studies in New Haven, but he never marched.) They meant that Hart, unlike his younger compatriots, *didn't* see the personal as the political; to him, the personal was the personal, and nobody else's business, and it wasn't polite to ask too many questions. His grandfather sat silently on his front porch all day with a Bible in hand, and nobody badgered him about it. (When a neighbor finally did dare to ask what exactly he was doing out there, the old man answered: "Cramming for the finals.") Though Hart's father spent the war in Kansas, running through a succession of small businesses and houses, some of Hart's uncles had returned from the Battle of the Bulge as hardened, silent men who drank too much and rode the rails for months at a time. They were his boyhood idols, and he knew better than to ask where they'd been or what they'd seen.

Like the role models of his youth, and like the taciturn railroad men he met during his first summers in Denver, where an uncle helped Hart land a job driving spikes in the ninety-degree heat, Hart learned to value reticence and privacy. And like his political heroes, the Kennedys, Hart believed that the political arena was constructed around recognized rules and boundaries, much like the societal rules and boundaries that had governed his upbringing.

This belief had only been reinforced by his experiences in public life. As a young senator (too young, really, to have merited such a prized assignment), Hart had served on the legendary Church Committee, which investigated the intelligence agencies' secret activities on American soil. The committee had uncovered the first tangible evidence of John Kennedy's sexual escapades and even his connections to Mafia figures, none of which had ever been publicly reported, despite its obvious availability. From his days at the McGovern campaign, Hart knew all the big-time reporters in Washington well enough to drink with them late into the night, but in his experience what was said at the hotel bar always stayed at the hotel bar.

It was well known around Washington, or at least well accepted, that Hart liked women, and that not all the women he liked were his wife. After all, Gary and Lee Hart had fallen in love and married as kids, in the confines of a strict church where even dancing was prohibited. It wasn't just that Hart had never played the field before marriage; he'd never even stepped onto it. And so here he was, young and famous and sturdily good-looking, powerful in a city where power was everything, and friends knew that he and Lee—as so often happens with college sweethearts—had matured into different people, that she spent long periods back in Denver with the two kids, that she could drive him absolutely crazy at times. Twice he and Lee quietly agreed to separate for months at a time, and during one of those separations Hart had even moved in with his pal Bob Woodward and slept on the couch—at least when he wasn't gone for nights at a time. No one in Woodward's newsroom, or anyone else for that matter, ever thought to ask for details or to write a word about it. Why would they? Whose business was it, anyway?

A sense of remove from public life was crucial for Hart, and not simply, or even mostly, because of whatever women he was or wasn't spending the night with. You could see it in the way he'd walk into any room, maybe a Hollywood cocktail party or a Manhattan fundraiser, and immediately plant himself in a corner somewhere, or over by the fireplace, watching and waiting for others to approach, just as he had been impelled to do at the church mixers as a boy. Ideas and rhetorical flourishes came easily to him, but not celebrity. "I am an obscure man, and I intend to remain that way," Hart told the writer Gail Sheehy during the 1984 campaign. Hart was an introvert who needed space to breathe and think and be alone, and he had risen through a political world where such a thing was not antithetical to success.

Once, during that first presidential campaign, when the presidency had suddenly and miraculously seemed within reach, Hart had sat down the lead agent on his Secret Service detail and quizzed him. What if Hart were president, and one day he wanted to fly off to, say, Boulder, and wander through the downtown by himself, talk to some voters, maybe buy a few books, and then hop back on the plane and return to Washington? Would the cameras need to follow? Would "Redwood"—that was Hart's Secret Service code name—really need the motorcade and the full detail and the rest of the traveling show? Yes, came the solemn reply—he would need all of it. And it was hard for Hart to argue the point after the convention in San Francisco, when the agents had stopped the elevator of the St. Francis Hotel and hustled him back upstairs, because, it turned out, some kid with a loaded .22 in his backpack had been waiting outside. (Word came back from the Secret Service that the hapless gunman, apparently not much of a reader, hadn't gotten the word that Hart wasn't the nominee.)

Hart wrestled with this issue of privacy all the time, even after his friend Warren Beatty, who had come by such wisdom firsthand, told him flatly: "There is no privacy." Hart would say he felt called to the White House, in the way the Nazarenes spoke of a calling—compelled to serve, in the way the Kennedys had been compelled. He wanted the job as badly as any man, and he believed, as any good candidate must, that he was singularly qualified to hold it. But he did worry about being miserable. More and more, as time went on, Hart wasn't content with the idea of simply becoming president. He meant to become president his way.

3

OUT THERE

IT STUNG BADLY, that moment in 1984 when Hart's soaring campaign took a direct hit, when he started to lose altitude and never fully recovered. It was March, less than two weeks after his stunning, ten-point thrashing of Walter Mondale in New Hampshire, and the two men were seated next to each other during a televised debate at Atlanta's Fox Theatre. A confident Hart was giving it to the former vice president pretty good, going on about the younger Americans who had entered the process in the previous decade, how weary they were of an aging Democratic establishment that cared only about keeping its interest groups happy, how badly they wanted new ideas. It was a theme that Hart had been sounding since 1973, when he wrote, in the closing pages of his memoir of the McGovern campaign, that "American liberalism was near bankruptcy." Despite President Kennedy's poetry, Hart had written then, the torch wasn't passed from one generation to the next—it had to be seized.

The fifty-six-year-old Mondale was no rookie, though, and he was ready with a canned one-liner that had been written for him by Bob Beckel, his sharp-tongued strategist (and later another cohost of *Crossfire*). The laconic former vice president had to wind up and start delivering the line several times, since he couldn't get Hart to shut up already and let him do it the way he'd practiced. "When I hear your new ideas," Mondale finally said, in his flat Midwestern accent, "I'm reminded of that ad. 'Where's the beef?'"

It's probably hard for any American born after, say, 1980 to appreciate how devastating a line like that could be. This was before ubiquitous cable or DVRs or the phrase "audience fragmentation." Most American families watched one of the same three networks at the same time every night, so no one watching the debate at home could have missed what was then the most talked about advertising campaign in the country—that Wendy's ad where one old woman kept talking about how big the bun was on the typical fast-food burger, while her tiny, white-haired companion blurted out: "Where's the beef?" Mondale's laugh line instantly became one of the seminal moments in the history of American debates. It recast him, instantly, as somehow more current and less of a cardboard cutout. And, more important, it underscored how little Democrats really knew about this young interloper who was on the verge of upending their party.

Hart's 1984 campaign had been, from the start, something of an amateur enterprise; he had hovered around 3 percent in the polls for most of the campaign before New Hampshire. He hadn't yet figured out a facile way of communicating his worldview in a few sentences, and even if he had, his campaign lacked the funding and sophistication needed to get it across. Mondale had seen Hart's vulnerability and struck at it. The blow didn't stop Hart from going on to win most of the remaining states, including California on the final day of voting before the convention. But Mondale's one great debate moment did arrest his precipitous slide long enough to keep the party regulars—and most notably the newly created "superdelegates"—in line, and it was they who ultimately ensured his path to the nomination.

There was never any question that Hart would run again, nor was there any question that he would be the presumed nominee, especially after his warnings about the party's dying establishment proved well founded. The first thing he did, the day after Reagan thoroughly humiliated Mondale at the polls that November by taking every state but Mondale's native Minnesota, was to call Bill

"Where's the beef?": Hart and Mondale share a laugh before the 1984 campaign. Mondale would use the phrase to devastating effect. CREDIT: KEITH WESSEL

Dixon, Wisconsin's banking commissioner and his old friend from McGovern days, and ask him to come to Washington. The plan was for Dixon, a Wisconsin lawyer who had worked on several presidential campaigns and run the 1980 convention for Jimmy Carter, to run Hart's Senate office until his second term expired at the end of 1986. Then Hart would retire from the Senate to focus his energy on running, and Dixon would be charged with doing what he was really there to do in the first place, which was to build a truly top-flight presidential campaign for 1988, the kind that couldn't be so easily caricatured by well-paid consultants with a single well-placed zinger.

In the more than thirty years since the ratification of the Twenty-second Amendment, which limited the president to two full terms in office, neither party had yet managed to win a third consecutive election, as Republicans would need to do in order to deny Hart the White House. Everyone agreed: it was Hart's race to lose. And he was going to have the campaign he needed in order to beat the sitting vice president, George H. W. Bush, and end the Reagan era once and for all.

By the time 1986 rolled around, though, Hart was deeply ambivalent about his new status as the party's leading man. In part, his concerns were temperamental. For the first time in his political life, going back to the 1960s, Hart was now the Man, rather than the insurgent, and the role was unfamiliar and uncomfortable for him. No one had ever accused him of telling ward leaders or union bosses what they wanted to hear, or of cozying up to other powerful interests; if anything, he leaned too hard toward the opposite approach. But now that he was assumed to be the nominee, everybody wanted a sit-down meeting or a quick grip-and-greet, some commitment to protect steel jobs or oppose nukes or whatever. Now all the influential organizers and fundraisers in the early primary states, the guys who had shunned him last time around, were looking for a lunch with the candidate and a photo with the kids. Like so many other Americans whose self-image was grounded in the sixties, Hart in his middle age found himself struggling not to become the very thing he had once disdained.

And it wasn't simply the mechanics of the thing, this process of whoring himself out like any other cheap politician, that seemed untenable. It was also the idea that if he ran for president like a front-runner, he wouldn't actually be able to *be* president, or at least not in the way he intended. From the early 1980s, Hart had been thinking at least as much about how he would govern as how he would get elected. For example, his chief foreign policy aide, Doug Wilson, had set up something called the "New Leaders" program, which was essentially an annual meeting of up-and-coming politicos from countries around the world; Hart's idea was that a president should come into office with a network of highly placed friends in other governments, rather than investing the first two years of a presidency in getting to know them. Hart saw himself as a transformational figure who would free the country from the stifling, left-right orthodoxies of the Cold War era. If he campaigned as the vehicle of everyone who wanted to protect the party's status quo, he complained, then he wouldn't be able to claim the public mandate he needed to govern like a reformer.

Then there was the tactical problem inherent in being the front-runner. Alone among major candidates of the modern era, Hart had, by that time, experienced presidential campaigns as both a lead strategist and as a candidate. So however much Hart may have liked to project an image of rising above the media's game of electoral chess, in truth he was already thinking several moves beyond his younger advisors. Having played a fundamental role in creating the modern primary system, Hart had now seen two long-shot candidates—McGovern and Carter—use it to shock better-known and better-funded opponents, and he himself had come impossibly close to doing the same thing in 1984. So no one understood better than Hart that the most perilous place to be in Democratic politics in the post-reform era was at the pinnacle of the primary field, as the anointed candidate of the establishment. Hart felt sure that if he were to embrace his role as the presumed nominee, he would become as vulnerable in '88 as Mondale had been in '84.

It didn't help that the emerging group of candidates who hoped to exploit Hart's vulnerability as the obvious front-runner looked—to use the term privately employed by Hart's campaign staff—like a bunch of "new Garys." In 1984, Hart's chief advantage had been his relative youth, the way in which he marked the arrival of the sixties generation. What his success had done, though, was to clear the path for a new group of his contemporaries, who were already testing their own presidential ambitions—Washington prodigies like Joe Biden and Al Gore in the Senate and Dick Gephardt in the House. (A little known Southern governor named Bill Clinton, whom Hart had once hired to work on the McGovern campaign, was also said to be exploring a run, although he would ultimately demur.)

Suddenly, these guys, too, were touting their comparative youth and rejecting the liberal orthodoxies of the postwar generation, embracing military reform and the potential of high-tech industries in Hart-like fashion. Known throughout his career as a reformer, Hart, who would be fifty by the time he announced his candidacy, now faced the danger of becoming another establishment retread.

The extent to which Hart was wrestling with this question—how to be the party's recognized front-runner without forfeiting his credentials as an antiestablishment Democrat—is evident from a memo he wrote sometime in 1986. At Hart's request, two of his most trusted aides, Billy Shore and Jeremy Rosner, had written their boss a secret memo laying out an overarching strategy for securing the nomination and then the White House in 1988. That memo is lost to the ages, but Hart's point-by-point response, written in longhand and all capital letters on a legal pad, offers a fascinating window into the political calculations he was trying to make—and into the depth of his personal involvement in campaign strategy. In the first of his twenty-seven "comments and critiques," Hart wrote: "I am not an 'outsider' out to defeat the party establishment. I am independent from the establishment, uniquely positioned to re-position it and move it forward (c.f. FDR, JFK)." In other words, he intended to make the convoluted argument that he was inside the establishment, but not of it.

"I have a strong regional base (west) and demographic base (young)," Hart wrote. "Plus my greatest strength *as a Democrat* is among independents. We must get analysts to understand that. I can broaden the party's base." He made it clear that he had no intention of retooling his own political argument. "I do not need to distinguish myself from the 'new Garys'—they have to distinguish themselves from me," he wrote. "In every case it will make their nomination less likely. Let's not go on the defensive!"

In fact, Hart intended to be very much on the offensive, and he had in mind his own strategy for putting some distance between himself and the Democratic establishment, while simultaneously making all the new Garys seem small and conventional. The big idea was to focus almost exclusively on big ideas, rather than on the usual political machinations. To start with, over three days in June 1986, Hart gave a series of three foreign policy lectures at Georgetown University, in which he outlined, with unusual technicality, the new approach he called "Enlightened Engagement." Essentially, Hart argued that in the world after the Cold War, where nations would inevitably rise up to determine their own futures, the United

States would no longer be able to protect its interests by deploying missiles and propping up repressive states; now it would need to retool its military to respond to stateless threats, and it would have to nurture democratic movements, mainly through economic assistance.

Twenty-five years later, that all sounds pretty routine. But in the context of 1986, especially for a Democrat, it was both provocative and prescient. Among those who bristled at Hart's pragmatic vision was his old mentor George McGovern, whom Hart asked to preview the lectures. In a private letter to Hart written in May 1986, the dovish McGovern, echoing other liberals, listed his "reservations" about Hart's worldview, most notably that he thought Hart overstated Soviet aggression and was too harsh toward Nicaragua's Communist government. McGovern also objected to a proposal to expand NATO's conventional forces in the waning years of the Cold War, in order to ease Europe's reliance on America's nuclear arsenal. "Is the concept of mutual force reductions dead?" he despaired.

On the domestic front, Hart countered Reagan's "Strategic Defense Initiative"—the missile shield more popularly known as "Star Wars"—with his own "Strategic Investment Initiative." The notion here was that the country should take the savings from scaling back its Cold War military buildups and invest it in education, job retraining, and infrastructure programs—all of which would be needed to compete in a more information-based and international economy. ("If you think education is expensive, wait until you find out how much ignorance costs," Hart was fond of saying.) Hart also proposed higher taxes on corporations and wealthy citizens, as well as a tariff on imported oil, as a way of raising revenue for investments and closing deficits.

Policy aides went to work on crafting an alternative federal budget, which Hart planned to release after the campaign launch. In the meantime, Hart's team took both the Georgetown lectures and the investment plan, along with his detailed argument for remaking the military, and bound them together in a ninety-four-page, small-type, heavily footnoted booklet called *Reform, Hope, and the*

Human Factor: Ideas for National Restructuring. Never again would anyone have to ask where the beef was.

As part of this plan to run on ideas, and not as the usual front-runner would run, Hart informed his team that there were things he simply wasn't going to do. He wasn't going to attend all the must-do fish fries and barbecues in the early primary states that he found about as gratifying as the flu. He wasn't going to spend time pleading for the endorsements of local party leaders, which he considered meaningless anyway, when he could be sitting with groups of actual voters and making his substantive case, instead. And he wasn't going to lower his stature by competing in Iowa's silly straw poll. "Very early in '87 I must (or Dixon) announce against straw polls—perhaps in a letter to state chairs," Hart wrote in his comments on the strategy memo.

He wasn't going to schmooze the urban bosses who hadn't died off yet, or the various interest groups who felt they had the right to blackmail a nominee before signing off on him. Hart even went to Boca Raton, where the top union leaders were holding an annual gathering, to make sure they understood he opposed the tariffs and quotas they were demanding on steel and other threatened industries—and to make sure the rest of the world understood that he wasn't going to bow before Labor.

Oh, and one more thing: Hart let it be known that he wasn't going to be covered like a presumed nominee, either. He would answer questions, sure—about Enlightened Engagement or the Strategic Investment Initiative. But he wasn't about to submit to a series of never-ending sit-downs about the latest polls or what the strategy was in Florida. He wasn't open to blocking off hours for portrait photographers who would stand him up under a white umbrella and tell him to lean this way or try a few more with his hand in his jacket pocket, all so they could put him on the cover of *Time* and *Newsweek* and *Rolling Stone,* again. He wasn't going to fall into the classic front-runner's trap of lapping up all the attention while the new Garys drove the Iowa countryside and camped out on couches like a little band of Che Guevaras.

You can imagine how this felt to the fortunate reporters from major papers around the country who had managed to get themselves assigned to Hart in those months leading up to his announcement, the rising stars who were now scrambling to write major profiles and previews to mark the start of Hart's presidential journey. (Other candidates, of course, would have killed for a slew of stories about them and would have sat for interviews until the plane ran out of gas and crashed.) Hart's high-handedness may not have caused his eventual collision with the media, but it probably eliminated any benefit of the doubt he might have gotten, any perspective to which he might have been entitled. If Hart was acting out of some profound reluctance to become a traditional front-runner, it felt like something different to the reporters, who had a job to do. It felt like arrogance and self-seriousness. It felt like contempt—for the process, and for them.

In fact, Hart could be plenty arrogant and self-serious. ("I despair, profoundly," he wrote to his aides in response to a draft op-ed, a line that instantly became legend in the headquarters. "It is absolutely ludicrous for me to consider national office if the people I depend on think *this* is presidential caliber.") But he did not have contempt for the media, or at least not for the media as a whole. Like a lot of liberal intellectuals shaped by the sixties, he had long been in awe of what he considered serious journalists, and he enjoyed their company more often than he did the companionship of his fellow senators.

A telling example concerned Sydney Gruson, who started as a foreign correspondent with *The New York Times* in the 1940s and eventually rose to become one of the paper's top corporate executives. Near the end of 1972, Gruson called Hart, who was just then packing up his things at McGovern headquarters, and said that if Hart really was planning to write a book about the campaign (which he was), he should come to New York to meet with editors at the paper's book division. Hart, who was now a national celebrity in his own right, was nonetheless honored and intimidated by having picked up the phone to find such a well-known *Times* editor on the line—so much so that, even in retelling the story many years later, he still seemed floored by it. Hart traveled almost immediately to New York, nervously carting along stacks of documents to demonstrate his seriousness of purpose, and he was elated when the *Times*'s book company agreed to publish his memoir, *Right from the Start*. He and Gruson forged a lifelong friendship; had Hart won the White House in 1988, Gruson, who was seventy by that time, would have occupied a senior communications role in the administration.

No, Hart's complicated relationship with the media, like so much else about his political persona, broke down mostly along generational lines. He felt comfortable dining with guys like Gruson and Woodward and the columnist Jack Germond, old friends he knew from McGovern days or from his early years in the Senate, most of whom still called him "Gary." (The night after the "Where's the beef?" debate, for example, found him eating with Germond and a group of other longtime reporters, who spared little of his feelings in telling him just how miserable his performance had been.) He thought these journalists to be genuine truth seekers, and he respected their intellects.

But now there were these younger reporters, too, the boomers who had first been drawn to journalism watching Redford and Hoffman in *All the President's Men,* thirty-something men and women who had recently graduated from the police beat or City Hall to the pinnacle of political coverage. And Hart could find no sure footing with this crowd, no easy rapport or rakish bonhomie. As Richard Ben Cramer noted in *What It Takes,* the younger cohort continually referred to Hart in print as "cool and aloof" and a "loner," much as you might describe a serial killer after he is discovered to have plotted his murderous spree in some isolated shed decorated with creepy cutouts of his victims. But the word they used more than any other to summarize him, particularly among themselves, was "weird."

It had started in 1984, when Hart suddenly went from marginal candidate to national sensation, and the younger reporters and editors—the ones who hadn't been around in the early seventies—

realized they knew next to nothing about him. In a frenzied effort to vet this guy who suddenly seemed like a possible nominee, the reporters descended on Colorado and Kansas and the halls of the Senate, looking to unearth relevant clues. As Cramer told it, they came away with three crucial fragments of evidence.

First, it emerged that Hart had shortened his name. In fact, his family had changed it, from "Hartpence" to "Hart," which is what some of his relatives used, but according to Hart's sister it was Gary who had talked everybody into it. (As if this weren't weird enough, Hart had also changed his signature at some point, so that his name in the letters he signed in his forties looked different from the way it had twenty years earlier.) Then there was some question as to when Hart was really born. His official Senate documentation said 1937, but his birth certificate said 1936. Was he forty-seven, or was he forty-eight? Hart himself didn't seem to think it mattered, until they asked him about his mother and her batty religiosity and what might have led her to obfuscate the circumstances of his birth, and then Hart got angry and said he wasn't going to talk about his mother when he was in the middle of trying to make an argument about the future of the country. And this struck everyone as completely and incontrovertibly weird.

"Name, age and momma"—this is how Cramer slyly referred to the holy trinity of questions that surfaced in all the stories about Hart. The constant implication was that Hart was like that doctor in *The Fugitive*, on the run from something murky and irredeemable in his past, constantly looking over his shoulder for the cops or a one-armed man.

In retrospect, of course, nothing about the trinity sounds terribly sinister or alarming. Yes, Hart had reinvented himself. However much he might deny it, then and later, it was clear that Hart had wanted to put some distance between the poor, jug-eared, Bible-toting youth he had been in Kansas and the secular, Yale-educated reformer he later became. But that didn't make him different from a lot of other Americans who grew up in claustrophobic small towns with overbearing parents and later found themselves caught up in the cultural upheaval of the sixties, where personal identities were always evolving. It didn't make Hart some shadowy, Gatsby-like figure; the salient facts of his upbringing had been well established since he entered public life.

True to form, Hart himself saw the relentless focus on his biography—and the supposed oddities contained therein—as a kind of autoimmune response of the media establishment, mobilized to repel the political outsider from the body politic. "I'm the only person who's bucked the system twice," he told *The Washington Post*'s David Maraniss just before the 1984 convention, referring to the McGovern campaign and to the one he was about to concede. "I think there is a strong desire to punish the person who does that, to make him appear odd. That's the only reason I can figure for all the attention on my personal life. You can't find one article that did that to Walter Mondale. Anywhere in his career. I challenge you to find one article. Can you find one? The answer is no! You can't find one because they weren't written. Nobody would care about it. Do you think anybody would care if they found out Walter Mondale was a year older? Do you think anyone would care if Ronald Reagan was a year older? Of course not. The entire focus is on the person who upsets the odds."

There was a lot of truth to this rant. The grandfatherly Reagan, after all, had baldly revised entire chapters of his youth, sometimes seeming to confuse himself with the characters he played in the movies, and the boomers in the media seemed unable to summon much outrage. But the real reason reporters latched on to Hart's dark trinity was probably because it was the best supporting evidence for what they knew in their gut to be true about Hart, what they discussed openly among themselves and would continue to believe decades later. Sure, he was brilliant and dynamic, but there was no escaping it: something about the guy just seemed *off*.

The same could have been said of just about any presidential contender, then or later; the vocation does not attract personalities most people would consider essentially normal. But the boomers hadn't known enough presidential candidates to reach that conclusion, and in any event, they experienced a kind of cultural disconnect when it came to Hart. He had become—by his own design, as much as anyone else's—a symbol of the boomers' inevitable ascendance. And so the reporters expected him, reasonably enough, to be a lot like them. Politically that was true enough. But as the young idealists who worked for Hart well understood, temperamentally he belonged to the generation born in 1936, not 1946, and he had never shed (and never would) the reserve and formality of post-Depression Kansas. As Cramer noted, he still called the TV anchors his own age "Mr. Rather" and "Mr. Brokaw," just as he still referred to his own wife as "Mrs. Hart." He didn't swear (ever) or smoke or rock out to the Doors or the Stones.

And while this younger cohort expected a politician molded by the sixties to reflect and emote easily—to "share," in the parlance of the age—Hart found their personal questions distasteful, as most politicians of an earlier generation would have. Every time Hart got near them, it seemed, they wanted to know about his parents' piety and itinerancy, his spiritual journey—or, worst of all, his marriage. Hart made it clear that he'd rather dangle from the campaign plane.

For the younger reporters, there must have been a kind of cognitive dissonance in hanging around Hart, who was supposed to be their hip contemporary but who insisted on acting and talking like their dads. He seemed to them perpetually unable to be himself, mainly because the boomers expected "himself" to be someone entirely different from who he was.

"Gary Hart constantly pushed toward the cerebral and away from the emotional," is how E. J. Dionne, who was the top political correspondent at *The New York Times* then, described him. When Dionne and I talked, it had been more than twenty-five years since the events in which Dionne himself played a pivotal role, and he still sounded dubious about the presidential timber of such a man. "That's who he is in some deep way. And that created questions—legitimate questions, I would say—in a press corps accustomed to politicians being much more gregarious and emotional."

Hart may have been personally annoyed by such characterizations, but politically he was unfazed. What others described as aloofness or remoteness seemed to him like traits associated with the classic cowboy heroes of his youth—a romantic ideal that Reagan embodied and that Hart, who would have been his party's first Western nominee, imagined to be compelling in himself. "These characteristics demonstrate strength, not weakness," Hart insisted in his memo to Shore and Rosner. "They are attractive to people—if not reporters stuck in the old political categories. Me being a 'loner' is like the myth that Reagan couldn't win because he was too old."

And yet, by the time Hart was planning his big announcement speech for the first week of April 1987 (the speech he insisted on delivering alone at Red Rocks, which the reporters thought to be beyond weird), the constant questioning of his past and his temperament had become something more than an annoyance. Even with a double-digit lead over his rivals, this notion that Hart was somehow unknowable was now threatening to overwhelm all of the substance in his campaign. The prevailing mood among the media was nicely captured by a *Washington Post* editorial that ran the day after the announcement. "Mr. Hart has some basis for claiming that he is the candidate of ideas," the *Post* grudgingly acknowledged, ticking off some of his proposals on trade and military restructuring. "But ideas are not all there is to a campaign: human beings choose which ideas will govern. And there apparently still is some unease with Gary Hart the person."

The newspaper then trotted out the mysterious trinity and noted that Hart had managed to win little support among his peers in the Senate—the clear implication being that this was because he was some kind of loner, and not because he routinely challenged the ideological orthodoxies of his party's establishment and its interest groups, or because he actually wasn't seeking such endorsements. "Since November's elections he has been a sure-footed spokesman for his party and his own candidacy," the *Post* allowed. "Now comes the examination of his ideas, which he welcomes, and the relentless analysis of his character, with which he still seems uncomfortable."

Hart's advisors—most of them in their late twenties or early thirties, children of the sixties who could hear the vortex humming— had long warned him, with increasing urgency, that the new generation of reporters was coming for him, and for the details of his private life, about which they themselves would never have been

Surrounded: Hart (trailed by Billy Shore) after officially announcing his second presidential campaign at Red Rocks in April 1987 CREDIT: KEITH WESSEL

foolish enough to ask. Now, sensing that they might soon lose control of the story line, Hart's closest aides—notably Shore, whom the candidate trusted most, and Kevin Sweeney, the earnest twenty-eight-year-old press secretary, a true believer who had been waiting tables in San Francisco only months before—prevailed on him to deviate somewhat from his all-about-the-ideas strategy. Specifically, they wanted him to make two exceptions to the list of things he didn't want to do; nothing radical or humiliating, just two eminently tolerable things that a normal front-runner could be expected to do. The first thing they had in mind, immediately following the announcement, was for Hart to lead the entire press corps on a tour of his hometown. This could not have been easy for Hart, who had come a long way from his upbringing in Ottawa, who could barely remember most of the Hartpences who lived there, and who detested the idea of descending on this unsuspecting Kansas town with the entire media carnival in tow. But that is exactly what he did, and as Cramer would later recount it, Hart managed to deliver a deeply moving and heartfelt speech at the Ottawa University chapel. He expressed his gratitude for the hardworking community that had raised him—the schools and the railroad, the downtown businesses and the local radio station. Then he talked, finally, about his now dead mom and dad, and the assembled reporters found out that Hart had avoided the topic not because he felt too little for his parents and the life he'd left behind, but because he felt too much.

"I don't think there's anyone in this country who's ever had better parents than I had," Hart told the crowd, pausing for long stretches as he struggled to maintain his composure. He called his father, Carl, "as honorable and decent a man as I think ever walked the face of the earth," and described his much maligned mother, Nina, as a woman who loved life and a good joke. "You often hear the term 'salt of the earth,'" he said haltingly, trying to hold himself together. "And I think that's what they were. Between them, they represented about the best this society has to offer. And what they gave me I don't think I can ever repay, except to try and raise my children as well as they raised me." After that, Hart's team figured, no one could accuse him of being unable to emote.

The second thing the team needed was Hart's cooperation with a single, intimate profile, one lengthy treatment, where he would at last sit down and discuss anything the reporter wanted to discuss, up to and including his upbringing and his marriage. If Hart would just open up to one of these younger hotshots, someone he felt he could basically trust, then readers and other reporters (who were an important audience, too) could be reassured that Hart wasn't actually hiding anything, that he was in fact a relatively normal guy who just happened to prefer talking about his ideas for the country to dissecting his personal life. And Hart would be able to say, ever after, that he had already answered all the *People* magazine sorts of questions, and it was time to move on to what mattered.

The idea to channel all of this into a definitive magazine profile, rather than cooperate with a book or perhaps submit to a grilling on national TV, may have emerged from Hart himself, although later it would seem to have been a collective decision. Hart's response to Shore and Rosner contains an intriguing note that looks ominous only in the context of history.

Under point number 20, Hart wrote: "Forget a book length biography. Let's plan a friendly—but critical—long feature piece. Suggestions?"

Warren Beatty had advised Hart, months earlier, that the longer he avoided giving in-depth interviews to reporters, the more valuable such an interview would become. Beatty knew his public relations. By early 1987, Hart's aides could have chosen just about any writer or venue for their big curtain-raising profile, since everyone wanted to be first with the big interview. That they chose E. J. Dionne made perfect sense. It wasn't just that Dionne, who was about to turn thirty-five, was perhaps the most obvious star of the new generation, having already reported from Paris, Beirut, and Rome, while somehow making time to cover two presidential campaigns. Nor was the main factor in the decision that Dionne would write his profile for the cover of *The New York Times Magazine,* which combined a more literary gravitas than the newsweeklies with the influence of a large national circulation.

What made Dionne special among the younger crowd, more than any of this, is that Hart actually respected him. Nerdy and sputtering with energy ("harried like a border collie with a bad herd," in Cramer's inimical description), Dionne wasn't just another privileged dilettante in search of some wry observation he could peddle on *Nightline.* A Catholic school kid from Fall River, Massachusetts, which was no one's idea of a patrician paradise, he was a Phi Beta Kappa graduate of Harvard and a Rhodes Scholar at Oxford, where he had earned a doctorate in sociology. He was a serious, first-rate intellect, and to Hart that meant Dionne could be, if not quite co-opted, then at least made to see the relevance and urgency of Hart's agenda. At least Dionne didn't go dead in the eyes when you talked about economic transformation or the decline of the nation-state, which is more than Hart could say for most of the boomers on the bus.

For his part, Dionne felt conflicted about Hart. As a fairly traditional Northeastern liberal, Dionne was put off by Hart's larger argument against orthodoxies and interest groups, particularly the way he seemed ready to jettison Labor in the name of some new economic order. He resented Hart's famous quote from his 1974 Senate campaign, when *The Washington Post*'s David Broder had posited to Hart that traditional liberalism was about to be vindicated by the election of a new class of young Democrats. "We are not a bunch of little Hubert Humphreys," Hart said then—a comment for which a lot of liberals, Humphrey among them, would have trouble forgiving him.

In a sense, Dionne and Hart personified the geographic rift in the party—between the old urban centers, with their New Deal ideology and their reliance on industrial and political machines, and the emerging Western and Southern states, where Democrats were more independent-minded and more hopeful about the new economy. It was a divide that would preoccupy the party for much of the next decade and beyond, as "New Democrats" and old ones sought to control the agenda.

And yet Dionne was thoughtful enough to accept the premise that both government and the party were in dire need of modernization. And he genuinely admired Hart, with whom he shared a bookish and theological bent. "There was a part of him I found utterly engaging and totally comprehensible," Dionne told me. Hart ranked right up there in sheer brilliance with the Harvard and Oxford professors Dionne had known—and he was funny, too, in a mischievous and endearing way. Dionne kept asking Hart, for instance, about the mystery novel he had cowritten with a Republican colleague in the Senate, William Cohen. (It was titled, perhaps ironically given all the questions about Hart's past, *The Double Man*.) But every time

Dionne raised a passage from the book, Hart would shut him down with that flashing of the eyebrows and a wry: "Oh, Cohen wrote that." Dionne soon realized that Hart was playing with him and would never own up to having written a word of the book, and after a while it became a comic routine between them.

However much Dionne may have been a man of ideas, he counted himself among a generation of reporters who had been heavily influenced—whether they were scholarly enough to know it or not—by the work of Erik Erikson. The German-born psychologist, who immigrated to the United States when the Nazis came to power and ended up on Harvard's faculty, is most famous for having pioneered the concept of "identity"—and what he called the "identity crisis"—in the 1950s and 1960s. "If Teddy White can be credited with opening the back room of American politics to the public view," Dionne said, "a writer like Erik Erikson could be credited for opening the back room of the psyche."

The most thoughtful works of what came to be known as the New Journalism, books as varied as Garry Wills's *Nixon Agonistes* and Hunter S. Thompson's *Fear and Loathing: On the Campaign Trail '72*, had this in common: unlike White's work, which dwelled on the surface of the political process, they burrowed deeply and relentlessly into the subconscious of their subjects, playing psychoanalyst to politicians, sifting through childhoods or scrutinizing mannerisms for the most tenuous clues to their underlying motives and insecurities. What good was it to know a candidate's stated positions if he had learned from a young age to dissemble or evade? What was the point of dissecting his agenda if he didn't have the strength of character to follow through?

Dionne found himself fascinated by the obvious tension in Hart's upbringing and education. He felt certain that if you could understand what had propelled the journey from Ottawa and Bethany College to Yale and Washington, the journey from Hartpence to Hart, then you could understand the inner turmoil that made Hart so confusing a character. "I was trying to figure out, What does it mean to be an existential politician?" Dionne would recall. This is a word that younger intellectuals had been throwing around since the early sixties, when Norman Mailer used it to describe John Kennedy, and while it had an erudite ring to it, Dionne still had some trouble defining it a quarter century later. An existential politician, Dionne told me, is "someone who is detached from traditional forms of faith, whether in God or in the political system, but nonetheless feels an obligation to act, whether the faith exists or not. And I think that Hart had some of that in him."

It was, for me, a sort of time-bending experience to hear Dionne describe his methodology, or what he could remember of it, more than twenty-five years later—the story behind the famous story that had been written while I was still a freshman in college. I could see myself doing all of the same things the young Dionne had done, the things that anyone writing for an elite, intellectual magazine would have tried to do. Dionne knocked around Ottawa, an explorer in a strange land, searching for the significance of Hart's origins. He spent a night in southern Illinois engrossed in deep, esoteric discussions with Hart's favorite philosophy professor from Bethany, Prescott Johnson, whom Hart would always credit with having had a profound effect on his life.

Industriously, Dionne spent many hours delving into the works of some of Hart's favorite writers and philosophers—Kierkegaard, Dostoyevsky, Plato. "The cave!" Hart exclaimed, laughing, when Dionne brought up Plato's famous concept in one of their conversations. "Let's don't start that. That ain't going to play in Iowa." At one point during their travels together, Hart gave Dionne a copy of one of his Kierkegaard texts, a gesture made, you can imagine, as much in frustration as in friendship. (As in: Here, read it for yourself if you're so damn interested, and stop pestering me.) Dionne held on to the book—*Purity of Heart Is to Will One Thing*—for all the years after.

At his first of two interviews with Hart, aboard a small plane en route from Austin to Denver, Dionne posed precisely the question I might have posed, too, though maybe not as artfully. "Why do *you* think that *we* think you're weird?" he asked. Note the use of the word "we," rather than "they," with its implication that it wasn't just a few cranky journalists who found Hart impossibly strange, but everyone, Dionne included. Note how the question was designed to elicit exactly the kind of response Hart provided, which was to ratify its basic premise. "Please," Hart replied, "keep your mind open to the possibility that I'm not weird." That, of course, became Dionne's lead.

In that interview and in the subsequent one, in the café of a Howard Johnson's hotel in New Hampshire, Hart went to heroic lengths to take on and conquer, once and for all, questions about his temperament and what urban reporters considered his exotic upbringing. Again and again, Dionne, surrounded by the imposing stacks of paper that represented his atlas of Hart's intellectual pilgrimage, threw Hart's own past quotes back at him, like the time in 1972 when, as a thirty-five-year-old operative attracting all kinds of media attention, Hart had mischievously said of himself: "I never reveal who I really am."

"Do you want a record kept of everything you've ever said in your life to anybody and have it thrown back at you fifteen years later?" Hart demanded. "My problem is that I've revealed too much about myself.

"See, I think you've got the coin reversed," Hart told Dionne. "I think I'm the healthy one. I think you ought to be asking all those other guys who have done nothing but hold public office and have no other sides to their personalities: Why they don't write novels and why they don't read Kierkegaard? Why they don't broaden themselves out? Why is it that somebody like me is thought the oddball?"

Inevitably, by the end of the second interview, Hart was growing testy and impatient. Questioned yet again about his childhood among the Nazarenes, Hart warned Dionne, "I'm going to answer about three more of these, and then I'm not going to answer any more. I was thirteen at the time. It's nonsense. Who cares what Ronald Reagan was thinking when he was thirteen? Or Joe Biden?

"My struggle was with the institution," Hart said of the church, trying yet again to be understood. "Thomas Jefferson had that struggle, and so have more than half or more of the thoughtful people in the world. It's not unique to me. And is it something that plagues me today? No. I am very normal and very healthy."

Then Hart heard his own words echo, saw Dionne writing in his notebook, and laughed. He laughed heartily, because the conversation seemed absurd, and because he was beginning to realize he could win neither by staying silent nor by trying to explain himself—a conundrum that would grow more pronounced in the weeks ahead. "I can see this," Hart said, imagining out loud the finished story Dionne would write. "'Hart insists that he is very normal. In a wide-ranging and lengthy interview, Hart insists that he is not weird.'"

Dionne never had any reservation about grilling Hart on his well-known weirdness, because the issue was out there already; it was all anyone talked about—which is to say, it was all other reporters were talking about on the bus or on TV. It was the main thing, Dionne assumed, that people wanted to know about Hart, and the reason Hart had granted him access in the first place.

In this sense, Dionne was offering what would become, in the ensuing years, the standard rationale for the slew of candidate profiles revolving around psychotherapy and personal behavior, rather than ideas and worldviews. (I myself would employ the same rationale on many occasions.) It wasn't really up to the writer to decide what questions were relevant. The conversation "out there" had already done that, and all the poor writer could do was to shake his head sadly and try to bring some clarity to it. Surely politics would be better if we could all just refocus the debate on the things that *really mattered,* but it never seemed to be the journalist's job to do the refocusing. The given issues were the given issues, in the same way that rivers just flow the way they flow, and all the helpless reporter could do was selflessly hurl himself into the murky current and try to help his readers navigate their way through.

What did bother Dionne, though, was the far more unseemly question of Hart's marital fidelity. Like other Washington insiders, he had long assumed that Hart was sleeping around. "Oh, everybody knew who Gary Hart was," Dionne told me. Asking him about it was something else. Dionne may have fancied himself something of an amateur Erikson, but he was not a trivial guy; he didn't earn a Ph.D. and survive Beirut only to come home and join the Hollywood paparazzi. He was well aware that no one in his position had ever before pestered a presidential candidate about rumored affairs, let alone written a major piece about it. But he was also well aware that the rumblings about Hart's sex life were out there, too. And if he ignored them altogether, then his colleagues might find him too credulous. His definitive profile might be derided as anything but.

"I didn't want to focus on his sex life," Dionne recalled when we talked. "I also did not want to write a naïve profile that acted as if I did not know this was potentially an issue. I always had the suspicion that this was the campaign in which it would blow up. And so my solution, as someone who really does not like candidates' sex lives being central to the dialogue, was to ask him about it in the interview. I probably asked three or four questions. I felt it should be there."

And so Dionne raised the issue during the second and final interview. Going back to the well of Hart's voluminous interviews as a younger man, Dionne reminded him of a painful learning experience. Back in 1972, the journalist Sally Quinn had come to interview Hart for a profile, and Hart, feeling either flirtatious or unnerved or a little of both, gave her an inexplicably dumb quote. "I have almost no personal life at all—I lead a completely political existence," Hart had said then. "If one party doesn't share the same interests, you've got a problem. Let's just say I believe in reform marriage."

It was, for Dionne, a deft way into the subject of Hart's so-called womanizing, slashing through the thicket of Hart's defenses with a machete of his own making. But this was what Hart had signed up for. He knew why they were doing the *Times Magazine* profile. He knew his marriage was going to come up, and he knew the subject made Dionne uncomfortable. He was ready.

"It was a very stupid thing to say," he admitted. "Lee was living in Denver, and I was living in Washington, and I was unhappy because my kids were little and I didn't see them much. I learned." Then, again, he turned the question back on Dionne, trying to shame him. "There's no reward for being candid," Hart said. "In fact, there are penalties for being candid. People say, 'Why are politicians such conniving, calculating S.O.B.'s?' It's because who knows what oddball thing you say is not going to come back fifteen years later to be some profound insight into your character."

As is the case with any magazine piece, then and now, Dionne's would take several weeks to write, edit, fact-check, and illustrate. (Hart, in keeping with his plan for the campaign, refused to set aside time for a cover shoot. "I will not pose, I will not pose, I will not pose," he told Sweeney.) Even after Dionne returned to Washington to write his 4,700-word piece, he continued to struggle with the questions about sex—how much to feature the material and where. "I felt it was very important that the piece not be dominated by that, but just tell the readers that this is out there," Dionne would remember. "I was very torn when I was writing that piece."

Dionne was taken with one of the other quotes he'd elicited from Hart, which nicely expressed Hart's frustration with the entire line of questioning about his marriage. Dionne thought the quote potentially explosive, and he made sure to weave it into the piece—not up high, but in the lower half, where he thought it belonged. When he got the edited draft back from the magazine, however, Dionne couldn't find that paragraph. As often happens, some less than impressed editor had cut the quote to make space for something else. It was gone, but only for now.

The Dionne interviews unsettled Hart. The tenor of the questions, coming from a reporter everyone agreed was as thoughtful and substantive as the campaign was likely to find, had the effect of confirming what his advisors had been telling him for months, and of making the campaign he had wanted to run seem futile. On a drive down to Denver from Red Rocks, where Hart had been walking through the announcement site and making final preparations, the normally pensive candidate suddenly unburdened himself to Shore. In a soliloquy both of them would remember long after, Hart said he had been visited by a "premonition," a sense of dread that the media would never let him campaign on the ideas he had laid out, but rather would insist on making the campaign about him and his persona. In 1987, it was still possible to find such a realization shocking.

Of course, by that time, Hart also must have known—subconsciously, if not consciously—that he had set events in motion that would make his "premonition" much more likely to come true. He had only recently exposed himself and his campaign to exactly the kind of relentless, trivial scrutiny he feared. But this was something Shore had no way of knowing.

Running for president in the modern age—like being president—is a uniquely isolating experience. You are surrounded, always, by supporters and handlers, and yet none can fully share in the constant absurdity of being the central figure in a campaign, and none can ever be entirely themselves in your presence. Often they lie to you outright—about next week's schedule, or about when you're stopping for lunch, or about how many people will show up at the next rally. You do not go home to your family or take the weekend off; if you're lucky, you get five hours in a hotel and thirty minutes to exercise before the sun comes up. (There is a surreal scene, in a long-lost *Frontline* documentary about his 1984 campaign, of Hart, dressed in suit and tie, frantically squeezing in some weightlifting while his aides brief him on strategy.) You become, in a sense, the CEO of your own life, the titular head of an existence that is said to be yours, but that is in every practical sense orchestrated and controlled by other people, some of whose names you can't remember or never knew.

And so candidates who reach a certain level of presidential politics tend to draw in someone—a "body man" who knows their flaws and keeps their secrets close, who can smooth over some messes and anticipate others, who can translate gestures and moods for exhausted staff members, and who can help the candidate relax, laugh, and generally feel moored to the world he knew before. (This is to be distinguished from the paid "body man" whom the new beat reporters love to write about every election cycle, the kid who carries around hand sanitizer and snack food and that kind of thing.) Nixon's number one body man was Bebe Rebozo. Clinton's traveling alter ego and fixer was Bruce Lindsey. Barack Obama leaned on a Chicago pal named Martin Nesbitt.

By 1987, Hart had not one, but two such body men. As coincidence would have it, each of them went by the nickname "Billy," and each embodied an opposing side of Hart's contradictory nature.

Billy Number One was Shore, the kind-faced and unassuming thirty-two-year-old, who ten years earlier, fresh out of Penn, had wandered into Hart's Senate office looking for an internship, because he had read about the new young senator who wanted to revitalize liberalism. Shore didn't meet the senator, or get the internship, but eventually he got hired in the mailroom, and then he worked his way up (because Shore was, if nothing else, immensely competent). And then one day in the early 1980s he found himself sitting at a table in the Senate Dining Room with the boss, whom he really didn't know very well, and Hart was talking about presidential politics, and he told Shore, "Maybe you ought to go up to New Hampshire and just take a look around." Just like that, Shore became the senator's one-man covert operation, gathering intel and recruiting soldiers for years before anyone really caught on.

Hart was like that. He would evaluate his personnel and formulate a plan gradually, keeping it entirely to himself, and then one day he would offhandedly utter a single line, and your life would be changed forever. It happened to Shore again, in New Hampshire, after the little grassroots campaign had suddenly ignited and grown much too quickly, and the Secret Service agents were getting into it with some of Hart's staff over logistics, right in front of the candidate, and if you knew Hart, you knew that he'd rather be digging his way through a landfill than referee something like that. "You know, you should probably just stick with me from now on," Hart said to Shore, almost as an aside, as if the idea had just occurred to him. And that was it. After that, if you wanted something from Gary Hart, everyone knew, it was best to go through Billy.

Shore's father had run a congressional office in Pittsburgh, so he had an innate sense for scheduling and staffing, the way the coach's kid instinctively knows how to turn the double play. But Shore's real skill and value were in enabling Hart to be the introvert he still was, at least much of the time. Shore provided a force field of protection around Hart's solitude, sitting nearby with a binder or a book, knowing how to be quiet, silently warding off others who didn't. And where Hart could be, as the writers never tired of pointing out, "cool and aloof," Shore was congenitally warm and considerate. Where Hart intended to remain above the indignities of cheap political theater, Shore understood that everyone around a campaign had a job to do; he was happy to help if he could, and genuinely apologetic if he couldn't. By filling in the gaps in his candidate's personality, Shore made it possible for Hart to go on being Hart without leaving a trail of scorched egos and resentment in his wake.

If Billy Number One played to Hart's pensive side, then Billy Number Two had a different brief. Throughout his adult life, Hart had been inexorably drawn to what he would call "colorful characters"—outsize personalities and raconteurs who seemed to relish the moment and knew how to have fun, which is something the Nazarenes hadn't taught. Warren Beatty was like that, and so was Hunter Thompson; Hart loved telling the story of sitting in the famous writer's living room while a wild turkey paraded around the house. Hart had a similar fascination with the blustery Russian poet and dissident Yevgeny Yevtushenko, with whom Hart spent a good deal of time during his 1986 visit to the Soviet Union, and even with world leaders like Fidel Castro and Muammar Gaddafi, both of whom cultivated an air of danger and mystery. In ways he wouldn't have cared to consider, Hart was still the boy who had learned everything he knew of the outside world sitting in the Carnegie-endowed library back in Ottawa. But if Shore appealed to the side of him that had happily passed those afternoons reading alone, these other figures reminded him of the worldly spies and swashbucklers whose adventures on the page he could only imagine.

Billy Broadhurst wasn't a famous actor or a defiant dictator, but he fit this mold nonetheless. Ray Strother, Hart's adman from 1984, had introduced Hart to his fellow Louisianan—a smooth-talking, silver-haired lobbyist who was an intimate of Louisiana's roguish governor, Edwin Edwards. Broadhurst would bring New Orleans cuisine back to Washington, where he lived part-time, and would host what he called his "Cajun kitchens" for a group of senators, Hart included, who would drop by after the day's final votes were cast. He was a voluble storyteller and repository of dirty jokes. Hart found him vastly amusing.

Broadhurst had a talent—an extremely valuable talent in politics—for discerning what other people wanted, without their having to ask for it. At the time, for instance, Broadhurst was carrying around one of those first-generation cell phones, the size of a woman's purse, with the pullout antenna and a battery that lasted an hour. Billy Shore wasn't a guy who cared much about the latest gadget, and he certainly never asked anybody for anything, but for some reason he did secretly covet that phone. And somehow Broadhurst must have noticed him eyeing it, or maybe Shore asked him about it not quite as offhandedly as he'd meant to, because one day Broadhurst showed up with another one. Shore needed it for the campaign, Broadhurst explained. It was a political necessity.

And so Broadhurst figured out, pretty quickly, that with Hart, when you were out to dinner or on a plane, it was often best to say nothing, to let the man simply be. If Shore wanted nothing so much as that clunky phone, then Hart wanted only respite from the endless, droning small talk, which probably no top-tier candidate since Nixon had found so profoundly draining. Broadhurst was acute enough to know when to shut up and give Hart his room to think, and for this reason he became a near constant traveling companion.

Broadhurst did have some semiofficial duties on the campaign. Bill Dixon, the campaign manager, had figured that if Broadhurst was going to keep dropping by the Denver headquarters and going to staff meetings here and there, it would be nice to know what he was actually supposed to do, and so Broadhurst had written him a memo with some ideas. The two men agreed that Broadhurst would take some meetings to screen people who wanted to see the candidate, and he would raise some money down South, both of which he delivered on. (Broadhurst, as you might expect, had also taken it upon himself to furnish the headquarters with a nice coffeemaker and microwave oven, which endeared him to everyone.) But Billy Number Two's real and unspoken job, everyone at the top of the campaign knew, was to keep Hart laughing and relaxed, or at least as relaxed as a guy like Hart could be.

Broadhurst quietly took responsibility for the downtime Hart kept insisting he needed, and which the schedulers promised to give him but, let's face it, never would. Hart demanded one weekend off a month—that was it—to unwind and pace himself for the long campaign ahead. And that weekend on the calendar belonged to Broadhurst. If the arrangement raised any alarms with Dixon or Shore or Sweeney, or with any of Hart's aides, no one would remember it later. What they remembered, instead, was a certain feeling of security in knowing that someone connected to the campaign was keeping an eye on Hart while he was off relaxing. And anyway, there were schedules to set and arrangements to make, speeches to write and reporters to mollify, and long-standing campaign debts from 1984 still shadowing the campaign. (The week of the Red Rocks announcement, federal marshals tasked with collecting those debts raided a fundraiser hosted by Beatty at the Los Angeles home of Marvin Davis, an oil tycoon, carting away $30,000 in cash and creating embarrassing headlines.) No one really had time to wonder what kind of relaxing Hart and Broadhurst had planned.

It was Broadhurst who conceived of a weekend in Miami at the end of March 1987, a last gasp of rest and freedom before the official campaign announcement that was two weeks away. He accompanied Hart to a fundraising meeting on Friday night in Miami, and on Saturday the two of them went down to the dock at the swank Turnberry Isle resort and boarded *Monkey Business,* an eighty-three-foot yacht Broadhurst had chartered for the weekend. Hart would later tell me he had intended to use the time for some deep thinking about campaign strategy. "It wasn't just fun and sun," he insisted. Whatever the plan, dozens of locals had gathered around to gawk at Hart and shake his hand, when an attractive blonde came up and said she knew him.

Actually, Donna Rice was an attractive blonde only in the sense that the Sistine Chapel had some pretty good artwork. She was twenty-nine and positively breathtaking, a model and aspiring actress when she wasn't selling pharmaceutical products for Wyeth.

As fate would have it, she had been walking on the dock when she saw the crowd and decided to investigate.

Rice reminded Hart that she'd met him only three months earlier, on New Year's Eve, at the rocker Don Henley's house in Aspen. She and Henley had been a thing for a while, and Donna had been preparing some food in the kitchen, and that's when she'd chatted with the handsome older guy who was apparently some kind of big political star, although she'd had no idea until Henley and some of the others had told her. (Lee had been there, too, although Donna didn't seem to remember that part.) Rice was smart, engaging, and undaunted by celebrity, and she didn't know a whit about politics. And you can imagine how all of that appealed to Hart, who loved women and thoughtful conversation, but who was feeling suffocated by fame and was tired as hell of talking about New Hampshire and Iowa. He invited Rice to come back to the boat later on. He and Billy were taking a quick lunch cruise to Bimini, where Broadhurst's boat was being repaired, and it would be great if Rice could come along.

Rice wasn't up for joining the excursion by herself, so she called her friend Lynn Armandt, who owned a bikini boutique in Turnberry Isle and who would likely come aboard at a moment's notice. Of all the bad choices Donna Rice would make in the weeks ahead that would affect her life as much as they did Hart's, this would prove to be one of the worst. But Armandt said yes, and the four of them—Hart, Broadhurst, Rice, and Armandt—sailed to Bimini, drinking and lunching on lobster salad while Hart went through the plot of his next spy novel. (Rice later said she asked Hart, at one point, if he had ever been married, and he said yes—in fact, he *was* married.) When they got ashore, they all drank some more, and then all four of them sang and danced onstage at a bar.

Then they gathered on the pier, surrounded by tourists, where Rice handed Armandt her camera so she could have some photos by which to remember the trip, and she posed on Hart's lap. In the days ahead, she would give some of the shots to her pal Lynn, just for fun. This wasn't an especially sage decision, either, although it would only matter after the fact.

As Hart would later tell it, what happened next was that Broadhurst's newly fixed boat got stuck in Bimini, because the customs office had closed for the day, and so, as luck would have it, the four of them had to spend the night. Hart and Rice would later insist the men and women slept apart, with Donna and Lynn on *Monkey Business* and the men on Broadhurst's boat. But when Armandt told her story months later to *People*, which paid her many thousands of dollars for the privilege, she would say that she woke up to find Rice missing from the cabin and assumed she must have been with Hart. Whatever the sleeping arrangements, they all sailed back to Miami in the morning and said their goodbyes—at least for the time being. Broadhurst had talked to Armandt about maybe doing some work for him in Washington, because he had a job open. And he thought there might be a role for Rice, too, doing some fundraising for Hart. He said they should keep in touch.

In *What It Takes*, Cramer alluded to the "true believers" in Hart's camp who would posit, in the months that followed, that everything was Broadhurst's fault, and not Hart's—that it was Billy Number Two who stupidly set up the cruise in the first place, and who kept them in Bimini, and who couldn't just let the women walk off the boat and out of Hart's life forever. Decades later, Billy Shore would clearly remember a moment in an airport holding room in Iowa, just a few days before Hart met Broadhurst and the two women for a second engagement in Washington. Shore had a stack of those old pink message slips that used to say "While You Were Out" on them, and leafing through the pile, he handed Hart the one from Broadhurst, since he knew Hart would want to return that call. Then Shore left the room for a moment, probably to use the men's room. When he returned, Hart was on the phone, and Shore could hear only his side of the conversation.

I don't know, Billy, I really have to work on that speech this weekend, Shore recalled Hart saying, or something to that effect. (Hart had a major economics address scheduled for the following Tuesday.) *I appreciate the thought, but I'm just not sure it's a good idea.* Shore was too kind to blatantly point the finger at anyone all these years later, but the implication of that memory was clear: it was Broadhurst who had engineered a reunion between Hart and Donna Rice that weekend in Washington, and he must have brought Rice over to see Hart despite the boss's stated reluctance.

In the many years after Broadhurst disappeared back to the Bayou, never to be heard from in Washington again, this sentiment would intensify and darken, to the point where some Hart loyalists entertained elaborate—if not entirely implausible—conspiracy theories. Could someone have paid Billy Broadhurst or Lynn Armandt to set Hart up? Did the Republicans, whose soon-to-be-nominee was a former CIA director, want to get Hart out of the way, the way Nixon's guys had managed to knock off Ed Muskie with a dirty trick fifteen years earlier? Did the Mafia, still rattled by disclosures about their ties to Kennedy in the Church Committee report, want to make sure Hart didn't get to the White House? Hart had been, after all, the committee member most persistent in questioning the Warren Commission's official report on the Kennedy assassination, and he had publicly promised, several times, to reopen the investigation as president.

Monkey Business, as it turned out, was owned by a guy named Donald Soffer, who had bought and developed most of Turnberry Isle. Soffer's friends included the speedboat magnate Donald Aronow, who was in turn a friend and supporter of George H. W. Bush's. In February 1987, not two months before Hart stepped foot on *Monkey Business,* Aronow was gunned down in a Mafia-style execution. In *Blue Thunder,* a sensational investigative book on the Aronow murder published in 1990, journalists Thomas Burdick and Charlene Mitchell alleged that Armandt had been connected to Soffer and to people in the narcotics trade, and they reported that federal agents had found a sheaf of Hart's stump speeches in the safe of Ben Kramer, another local Syndicate figure, after he was arrested.

What did all of these disparate clues add up to? That was anyone's guess. Hart would never go as far as to say he believed in a conspiracy, but he didn't discount it, either; he declared himself "agnostic" on the question. "It was either the most unbelievable tragedy of errors," he told me once, "or it was a setup. And no one's ever going to know."

Once, an old supporter sent Hart, without comment, a video making the rounds on YouTube, which Hart forwarded to me. The video featured a long interview with Chip Tatum, who claimed, believably, to have been a high-level black-ops agent with the CIA in the late 1980s, and who disappeared in 1998. Tatum said he had worked with Oliver North and carried out orders from then Vice President Bush, including some to assassinate foreign nationals. About an hour into the video, he said he had been asked by the Republican administration to "neutralize" Hart's campaign, and while he had refused to take such covert action against an American citizen, he assumed someone else had accepted the assignment. (Tatum's allegation was undercut by his assertion that agents had subsequently taped Hart's affair with Rice and leaked it to the press, which never actually occurred.)

To the extent that such wild theories involve the complicity of Billy Broadhurst, though, they probably do him a disservice. Broadhurst was himself humiliated after the events of 1987—"Billy was more careful when he was pimping for me," his friend Edwin Edwards quipped, unhelpfully, after the scandal broke—and he genuinely seems to have loved Hart. Even when I tracked down Broadhurst twenty-five years later, long after Hart had stopped speaking to him, he sounded shattered by the whole episode. He told me Hart would have made a great president and that he would never publicly discuss anything that happened in 1987 unless Hart personally asked him to. (Hart wouldn't.)

And what's clear, no matter what you want to believe, is that no one could have set up Gary Hart without Hart's willing participation. It wasn't Broadhurst who invited Donna Rice to join the cruise to Bimini. And if Rice's account can be believed, it wasn't just Broadhurst, but Hart himself, who encouraged her to visit Washington, calling her several times from the road in the weeks after their cruise.

Why he did something so reckless is a question that no one—not the armchair Eriksons in the press corps, not the aides who were closest to the candidate, not even Hart himself, who had years of painful solitude in which to reflect upon it afterward—would ever be able to fully or persuasively answer. Maybe in his own mind, as he had hinted back in 1972, Hart considered his oft-troubled marriage to Lee more of a political necessity, for both of them, than an enduring commitment to monogamy—and if she didn't expect him to be faithful after all this time, how could anyone else? (In 1987, remember, it was probably easier to run as an adulterer than as a man who'd just split from his wife.)

Maybe, as some of his advisors later postulated, Hart saw the official start of the campaign as a kind of wedding night, and his dalliance with Rice was the bachelor party, a last stand before accepting the limitations of the life he had chosen. Maybe Hart had a genuine compulsion, an addiction to sex or at least to flirtation, that most men of his generation wouldn't have recognized or known how to handle—and that, up until that moment in the life of the society, probably wouldn't have prevented him from becoming president in any event. A Westerner born in the Depression years wasn't what you'd call an obvious candidate for addiction therapy, and certainly not in the 1980s.

What's certain is that, far from harboring some self-destructive instinct, Hart did not believe he would be caught or that his decisions would be catastrophic. He had been at the center of the media universe not three years earlier, besieged by cameras and skeptical reporters everywhere he went, and no one had even bothered to raise the rumors publicly, even though his escapades were common knowledge among Washington pundits. He knew for a fact that Mondale had been the subject of similar speculation, because some of his own consultants had come to him claiming to have evidence, but there was no way Hart was going to start that kind of thermonuclear war, and no reporter had followed up on the lead, either. Hart may have credited the aides and friends who warned him that things were different now, that even the appearance of adultery could ruin him, but he could not believe for a second that any creditable reporter would actually go hunting for the evidence.

Days after the cruise to Bimini, and just a few weeks after his conversations with Dionne, Hart took his first major campaign trip, touring the rural South with a small contingent of aides and reporters. (Hart firmly believed he could win some Southern states in a general election, and he had pointedly rejected Shore and Rosner's advice to ignore the region.) At dinner one night in Atlanta, where Hart stopped in to see Jimmy Carter, Lee sat at one end of a long table near the two Billys and John Emerson, who had run California for Hart in 1984 and was now his deputy campaign manager. At the other end, out of earshot, Hart sat with his old friend Jack Germond, the columnist and TV commentator who had been a frequent dinner companion since 1972.

It seemed to Germond on that trip that Hart had at last become an unstoppable force in presidential politics—at ease as a candidate, focused and passionate. And yet he worried about one thing, and he shared it with Hart in a whisper no one else at the table could hear. Personally, he didn't care whom Hart did or didn't sleep with, but this stuff about a "zipper problem" was out there, Germond said. What was Hart going to do about it?

Hart assured Germond, as he had his campaign aides, that he had nothing to worry about there—his adventurous days were in the past. Only later would Germond learn that, on that very trip, Hart had called Donna Rice from a pay phone in Alabama.

4

FOLLOW ME AROUND

IT WAS AROUND 8 P.M. on Monday, April 27, when the phone rang on Tom Fiedler's desk. If the caller had intended to get his answering machine, then she didn't know much about Fiedler. He was still in the *Miami Herald* newsroom, rereading a bunch of notes and campaign speeches.

"You know, you said in the paper that there were rumors that Gary Hart is a womanizer," the woman on the other end said. Fiedler would later describe her tone as one of "strained jocularity," as if she wanted all this to sound absurd and lighthearted, but they both knew it wasn't. "Those aren't rumors," she told him. And then a stunning question: "How much do you guys pay for pictures?"

The call had come to Fiedler—and not to any of the other dozens of reporters who were following Hart—for two reasons. The first was just good fortune: Fiedler was the top political reporter in Miami, where Hart happened to have hooked up with Donna Rice, and where the caller lived. In those days, before websites and multiple cable news channels, your local paper was your main connection to the world. So if you had a tip, that's who you called.

The second reason had to do with Fiedler himself, who had added his own dispatch to a series of controversial media stories since Hart's formal announcement two weeks earlier, each one affecting the next, setting in motion a cascade of events that would quickly and imperceptibly change the flow of American history.

It had started, everyone would later agree, with Howard Fineman, who was *Newsweek*'s top young political writer. The newsweeklies—*Time, Newsweek,* and to a lesser extent *U.S. News & World Report*—were still a huge deal in 1987, and they prided themselves on getting to what *Newsweek* editors called the *zeitgeist* of a story, as opposed to its more restrictive set of facts. Newspaper reporters, back then, were almost always tethered to the format of "objective" coverage—the who, what, when, where, and why, with little of the analytical voice that later generations would take for granted. For that kind of analysis, you generally had to read one of the glossy "newsmags," whose editors didn't mind veering widely into the lane of speculation. There was nothing a *Newsweek* writer liked better than getting out in front of a story (and generating "buzz" for the magazine) by writing what all the daily guys knew to be obvious but couldn't actually say.

And so it made sense that it was Fineman, a sharp and competitive reporter, who went where others on the bus were dying to go, and whose editors let him. "The Harts' marriage has been a long but precarious one," he wrote in his story that would be on newsstands when Hart made his announcement at Red Rocks, "and he has been haunted by rumors of womanizing. Friends contend that his dating has been confined to marital separations—he and Lee have had two—nonetheless many political observers expect the rumors to emerge as a campaign issue." Having thus liberally sprinkled the kerosene, Fineman lit the match with a quote from John McEvoy, who had been one of Hart's senior aides in the 1984 campaign: "He's always in jeopardy of having the sex issue raised if he can't keep his pants on." (Soon after, *Newsweek* published a "clarification" from an irate McEvoy, who contended that the quote "was made in a speculative and purely hypothetical context, contrary to the actual facts as I know them." Which didn't clarify much, really.)

What Fineman's story did, more than anything, was to open the door for everyone else. Stories of Hart's "womanizing"—a strange word, which made him sound as if he were running through random women and then discarding them on the side of the highway, rather than having squired around some of the better known social- ites in Washington—were no longer "out there"; now they were in print, and by the arcane logic of political journalism, that meant they had been legitimized as a campaign issue. And so what hap- pened next is that every reporter who scored a sit-down with Hart in the hours after his announcement, on what was supposed to be a triumphant cross-country tour, kept asking him about the long- standing rumors of his unspecified affairs, which in fact had been just as long-standing and unspecified the week before, but were only now—thanks to *Newsweek*—considered to have met the definition of news.

When it got back to Hart that operatives for some of his rivals had been calling reporters in the days leading up to his announcement to fan the flame (what would happen to the party if this stuff came out after he was nominated, when it was too late to get someone else onto the ballot?), Hart couldn't manage to contain his aggravation. "All I know is what reporters tell me," Hart seethed in an interview with a *Time* correspondent aboard the plane. "If it's true that other campaigns are spreading rumors, I think it's an issue."

This mini-outburst constituted, as Cramer would later put it, a "fatal mistake." If *Newsweek* had made it okay for the reporters to interrogate Hart about his legendary infidelity, then Hart's quote had now made it okay for them to write their own stories on the subject. A candidate accusing rival campaigns of defaming him was a story any day of the week, no matter what the issue—that the issue here was sex, rather than, say, a proposal to tax foreign oil, only made it irresistible.

It was not the last time Hart would find himself trapped inside a box that candidates and their experts in "crisis management" would try ever after to escape, desperately and in vain. If you refused to answer the questions, you were hiding something, and the story wouldn't die. But if you tried to refute the premise of the story, you only succeeded in giving it new life, by virtue of the fact that you had "responded" to the allegations. Either way, it was impossible to change the subject. If there were any doubts that the campaign, officially in its first week, was getting away from Hart, the *New York Post* put them to rest with its front page the next day. GARY: "I'M NO WOMANIZER," it screamed from the newsstand.

The following week—exactly fourteen days after the announcement, to be precise—was when Fiedler decided to weigh in. He'd been on the plane, too, and he was troubled. The dinosaurs on the trail, the ones who started as copy boys and learned to write on the job, were mostly "know it when you see it" types—as in, you know a story when you see one, and you know something's horseshit when it's horseshit, and you don't need a graduate seminar to figure it out. But Fiedler, who was forty-one at the time, was one of these younger, more professional reporters—the kind who learned the business in a classroom and called himself a "journalist." Fiedler was a guy who thought there should be rules about when something was news and when it wasn't, codes of ethics that governed the behavior of responsible and objective journalists, just as there were in any licensed profession. And he thought it raised some serious issues, this trafficking in sheer rumor about Hart's sex life.

Specifically, Fiedler objected to the kind of innuendo that bled through the *New York Post*'s piece: "whispers" and "rumors" and "wagging tongues." If you have the evidence, then by all means produce it, Fiedler thought. But it didn't seem ethical for reporters to pass along gossip to their readers like some high school cheerleader giggling with her friends.

Fiedler's piece on April 27 had run under the headline SEX LIVES BECOME AN ISSUE FOR PRESIDENTIAL HOPEFULS. The piece was a classic of the "news analysis" genre that enabled daily reporters to stray, though not very far, from the constraints of your basic news story. Fiedler opened with an anecdote about Hart wandering to the back of the plane during the announcement tour, to face the reporters who were demanding he refute the rumors about affairs. "Anybody want to talk about ideas?" Hart had asked them, sardonically. (They didn't.)

"This vignette may tell us something about Gary Hart, a man with an opaque past," Fiedler wrote. He went on to list a series of "real and serious" questions related to media ethics that he felt the Hart case had raised:

> Is it responsible for the media to report damaging rumors if they can't be substantiated? Or should the media withhold publication until they have solid evidence of infidelity?
>
> Even if sexual advances can be proven, do the media have a legitimate interest in a candidate's private sex life, assuming it doesn't interfere with doing the job?
>
> Finally, to go back to Hart's question, can't the media stick to analyzing his ideas?

As was (and is) the style with such news analysis pieces, Fiedler didn't actually endeavor to answer these questions. "In a harsh light, the media reports themselves are rumor mongering, pure and simple," he wrote. And yet, he consulted with some professors who suggested that now that such rumors were "out there," reporters had a duty, really, to investigate them. "You aren't protecting the people of Miami by refusing to report the rumor," Bruce Swain, a journalism professor at the University of Georgia, assured Fiedler. The analysis ended with a quote from Hart himself. "No one has suggested what you do about vague, unfounded, and unproved rumors," Hart said in an interview. "I think people are going to get tired of the question."

Fiedler couldn't have known that his anodyne analysis of recent events would, in itself, become a critical part of those events, another step down in the cascade that was carrying political journalism into dark and unexplored waters. When the woman who refused to identify herself called him at his desk on the twenty-seventh, having just read the piece, she said, "Gary Hart is having an affair with a friend of mine," according to the account Fiedler and his colleagues later wrote. "We don't need another president who lies like that."

Fiedler described himself as being somewhat indignant at the caller's "mocking" tone. This was the presidency they were talking about, after all, and a man's career to boot. He said he advised his tipster to sleep on it and call back in the morning if she had any use-ful information. When she called back the next morning, at 10:30, her tone was more serious. She said she was a "liberal Democrat," but she was sickened by a candidate who would say one thing and then so blatantly do another. She and Fiedler talked for ninety min-utes, during which the caller described to Fiedler the party aboard the chartered boat at Turnberry Isle, her friend's crush on Hart, the way her friend had flashed around the pictures she had taken of the two of them together. She did not name Donna Rice.

Then she said there were phone calls. Somehow, she knew from where they had been placed—Georgia, Alabama, Kansas—and pre-cisely when. She claimed that Hart had invited her friend to visit him in Washington, and her friend was going to see him that Friday night. "Maybe you could fly to Washington," the anonymous caller helpfully suggested, "and get the seat next to her?" She said she'd get him the flight information if she could.

For decades after Fiedler received that call, just about everyone close to the events of that week—and everyone who wrote about them later—assumed that the caller was Lynn Armandt, the girlfriend Rice brought along on *Monkey Business*. This was a logical deduc-tion, since it was Armandt who later profited from the photos taken aboard the boat, which the caller offered to sell. When I asked Fiedler about this, however, he told me that while he would continue to pro-tect the identity of his source, which he had learned soon after the fact and had kept secret for twenty-six years, he was willing to say flatly that it was *not* Armandt. Fiedler volunteered that he thought Rice knew who the tipster really was.

When I spoke to Rice a few months after that, during the first of two long conversations, she told me that she had never figured out with any certainty who it was that had set all of this in motion back in 1987. But she had come to believe that Armandt was in cahoots with another friend of theirs in Miami—a woman named Dana Weems—who had somehow escaped notice in most contemporary accounts of the scandal. Rice had talked to both Armandt and Weems about her dalliance with Hart, and she had shown them the photos taken at Bimini.

Dana Weems wasn't especially hard to find in the age of Google. A clothing designer who had done some costume work on movies in the early 1990s, she sold funky raincoats and gowns on a website called Raincoatsetc.com, based in Hollywood, Florida. When she answered the phone after a couple of rings, I introduced myself and told her I was writing a book about Gary Hart and the events of 1987.

"Oh my God," she said. There followed a long pause.

"Did you make that call to the *Herald,* Dana?" I asked her.

"Yeah," Weems said with a sigh. "That was me."

She then proceeded to tell me her story, in a way that probably revealed more about her motives than she realized. In 1987, Armandt sold some of Weems's designs at her bikini boutique under a cabana on Turnberry Isle, which is how the three women met. Like Rice, Weems had worked as a model, and even now, through the phone line and all the intervening years, the jealousy she felt for Rice was hard to miss. Weems told me Rice wasn't nearly as successful a model as she was, that Rice was an artificial beauty who was "Okay for commercials, I guess." Weems recalled going aboard *Monkey Business* on that last weekend of March for the impromptu party that Hart was at, but in her version of events, Hart was hitting on *her,* not on Rice, and he was soused and pathetic, and she had wanted nothing to do with him, but still he followed her around the boat, hopelessly enthralled . . .

But Donna! Donna had no standards, is how Weems remembered it. Weems figured Donna wanted to be the next Marilyn Monroe, sleeping her way into the inner sanctum of the White House. After that weekend, Donna wouldn't shut up about Hart or give the pictures a rest! It all made Dana Weems sick to her stomach—especially this idea of Hart getting away with it and becoming president. "What an idiot you are!" Weems said, as if talking to Hart through the years. "You're gonna want to run the country? You moron!"

And so when Weems read Fiedler's April 27 story in the *Herald*, she decided to make the call, while Armandt stood by, listening to every word. "I didn't realize it was going to turn into this whole firecracker thing," she told me. It was Armandt's idea, Weems said, to try to get cash by selling the photos Rice had lent her, and that's why she asked Fiedler if he might pay for them (though she couldn't actually remember much about that part of the conversation). Weems said she hadn't talked to either woman—Rice or Armandt—since shortly after the scandal. She lived alone and was confined to a wheelchair because of multiple sclerosis. She was surprised that her secret had lasted until now.

"I'm sorry to ruin his life," she told me, offhandedly, near the end of our conversation. "I was young. I didn't know it would be that way."

After he talked to Weems, Fiedler spent the next few days checking the dates she had given him against Hart's schedule during the previous weeks. It all matched up. He was more dubious about the supposed rendezvous that coming Friday, because Hart was scheduled to be in Kentucky for a Derby party that weekend. But on Friday, not having heard back from his source and "tormented" by the silence, Fiedler called Hart's headquarters again and found out that the Kentucky event had been scrubbed; Hart would instead be returning to his townhouse on Capitol Hill. He planned to work on that big economics speech he was to deliver in New York the following Tuesday, one of the last major bricks in his wall of ambitious policy ideas. As fate would have it, his audience would be the American Newspaper Publishers Association.

Fiedler later wrote that what crossed his mind at that moment was the image of a slot machine, with all of the jackpot signs suddenly lining up. That Friday afternoon, he conferred with his editors, who decided that the information he had was enough to go on. They summoned Jim McGee, the paper's top investigative reporter, into an office at about 5 p.m., and a few minutes later McGee ran out of the building with nothing but his wallet and the clothes he was wearing, and hailed the first cab he saw. In those days before TSA security checks, he just did make it onto one of the last two nonstop flights bound for Washington.

Fiedler stayed behind for the time being. He worked his phone in the *Herald* newsroom, trying unsuccessfully to dig up an address for Hart's Washington townhouse. He was still at it when he happened to get a call from Ken Klein, the press secretary for Bob Graham, Florida's junior senator. Klein, as it turned out, knew exactly where Hart's townhouse was, because Graham's chief of staff rented the basement. That's the kind of reporter Tom Fiedler was—the kind who constantly seemed to be lucking into breaks in a story, mostly because he never for a minute stopped hunting for them.

In some ways, despite his passing consideration of all the deeper questions related to rumor and privacy, Fiedler was a very different kind of reporter from E. J. Dionne, who gravitated toward philosophical questions more than he did breaking news, and who liked to get lost in the esoteric undercurrents of a subject. Soft-spoken and methodical, with a mop of brown curls, Fiedler could seem unimposing, or even meek; his colleagues compared him, not unkindly, to Clark Kent. But to write Fiedler off as some Hollywood-cast pipsqueak would have been a gross underestimation. Fiedler was a bulldog, possessed of the quiet intensity and unflagging persistence one might expect from a descendant of the Puritan leader John Winthrop. Had things gone a different way, he would have been just as happy covering cops or corporate takeovers as he was politicians; the point of the job, for Fiedler, was to find out whatever it was they didn't want you to know.

In fact, he had set out to become, of all things, a boating writer. Or rather, that had seemed the most sensible path after growing up on Cape Cod and attending the Merchant Marine Academy, whose graduates were promised a navigable route around combat assignments in Vietnam. The life of a merchant marine had to be served at sea, though, whereas journalism seemed like a perfectly manageable, land-bound existence for a new husband and father. So Fiedler went to graduate school at Boston University and then joined the *Sentinel* in Orlando, where he was immediately assigned to the paper's brand-new "Mickey desk," covering Disney World.

Then, in 1972, the paper's editors, short of reporters to cover the competitive Democratic primary in the state, sent Fiedler out to follow the peripheral candidacy of George Wallace. (It was at that point that Fiedler first met Hart, at a McGovern news conference, though Hart would never have remembered an isolated encounter with a small-time reporter like that.) Wallace went on to win the Florida primary, and suddenly—here was that irrepressible luck again—Fiedler woke up to find that he had gained something of a reputation as a fine political writer. The *Herald* hired him away, shipping him out first to its West Palm Beach bureau, and then, after the 1976 campaign, sending him to Washington as a junior member of its well-staffed bureau there. Doggedly and with understated ambition, Fiedler kept climbing the ladder.

By 1987, Fiedler hadn't quite joined the exclusive cadre of bigfoot reporters from larger regional papers—like Tom Oliphant at *The Boston Globe,* or Larry Eichel at *The Philadelphia Inquirer,* or Carl Leubsdorf at *The Dallas Morning News*—whom any presidential candidate had to know and cultivate. But he was a known presence on the campaign trail, capable of landing major interviews and writing a story to which the rest of the media would have to pay attention. And when it came to the questions he had raised in his piece, Fiedler himself never had any doubt, not for a second, that Hart's marital infidelity, if it could be substantiated, was a story. Nor, it seems, did anyone else at the *Herald,* where the question of newsworthiness was raised but quickly dispatched. In the reconstruction of how the story unfolded that Fiedler and his colleagues at the paper later published, there is not a single mention of any debate about whether a candidate's private life merited investigation.

As far as Fiedler was concerned, the sex in itself wasn't newsworthy—or at least that was how he would always frame the argument. Hart could sleep with whomever he wanted. What mattered was that if Hart were indeed cheating on his wife, then that would make him not just a philanderer, but also a liar and a hypocrite. Just fourteen days before Fiedler's phone rang portentously, Hart had stood up at Red Rocks and promised American voters that he would hold himself to the "very highest possible standards of integrity and ethics." Never mind that he had been talking about something entirely different, that he was drawing a direct contrast with the Reagan administration, whose ill-advised foray into illegal arms sales to the Iranians was playing out daily in congressional hearings. If he wasn't being faithful to his wife, and if he was purposely misleading the reporters who questioned him about the rumors, then how could Hart claim to be a moral leader?

"He was holding himself out to be a person of high ethical standards," Fiedler told me, looking back later. "And if he wasn't outright denying it, he was certainly very ambiguous about the idea that he was a womanizer." (Twenty-six years later, that word sounded oddly retro, as if it had just been exhumed from some archive and dusted off.) "So I think our view was largely shaped on that. There was a contradiction between how he was holding himself out publicly and how he was behaving privately."

Fiedler was well aware that no one in his position had ever breached this territory before. Certainly no reporter had even contemplated staking out the home of a presidential contender as if he were some drug runner on an episode of *Miami Vice*. But Fiedler had developed a theory of the case, a reason for changing the rules. The way Fiedler would explain it, the role of the political press had been dramatically and forever changed by the party reforms that began in 1968—ironically, the very same reforms on which Hart, as a young activist, had made his name and career. Before 1968, the Democratic and Republican nominees had been chosen predominately by party bosses and wealthy patricians, respectively, men who gathered in the proverbial back rooms of American politics and vetted the candidates themselves. These party leaders knew their own candidates intimately, and they were perfectly capable of deciding which of them had the mettle and integrity to be president and which didn't. The bosses had no need for meddlesome reporters who could present them with exhaustive dossiers on potential nominees.

What the reforms had done, though, was to create the modern system of primaries and caucuses, in which voters, and not activists, had the ultimate say. And unlike the bosses, the voters had no real familiarity with the candidates who beseeched them, aside from what they saw on television. *Someone* had to give these candidates a thorough vetting. *Someone* had to be responsible for making sure the voters didn't choose a deeply flawed potential president. And the only institution in American life that could move in to fill that vacuum was the media.

Did it matter if Gary Hart was lying about his sex life? Did it make him less of a leader than, say, Jack Kennedy? On these questions, Fiedler claimed to be disinterested. As far as he was concerned, the relevance of any given data point was entirely up to the voters. Fiedler's job was simply to offer up as much information as he could that might reasonably pertain to a man's character and moral fitness, and then let the public decide whether that information disqualified him or not. Fiedler was a hired investigator, paid not to judge the value of whatever unpleasantness he uncovered, but simply to compile and present it.

You could argue that this theory represented a startling abdication. After all, the role of the media had always been to make choices about which information mattered and which could be overlooked—which belonged on the front page, or inside the paper, or nowhere at all. At its most basic, any newspaper or newscast—or website, for that matter—is one big exercise in prioritizing information; the core role of any reporter or editor is to adjudicate the value of a story, relative to other stories. Floridians didn't get the *Herald* dropped in their driveways so they could be assaulted with all the facts that could possibly be considered about a presidential candidate, in no particular order of importance—how he viewed the Soviets, what kind of shampoo he used, whether he changed his name. They expected journalists to exercise a little judgment about whether the information they happened upon was important—or even germane—to the arguments in a campaign.

To understand where Fiedler was coming from, though, you have to view his rationale through the lens of Watergate, which was still very recent history in 1987—and which probably had a lot more to do with the shift in journalistic mores than the electoral reforms of 1968. It wasn't just that reporters like Fiedler, who had started covering politics in the same year as the break-in at the Watergate, looked to Woodward and Bernstein as examples of the accolades a good scandal story could bring you (although they surely did). It was more that Watergate left the entire country feeling duped and betrayed. Sure, the whole thing ended up elevating the media, as personified by *The Washington Post,* to heroic stature in much of America. But political reporters had to ask themselves some hard questions in the aftermath of Nixon's resignation. How had a man so deficient in character, a man whose corruption and pettiness were so self-evident on those secretly recorded White House tapes, been able to win two presidential elections? Why had it taken a couple of no-name metro reporters to expose what the elite White House and campaign journalists had somehow missed after covering Nixon for twenty years?

The new generation wasn't going to let that same thing happen to them. (And their elders at papers like the *Herald* were sufficiently chastened that they weren't about to argue the point.) If reporters like Tom Fiedler were going to err, they were going to err on the side of disclosure, not propriety. The voters might consider the story of a president's private behavior to be relevant, or maybe they wouldn't, but never again would they have to wonder ruefully what kind of person they had elected.

Had Hart been just another of the unknown and uninspiring Democratic hopefuls whom pundits on the new genre of news shows had taken to calling the "Seven Dwarfs," the rumors about his sex life might not have had so much currency. But Hart wasn't just another candidate; he was crushing the rest of the field and running comfortably ahead of Bush in the polls, and he had already moved on to an ambitious governing agenda for the next eight years, as if the election itself were a formality. He was, for all practical purposes, a president in waiting. For Fiedler, when it came to this question of whether to find out if the guy was cheating on his wife, it really wasn't much of a question at all.

. . .

Fiedler's phone rang again late Friday night, May 1, this time at home. It was McGee, and he was excited. McGee, who at thirty-four could fairly be called one of the finest investigative reporters in all of American journalism, had spent the flight to Washington stalking his fellow passengers, walking up and down the aisle in search of women who looked as if they could plausibly be on their way to sleep with a presidential candidate. "He wondered how he would decide which woman to follow," the *Herald*'s reporters later wrote, without a hint of realizing how creepy that sounded.

On the ground in Washington, McGee drove to Hart's home on Capitol Hill and took up a position on a park bench that afforded a clear view of the front door. It was 9:30 p.m. when he saw Hart leave the townhouse with a woman he recognized from the ticket counter in Miami. McGee later described Rice as a "stunning" blonde and reported that when he first spied her at the airport, she had been in the company of another blonde who was "not as attractive."

Hart and the young woman promptly drove off, and McGee rushed to a pay phone across the street. He called his editors and Fiedler to ask for backup; the story was unfolding rapidly, and he needed more bodies to help with the surveillance. McGee was still stationed on the street when, about two hours later, Hart and Rice returned from dinner and could be seen reentering the townhouse. McGee didn't dare leave to get some sleep. He had to make sure the woman spent the night.

Fiedler later described himself as "dumbfounded" by McGee's report from the townhouse that Friday night. He awoke Saturday morning and hopped the first flight to Washington. He brought with him McGee's editor, Jim Savage, and a photographer, Brian Smith. When you added in Doug Clifton, an editor in the paper's Washington bureau who had joined McGee for part of the stakeout Friday night, the *Herald*'s crack undercover team now numbered five, along with at least two rental cars, on a block where maybe one or two residents could be spotted on the sidewalk at any given time

in the afternoon. The odds of this kind of surveillance going undetected were not especially high.

Indeed, the covert operation did not go undetected. At about
8:40 p.m. Saturday, Hart and Rice left the house and emerged
into the adjacent alleyway, heading for the senator's car. The idea,
apparently, had been to meet Broadhurst and Armandt for dinner.
It was then that Hart noticed things were amiss. The first reporter
he spotted in the side alley was McGee, a two-hundred-pound
man who for some reason had decided to make himself incon-
spicuous by donning sunglasses and a hooded parka. At night.
In May.

McGee, sensing he'd been made, turned on his heels and ran
into Fiedler, who, being the only reporter on the scene whom Hart
actually knew from the campaign plane, had disguised himself in
a tracksuit and was pretending to jog around every so often. "He's
right behind me," McGee whispered urgently. Fiedler immediately
changed direction and jogged across the street, like a disoriented
sprinter.

Jumpy and alarmed, Hart abandoned the dinner plan and led Rice
back inside. He was certain he was being watched but mystified as to
who might be watching. He peered out of his second-floor kitchen
window and surveyed Sixth Street. Hart was by no means an expert
in counterintelligence, but he had traveled behind the Iron Curtain,
where Americans were routinely tracked by government agents,
and he had spent considerable time in the protection of Secret Service agents who were always scanning the periphery for threats. All
of this was more than enough training for Hart to recognize the
clownish stakeout that had all but taken over his street. He saw the
five participants milling around, pretending to be strangers but
then talking to each other, ducking into cars, or—at least in Hart's
telling, though the *Herald* guys disputed his account—disappearing
behind his bushes. *His bushes.* He thought they had to be reporters,
but how could he be sure? Maybe they worked for another campaign, or for the Republicans.

Hart would later tell me what he had told Cramer not long after the event had taken place, that he felt nothing at that moment so much as sadness, a gloom that descended on him when he realized that this would never stop, that even in his own home he could not be free from the constant invasiveness and speculation. But he must have realized something more than that, too; he must have known, instinctively, that he had wandered into some new frontier and would not be able to retrace his steps. He had stubbornly clung to the idea that the accepted boundaries of privacy would hold, that certain of the old rules he had known would not suddenly disintegrate, as his advisors had warned. But in that moment, staring down at a sidewalk bathed in the floodlights of his own security system, Hart must have known he had been disastrously wrong. The exact ramifications of that miscalculation weren't clear, and wouldn't be clear for many days after. That there would be severe ramifications, however, could not have escaped a man as preternaturally intuitive as Gary Hart.

Hart's first thought was to call the police. For decades afterward, he would second-guess himself for not having made this simple decision. But what was he going to say, exactly? That people were congregating on his sidewalk and looking through his windows? That he, Gary Hart, was being stalked? That reporters were standing outside the home of a presidential candidate, on a public street? All roads here seemed to end in the same desolate place, which was a spate of stories about how weird Gary Hart was calling District cops and pleading with them to keep the media or his opponents at a comfortable remove.

Instead, Hart decided, at first anyway, to hunker down and wait. He called Broadhurst, and Broadhurst came over with Armandt and some barbecued chicken. Billy Number Two tried to ease the boss's mind, but Hart could not be easy now. He needed to be alone, to think, to take some kind of action. Later, when she sold her version of the story to *People,* Armandt would say that Broadhurst took this opportunity to tell both women what their story was going to be if they were asked—that Rice hadn't spent Friday night at Hart's place, that the four of them had been planning an innocent dinner so they could talk about jobs and the campaign. Rice would never discuss this supposed cover-up, but she did tell me, many years later, that Hart was present for the conversation. Afterward, he instructed Broadhurst to gather up the women and leave via the back door. He would never see Donna Rice again.

If everything leading to that point had been unprecedented in the annals of presidential politics, then what happened next was the stuff of pure fiction, the kind of thing a Hollywood studio might have rejected as straining the bounds of suspended disbelief. It might seem farcical, even now, had a man's career and the future of the country not been at stake.

Like a character in one of the spy novels he loved to read and write, Hart decided to outwit his surveillers and flush them into the open. It's not clear how he thought this was going to end, other than badly, but a cornered man does not think so clearly. Hart put on a white sweatshirt and pulled the hood up over his famous mane. At first, he got into his car and merged into the Capitol Hill traffic. He expected to be followed, and he was—Smith, the photographer, was tailing him close behind. Satisfied with this maneuver, Hart pulled over after a few blocks, emerged from the car and started walking back in the general direction of the townhouse. He detoured down a side street and walked twice around the block.

Next Hart walked past the rental car where McGee and Savage thought they were safely incognito. In Richard Ben Cramer's telling, Hart made a show of writing down the license plate number in full view of the two reporters; the *Herald* didn't mention this detail, but it did report that Hart seemed "agitated" and appeared to yell over his shoulder, at someone on the other side of the street, as he walked away. Probably both accounts are true. In any event, McGee and Savage cleverly deduced from Hart's behavior that their undercover stakeout had been compromised. They could not write a story, in any event, without at least trying to get his response. So after quickly conferring, they exited the car, followed Hart's path back up the alley alongside his row of townhouses, and turned a corner. Both men, according to their own account, "flinched in surprise." There was Gary Hart, the presumed nominee of the Democratic Party, leaning against a brick wall in his hoodie. He was waiting for them.

There were no press aides or handlers, no security agents or protocols to be followed. There was no precedent for any reporter accosting any presidential candidate outside his home, demanding the details of what he was doing inside it. It was just Hart and his accusers, or at least two of them for the moment, facing off in an oil-stained alley, all of them trying to find their footing on the suddenly shifting ground of American politics.

Eight days later, the *Herald* would publish its front-page reconstruction of the events leading up to and including that Saturday night. Written by McGee, Fiedler, and Savage, the 7,500-plus-word piece—*Moby-Dick*–type proportions by the standards of a front page—is remarkable reading, for a couple of reasons. First, it's striking how much the *Herald*'s account of its investigation consciously imitates, in its clinical voice and staccato cadence, Woodward and Bernstein's *All the President's Men*. ("McGee rushed toward a pay telephone a block away to call editors in Miami. It was 9:33 p.m." And so on.) Clearly, the reporters and editors at the *Herald* believed themselves to be reconstructing a scandal of similar proportions, the kind of thing that would lead to Pulitzers and movie deals. The solemn tone of the piece suggests that Fiedler and his colleagues believed themselves to be the only ones standing between America and another menacing, immoral president; reading it, you might think Hart had been caught bludgeoning a beautiful young woman to death, rather than taking her to dinner.

The other fascinating thing about the *Herald*'s reconstruction is that it captures, in agonizing detail, the very moment when the walls between the public and private lives of candidates, between politics and celebrity, came tumbling down forever. In a sense, the scene that transpired between Hart and his inquisitors in the alley on Saturday night, which at least two of the *Herald* reporters transcribed in real time, was the antithesis of Johnny Apple watching silently as the famous starlet ascended to President Kennedy's suite, or Lyndon Johnson joking with reporters about the women he planned to entertain. Even in the dispassionate tone of the *Herald*'s narrative, you can hear how chaotic and combative it was, how charged with emotion and pounding hearts.

"Good evening, Senator," McGee began, recovering from his shock at seeing Hart standing in front of him. "I'm a reporter from the *Miami Herald*. We'd like to talk to you." As the *Herald* relayed it: "Hart said nothing. He held his arms around his midsection and leaned forward slightly with his back against the brick wall." McGee said they wanted to ask him about the young woman staying in his house.

"No one is staying in my house," Hart replied.

Hart may have surprised the reporters by choosing the time and place for their confrontation, but it's not as if they weren't ready. They had already conferred on a list of questions intended to back Hart up against a wall—which was now literally the situation. McGee reminded Hart that he and the woman had walked right past McGee earlier that evening on the way to his car. "You passed me on the street," McGee said.

"I may or may not have," Hart replied.

McGee asked him what his relationship was with the woman.

"I'm not involved in any relationship," Hart said carefully.

So why had they just seen Hart and the woman enter the townhouse together a few minutes earlier?

"The obvious reason is I'm being set up," Hart said, his voice quivering. It was a cryptic comment, but telling. Hart was reeling, and at that moment his mind was already revving with possible scenarios. Did Donna Rice know how these reporters got here? Was her friend an operative for some other campaign? Good Lord: Could Broadhurst himself have been less of a friend than he seemed?

McGee wanted to know if the woman was in Hart's house at that very moment. "She may or may not be," is how Hart answered, evading again. Savage then asked to meet her, and Hart said no. For some reason, Hart volunteered that she was in Washington for the weekend, which was the first acknowledgment he gave that he knew her at all.

McGee offered to explain the situation, as if Hart had just woken up in a hospital or an asylum and might not have had any idea what was happening. He said the house had been under surveillance and that he had observed Hart with the woman the night before, in Hart's car. Where were they going?

"I was on my way to take her to a place where she was staying," Hart said, referring to Broadhurst's townhouse nearby.

Now Savage cut in and asked how long Hart had known the woman—"several months" was the response—and what her name was.

"I would suppose you would find that out," Hart said.

McGee demanded to know why Hart and the woman had come back two hours after they left the night before. Hart replied that they had come back to pick up some things she had left at the house, and that she stayed for only ten or fifteen minutes. He couldn't remember how she'd left his house to return to Broadhurst's place.

"Senator, this is important," Savage said now, as if somehow he and Hart were now in this together, trying to figure out what had actually happened while Hart was comatose in his hospital bed. "Can you remember how she left? Is it possible you called a cab for her?"

Hart said he didn't recall. McGee tried again to ask who the woman was. "She is a friend of a friend of mine," Hart offered, then corrected himself. "A guest of a friend of mine."

His voice was steadier now, and the reporters noticed that his composure had returned. As would happen several times throughout the ordeal of the next week, and for long afterward, Hart was lurching between conflicting instincts. There were moments where he thought that if he said just enough, if he issued enough of a denial to explain himself, then his tormentors would see the absurdity in what they were doing. But then soon enough he would grow defiant, the way he did when Sweeney or one of the other aides tried to explain that the reporters would not stop pressing into his personal life. The hell with them, he would think. They were not *entitled* to know.

.   .   .

"Hi, Tom," Hart said now. Fiedler had made his way into the alley and had joined his colleagues, making it three on one (or actually four on one, since Smith, the photographer, was there, too). The *Herald*'s contemporaneous account made no mention of Hart's tone of voice when he paused to greet the one reporter on the scene he actually knew. Perhaps his tone betrayed a sense of disbelief at seeing the paper's top political writer camouflaged in an alley. Perhaps at that point he was just glad to see a familiar face, someone who might listen to reason.

Looking back years later, Fiedler would recall Hart's besieged posture, the way he leaned back defensively, as if expecting to be punched. And he would remember his own sense of disbelief. "It was one of those things where I thought, how did I end up here?" Fiedler told me. "At that point, I was considering myself a pretty serious political writer, the kind of writer who grappled with issues of important public policy. And here I am, almost in a disguise, following a tip where I'm not really quite sure it's all going to come together, and knowing that the story I would write would be kind of a scandal sheet story. Which was so not only out of character, but it was out of my own sense of who I was and what I was doing."

And yet, for all that, Fiedler felt compelled to be there; he recalled no doubt about that. Hart's hypocrisy, the falseness of his moral posturing, was a vital political story, which the *Herald* had now been tracking for six days. Staking out the townhouse, however unseemly, was the only way for Fiedler to confirm everything he'd been told by the anonymous caller, and this confirmation was something he owed the public—and Hart. "Seeing them together at that point and confronting Senator Hart over it, it just seemed as if it were something we were almost obligated to do," Fiedler recalled. "As odd and surreal as it felt, it just seemed to us that we had to do it."

In fact, Fiedler would always remember that his overriding emotion in that alley was anger. He shouldn't have *had* to be there, asking about such tawdry details of a man's private life. He was a respected chronicler of national politics, for Christ's sake. It was Hart who had set all this in motion, who had dragged Fiedler and the others into the dirt and muck of tabloid journalism, by refusing to tell the truth about who he was. It was Hart who had disappointed and debased Fiedler, not the other way around.

"I think I felt I'd been deceived all this time," Fiedler would remember. "And suddenly here it is, and the allegations I was probably hoping would be disproved were turning out to be true. That this is the guy who only a few weeks before had stood up in front of the world—and, in a sense me, because I was there with the press corps—and talked about ethics, and said he wanted to be held to the highest standards and said he was going to run a campaign that exemplified all that. And here I am in an alley, late on a Saturday night, confronting him about a relationship that just seemed completely sordid. And I kind of felt angry about being in that position. I felt stuck, because I was going to end up doing a story that I maybe hoped I wouldn't do."

As Fiedler watched, McGee hit Hart with questions about the phone calls he had made to Rice, which they knew about from the tipster (even though they still hadn't figured out her identity). Hart, whose suspicions about being set up must have now seemed legitimized, didn't dare deny the calls, but he characterized them as "casual" and "political" and "general conversation." Then Fiedler jumped in. He asked Hart if he had taken this woman on a yachting trip in Florida.

"I don't remember," Hart said, dubiously. You can imagine the vertigo he must have been experiencing as the details of his private life, things he had not disclosed even to Shore or other close aides, just kept coming, one after the other. It probably dawned on him, right about then, that he should never have been in the alley, any more than he should have been on the yacht.

This had been going on for several minutes now, and to that point, the questions had been about the kinds of concrete details on which investigative reporters tend to fixate. Who was the woman? Why was she there? Why had he called her? Fiedler was after something else. He sought an acknowledgment of Hart's essential hypocrisy. He sought some deeper confirmation of the man's flawed character.

So now Fiedler stepped forward and reminded Hart that he had been at Red Rocks and had personally heard the speech. He quoted Hart's own words back to him, right there in the alley, the bit about running a campaign based on integrity and ethics and a higher standard. If that were so, Fiedler wanted to know, then why was Fiedler having to stand in this alley, at this moment, doing something so beneath him? He "implored" Hart, by his own account, to offer some kind of exculpatory evidence. "You, of all people, know the sensitivity of this," Fiedler said, adding that the *Herald* was prepared to print a story about what it had uncovered. He pleaded with Hart to be more forthcoming.

"I've been very forthcoming," Hart said.

Fiedler asked again about the nature of Hart's relationship with the woman.

"I have no personal relationship with the individual you are following," Hart replied, for at least the third time. (He still seemed not to get that he was the one being followed.) To Fiedler, this nonanswer was highly significant. If Hart had said she had some role in his campaign, that they had been talking about enlisting volunteers or fundraising (and, in fact, Rice hoped that the fundraising job Broadhurst had dangled might well be in the offing), then the *Herald*'s reporters would have had a problem. Fiedler would go as far as to say, years later, that if Hart had claimed she was a colleague in this way, there wouldn't have been a story to write—or at least not until the reporters had checked into it further. But Hart wouldn't connect Rice to the campaign. He wouldn't identify her at all, and that gave the *Herald* its story.

When McGee pressed him again about the yacht and whether he was denying having met her there, Hart grew visibly irritated. "I'm not denying anything," he said. They were missing the point. He wasn't going to confirm or deny knowing Rice, or having been on a chartered boat. Hart's stance was that none of it was anybody's business but his. When the reporters asked Hart to "produce" the woman, or this friend who was supposedly hosting her, Hart said other people had a right to privacy, too.

"I don't have to produce anyone," he told them.

McGee was an expert in ambushes. He had tried to shock Hart

into answering questions, and then he had moved seamlessly into conspiratorial mode, implying that he was there to help Hart out of this, but Hart really needed to help himself. Hart was far too sharp to be taken in by that. Now McGee could see that Hart was getting ready to bolt. So McGee pulled out his last question, the one you save for the moment when there is nothing to be lost by asking it. He put the question point-blank to Hart: Had the senator had sex with the woman in the townhouse?

"The answer is no," Hart said, more definitively than he had answered other questions. Then he added, "I'm not going to get into all that."

As Hart walked away, shaken and alone, and started back up the alley, Smith, the photographer, started clicking away. Hart whirled around. This yielded the shots of him that would appear in the next day's paper—rumpled and recoiling, hiding in a hoodie like some perp who was about to have his head forcibly lowered into the backseat of a cruiser.

"We don't need any of that," were Hart's parting words.

There was something else Fiedler had raised with Hart during their standoff in the alley, but so much was coming at him that it didn't really register. When Fiedler was chiding Hart for being a hypocrite, he reminded the candidate that he had just been quoted as saying that reporters should follow him around if they didn't believe his denials of extramarital affairs. McGee joined in and pressed the point, too. Hart didn't respond to this directly, and it's not clear he even knew at that point what they were talking about. He certainly didn't realize that night that those three little words—"follow me around"—would shadow him for the rest of his days, to the point where they would bury everything else he had ever said in public life.

In the history of Washington scandal, only a few quotes—"I am not a crook," "I did not have sexual relations with that woman"—have become as synonymous with a politician. Even when insiders and historians recall the Hart episode now, it is almost universally remembered in the same way: Hart issued his infamous challenge to reporters, telling them to follow him around if they didn't believe him, and then the *Herald* took him up on it. Inexplicably, people believe, Hart set his own trap and then allowed himself to become ensnared in it. In most ways, this received version of events, which I and many other chroniclers reinforced often in the years after the scandal, is technically accurate. In the most important respect, however, it turns out to be, really, an outright lie.

The whole thing goes back to E. J. Dionne's second interview, in the New Hampshire hotel restaurant, when Dionne was pressing Hart on the rumors of affairs, and Hart was growing exasperated. Finally, he told Dionne: "Follow me around. I don't care. I'm serious. If anybody wants to put a tail on me, go ahead. They'd be very bored." Hart said this in an annoyed and sarcastic sort of way, in an obvious attempt to make a point. He was "serious" about the sentiment, all right, but only to the extent that a man who had been twice separated from his wife and conducted numerous liaisons over the years, with the full knowledge of his friends in the press corps, could have been serious about such a thing. Hart might as well have been suggesting that Martians beam down and run his campaign, for all the chance he thought there was that any reporter would actually resort to stalking him.

Dionne certainly didn't take the comment literally. "He did not think of it as a challenge," Dionne would recall many years later. "And at the time, *I* did not think of it as a challenge." Dionne interpreted the comment as Hart saying that he understood that his private life had become a real political vulnerability, and he had shut down, at least for the moment, any activities that might provide fodder for a scandal. That's how Kevin Sweeney, the press secretary, interpreted it, too. Sitting at the restaurant table during the interview, Sweeney was elated when he heard Hart make such a categorical statement after weeks of refusing to address the rumors; it meant, he thought, that Sweeney and the others had finally gotten through to Hart, and that Hart now understood that the media's definition of privacy was evolving.

Nonetheless, Dionne was surprised when his editor struck the quote from the first draft of his profile. Dionne might not have considered it a literal challenge, but he suspected that some other reporter of his generation would—and that if Hart ever did get caught philandering during the campaign, those words would become the noose from which he was hung. Had Dionne simply shrugged at that point and decided to surrender the quote to his editors in order to contest some other disagreement he cared more about (something we aggrieved magazine writers are forced to do all the time), then Hart's "follow me around" moment would have been the proverbial tree falling in the forest, uttered but never actually heard. Instead, Dionne inserted the quote back into the body of the revised piece, closer to the end than to the beginning. It ended up sticking in the final version.

As it happened, Dionne's cover story wasn't set to appear until Sunday, May 3—the same day the *Herald* published its front-page exposé. No one at the *Herald* had a clue that Hart had issued any "challenge" on the Monday night when Fiedler heard from his anonymous tipster, or when he continued to chase the story. And though many years later the *Herald* reporters would say that McGee read the quote before he flew off for Washington Friday night and began prowling outside Hart's townhouse, there is nothing in their own contemporary account to suggest it.

In those days before the Internet, however, the *Times* circulated hard copies of its magazine to other media a few days early, so editors and producers could pick out anything that might be newsworthy and publicize it in their own weekend editions or Sunday shows. And so it was that when Fiedler boarded his flight to Washington Saturday morning, eager to join the stakeout, he brought with him the advance copy of Dionne's story that had been sent to the *Herald*. Somewhere above the Atlantic seaboard, anyone sitting next to Fiedler might have seen him jolt upward in his seat as if suddenly receiving an electric current to his brain. There it was, staring up at him from the page— Hart explicitly inviting him and his colleagues to do exactly the kind of surveillance they had undertaken the night before.

At a minimum, Hart's quote made the *Herald*'s hard choices, about whether to publish immediately or not, a whole lot easier. By the time Fiedler and his colleagues had finished confronting Hart in the alley that Saturday night and retreated to Fiedler's room at a nearby Quality Inn, it was after ten, and only a few hours remained until the last edition's final deadline. That wasn't much time to debate the merits of printing such an unprecedented story, or to edit it. The *Herald*'s editors and reporters knew they would face a lot of scrutiny from their own industry and the public for the way they had gone about tailing Hart, and were there enough time to nail down some of the elusive details (like, say, the identity of the woman involved), they would have been in a better position to defend their decisions.

Fiedler, though, was anxious to bang out what they had so the paper could publish it Sunday morning, and with good reason. He had in mind what had happened to Clark Hoyt and Robert Boyd, reporters for the Knight Ridder newspaper chain, in 1972, after they had uncovered proof of Senator Eagleton's depression. (They, too, had been tipped off by an anonymous caller.) Hoyt and Boyd had held off writing their story for more than twenty-four hours while the campaign promised them an interview with Eagleton to discuss the allegations. But they were double-crossed; McGovern's aides already knew what Hoyt and Boyd had, and they had no intention of producing the candidate. What they did, instead, was to hold a news conference and disclose the facts themselves, putting their own spin on the story and denying the two reporters the biggest scoop of their careers. (Hoyt and Boyd won a Pulitzer Prize for their story, anyway.)

McGovern's campaign manager at that time, of course, had been the same man Fiedler and the others had just accosted outside his home. And Fiedler's fear was that, given twenty-four hours to strategize, Hart and his team would figure a way to get out in front of the story before the *Herald* could publish. Probably they would do this by going on the attack against the *Herald*, accusing the paper of stalking the candidate at his home—an allegation that would quickly turn the story into an argument over the *Herald*'s tactics, instead of an exposé about Hart's infidelity. Given how politically adept Hart's team generally was, and what transpired in the hours ahead, Fiedler was almost certainly right to worry.

The discovery of Hart's infamous quote, which the *Herald* reporters stealthily appropriated from the advance copy of the *Times Magazine* on Saturday night and paraphrased at the end of their Sunday blockbuster—so that the two articles, carrying versions of the same quote, appeared on newsstands simultaneously—probably negated any reservations the editors in Miami might have had about pushing the story into print. By morning, everyone who read the *Times* would *know* that Hart had goaded the press into hiding outside his townhouse and tracking his movements. So what if the *Herald* reporters hadn't even known about it when they put Hart under surveillance? At a glance, Hart's quote appeared to justify the *Herald*'s extraordinary investigation, and that's all that mattered.

The difference here is far more than a technicality. Over the decades that followed, the narrative implied by the *Herald* story—that Hart had asked to be tailed, and subsequently was—became the dominant thing most Americans recalled about him, to the point where even political insiders of the period were certain that this is what happened. (When I spoke to Dana Weems, she repeatedly insisted to me that she had only called the *Herald* after reading Hart's "follow me around" quote, which was obviously impossible.) And this version of events conveniently enabled the *Herald*'s reporters and editors to completely sidestep some important and uncomfortable questions. As long as it was Hart, and not the *Herald*, who had set the whole thing in motion, then it was he and not they who had suddenly moved the boundaries between private and political lives. They never had to grapple with the complex issues of why Hart was subject to a kind of invasive, personal scrutiny no major candidate before him had endured, or to consider where that shift in the political culture had led us. Hart had given the media no choice in the matter—this is what everyone knew.

I had a chance to talk to Fiedler about this over lunch one day in the spring of 2013. We ate at a French restaurant near the campus of Boston University, where Fiedler, who had gone on to run the *Herald* before his retirement, was now installed as dean of the College of Communication. About five years earlier, Fiedler and I had sat on a panel together at the University of Florida, and I had watched beforehand as he regaled a small group of students with the story of how he and his colleagues had taken down Hart. Still, Fiedler struck me as a thoroughly gracious and gentle person who cared about doing the right thing. Nothing about him suggested malice, or even a lack of compassion. By the time we met again in Boston, he was an astonishingly young sixty-seven, with the same thicket of dark curls he had sported a quarter century earlier.

Fiedler readily acknowledged that the order of events in 1987 had since become jumbled in the public mind, and his expression was genuinely regretful. He blamed a lot of this on the way the TV news programs that weekend had juxtaposed the *Herald*'s reporting with the quote from the *Times Magazine,* as if one had led to the other. That had really been the beginning of the myth, he said, and from that time on, people were confused about which came first—"follow me around" or the *Herald* investigation. When I asked why he had never tried to correct the record, Fiedler shrugged sadly. "I don't know what I would need to do," he said.

Then I mentioned to Fiedler that I had Googled him recently and been sent to his biographical page on the BU website. And this is what it said: "In 1987, after presidential hopeful Gary Hart told journalists asking about marital infidelity to follow him around, Fiedler and other *Herald* reporters took him up on the challenge and exposed Hart's campaign-killing affair with a Miami model." Why did his own webpage explicitly repeat something he knew to be untrue?

Fiedler recoiled in his seat and winced. He looked mortified. "You know what? I didn't know that," he said. "Honestly. I'm serious." He stared at me for another beat, stunned. *"Wow."* I knew he meant it. When I visited the same site a month or so later, I was surprised to find that Fiedler hadn't changed a word.

The first person Hart tried to reach when he got back inside his home on Saturday night, his pulse racing from the confrontation in the alley, was Bill Dixon, his campaign manager, who was in Denver. Hart got a busy signal.

So Hart called Billy Shore, who was home alone on a Saturday night in Denver, at the house for which he had just signed an eighteen-month lease. Shore didn't get a lot of quiet time without the boss being quiet a few feet away, and so he was relishing the last pages of Sue Miller's novel *The Good Mother* when the phone rang. Hart's voice on the other end of the line sounded strained, but nowhere near panic. He said there was a problem: Broadhurst was there with two friends, and some reporters from the *Herald* had been skulking around, and Hart had just talked to them. Hart wanted Shore to find Dixon.

To Shore, who was used to fielding irritated calls from the boss at all hours, this didn't exactly sound like the approach of Armageddon. There was no mention of any woman. He went back to finishing his novel, figuring he could handle this latest annoyance in a few minutes. Five minutes passed, during which it must have occurred to Hart that, just maybe, he had undersold the severity of the situation. Shore's phone rang again, and this time, Hart's voice bristled with urgency. This was a big problem, Hart said. Shore needed to get to Dixon. Now.

Dixon was at home when Shore's car came roaring into the downtown apartment complex where Dixon lived, which functioned as a kind of second headquarters for the campaign's high command. Within minutes, several of Hart's top aides—John Emerson, the deputy campaign manager; Kevin Sweeney, the press secretary; Paul Tully, the political director—were assembled in the campaign manager's apartment, placing a flurry of urgent phone calls to Washington. Dixon, meanwhile, threw a few things in a bag, humped it down to Stapleton Airport, bought a ticket on the red-eye, and jumped aboard just before the doors closed. The hell with it, he thought—it's not like he was going to get any sleep, anyway.

In a lot of ways, Dixon was a man ideally suited to a challenge for which there was no existing playbook. Forty-three at the time, a true-believing child of the sixties, Dixon exuded Midwestern niceness and good humor. But he was also the son of an Irish Catholic cop, with a street savvy that made him one hell of a tough lawyer; in later years, as a partner in one of the Midwest's top civil rights firms, he would almost never lose a jury trial. (Among the lawyers who ended up working for Dixon and his partners in that Chicago-based firm was a prodigy named Barack Obama.) It was Dixon who, as a staff lawyer for the House Judiciary Committee in 1974, had written the memos compiling impeachable offenses against Richard Nixon that eventually leaked to the press. Dixon knew something about the ways of Washington and the media, and even more about how to prosecute a case.

And even before he hit the ground in Washington at dawn on Sunday, Dixon understood that this was precisely what Hart would require—not so much a vigorous defense of his own actions, but rather an all-out prosecution of his accusers. The rumors about Hart were at this point well established; proving his innocence of all charges would be a slog once the *Herald*'s sensational story got out. But in their zeal to expose Hart's faulty character, Fiedler and the others had crossed all accepted boundaries of privacy and professional ethics. Dixon intended to put them on trial for it.

He already knew that his client wouldn't be much help in this regard. In later years, through successive scandals that came to dominate ever shrinking news cycles, a central principle of the political canon would hold that the first thing you do in such situations is to get all the facts directly from the source. Some of Hart's aides, like Shore, would always regret not having pressed Hart immediately for that information. But when Dixon had talked to Hart on the phone Saturday night, after the alley confrontation, all Hart had said was that the *Herald* was wrong and there was no story.

In lawyerly fashion, Dixon was an inveterate, almost unconscious note-taker, and twenty-six years later, sitting on his back porch on Lake Mendota in Madison, Wisconsin, he shared with me the legal pad on which he had started scribbling that Saturday night and which he carried with him for the next forty-eight hours, creating the only contemporaneous record that endures. On it, Dixon had written that Hart's phone had to have been tapped, along with the woman's. "I don't know who's setting me up," Hart told Dixon, according to his notes.

But that was all Dixon got out of Hart. "Billy's got the facts," Hart snapped, before handing the phone over to Broadhurst and washing his hands of the whole fiasco. Hart had the economics address planned for Tuesday in front of the newspaper publishers, the first of what was to be a series of speeches in the same vein over the next month. He intended to hunker down and write. This, Dixon knew, was entirely in character for Hart—trusting in the inevitability of his superior ideas and leaving the tactics to others—and didn't indicate any special level of avoidance; at this point no one really feared that the campaign itself was in mortal jeopardy. When the reporters started showing up Sunday and pounding on Hart's door, Dixon arranged to move Hart to the Georgetown home of Steve and Kitty Moses, loyal supporters who were away at the same Kentucky Derby fundraiser Hart had originally been scheduled to attend. Eventually, Shore showed up to keep the boss company. Hart installed himself in Steve Moses's study, cowboy boots propped defiantly on the desk as he edited drafts in longhand.

The witnesses Dixon felt he needed to depose were all at Broadhurst's house, so it was to that address—on A Street Northeast—that he had the cab take him from Dulles Airport on Sunday morning. Broadhurst had been up all night. Within an hour or so of hearing Hart's story about the alley, Broadhurst had somehow managed to track down Fiedler at the Quality Inn and had offered him a deal: if Fiedler would come to Broadhurst's townhouse right away, Broadhurst would make the two women staying with him—Rice and Armandt—"available." He said he couldn't force them to talk, however—that was up to Fiedler—and Fiedler presumed, probably rightly, that the cagey Broadhurst was just trying to find a way to delay publication of the story. In the end, Broadhurst ended up meeting Fiedler and the other reporters at an all-night restaurant in Chinatown, where he insisted that all of this was a big misunderstanding. By then, however, even had Fiedler believed him (which he didn't), the *Herald* had literally stopped its presses and begun rolling out a new front page with the banner headline: MIAMI WOMAN IS LINKED TO HART.

"Gary Hart, the Democratic presidential candidate who has dismissed allegations of womanizing, spent Friday night and most of

Saturday in his Capitol Hill townhouse with a young woman who flew from Miami and met him," the story began. "Hart denied any impropriety." The piece noted that *Herald* reporters had seen Hart and the mystery woman leave and then reenter the house Friday night, and that neither had left the premises again until they reemerged together Saturday night. The story didn't need to speculate on what was going on inside all that time, although from the tone of things, one could imagine it involved bearskin rugs and lots of mirrors.

Broadhurst told Dixon the story wasn't true. As he had explained to Fiedler, Broadhurst had supervised the construction of a new deck at Hart's house, and so he had the codes to the garage and the back door and could come and go as he liked; he had shown both women the deck and had taken them home via the back door at about midnight Friday. Both women, he swore, had stayed in spare bedrooms at his place. (Dixon had no reason to disbelieve this, especially when he himself stayed Sunday night in the same room Rice had supposedly stayed in the night before, and he watched the housekeeper change the rumpled linen.) On Saturday, Broadhurst told him, he and the two women had driven around Alexandria, Virginia, so Armandt could look for a place to live.

Broadhurst disclosed that he and Hart and the two women had partied with a large crowd on a yacht in Miami, but at that point he said nothing about an overnight cruise to Bimini. Neither did Rice, who seemed to Dixon naïve and startled, a nice girl who genuinely liked Hart and couldn't really understand what was happening. Dixon went at her as hard as a lawyer could go after a friendly witness whom he didn't want to become a hostile one. She said she'd taken an interest in the campaign because she was impressed with Hart's positions (a line that would have given late-night comedians weeks of material had it been made public). Ever thorough, Dixon wanted to know which positions, and Rice cited "nuclear arms and his new ideas." She said she'd come to Washington hoping to work for the campaign.

By early Sunday afternoon, reporters were descending on Broadhurst's townhouse, rapping on doors and windows. It occurred to

Dixon that he would have to step outside and make a statement, something that might choke off the momentum of the story. "Recent accusations about Senator Hart's personal life are preposterous and inaccurate in their entirety," Dixon said when he confronted the small assemblage. "They have taken a casual acquaintance and a simple dinner with three friends and political supporters and attempted to make a story where there is none." Then Dixon got to the core of his case.

"The system, when reduced to hiding in bushes, peaking in windows, and personal harassment, has clearly run amok," he said. These were the specific phrases—"hiding in bushes" and "peeking in windows"—that he and the other aides had agreed to repeat until none of them could stand to say the words any longer. "Senator Hart accepts the scrutiny that comes with his leadership role in the Democratic Party and the country. But scrutiny and questions of character are one thing; character assassinations are entirely another. Those who cover politics have some duty of self-restraint; here the boundaries of journalistic ethics have clearly been crossed."

In addition to this ethical argument, Dixon was already developing a second plank in his case against the *Herald*. Many years before, he had worked his way through the University of Buffalo as a garbage collector by night and as a licensed private investigator by day. And so Dixon had actually done quite a few stakeouts, and once he got the facts as Broadhurst told them and took a look at Hart's townhouse, he concluded that even at twenty-one he would have known how to do a more credible job than the *Herald* had. Specifically, these geniuses had forgotten that townhouses have back doors; otherwise, they would have seen Broadhurst and Armandt coming and going. In fact, Dixon had good reason to think that even the front-door surveillance had been spotty, since Ron Elving, Hart's press aide in the Senate, had stopped by a few times that Saturday with revised drafts of the economics speech and had somehow evaded the *Herald*'s dragnet. No self-respecting private dick would have vouched for a surveillance report on a house that had only been half watched, at best.

So in Denver, Sweeney and the others started pushing back with the other reporters who were calling in a mad frenzy. Not only should the *Herald* never have been spying in the first place, they said, but this so-called surveillance was a joke. Someone needed to ask these guys why they hadn't been watching the blessed back door.

The two-pronged assault on the *Herald* story was as much for the benefit of the reporters—and their editors—as it was for their readers. In order to contain the damage, Hart's team knew, they needed to isolate the *Herald,* to make sure it became an outlier among reputable news organizations. After years of changing cultural attitudes about adultery and privacy, after more than a decade of considering Watergate's lessons when it came to the fitness of candidates, after months of building innuendo about Hart's flawed character, the *Herald* had at last taken political journalism into what had previously been tabloid territory. But on this question of whether presidential candidates should be given the same treatment as a Jim Bakker or a Fawn Hall, the soap opera stars of nightly newscasts in the spring of 1987, the rest of the media still hung in the balance.

Fiedler had made his choice. Now his colleagues on the campaign bus needed to make theirs.

5

"I DO NOT THINK THAT'S A FAIR QUESTION"

FOR MOST OF THE TWENTIETH CENTURY, information in America was controlled and disseminated by a select group of elite institutions. By the end of the 1970s, if you lived in a typical American city, you read about national events in your local paper (if you were lucky, you had a choice between two), or perhaps in the copy of *Time* or *Newsweek* that arrived in the mailbox every Tuesday. Any other newspaper would have to be purchased, probably a day late, at the out-of-town newsstand. The locally owned newspaper—whose status as a paragon of civic virtue would be mythologized by journalists and media critics in later years, after faceless conglomerates had gobbled up most of the American media—exercised as much of a monopoly over information in some cities as the power company had over transformers and wires. Thus was it possible, as late as 1968, for some Indiana voters to know little of the Democratic primary campaign being waged in their own state, simply because the *Indianapolis Star*—whose publisher, Eugene C. Pulliam, had been a Lyndon Johnson supporter—all but refused to acknowledge Robert F. Kennedy's campaign.

The most immediate means by which information traversed regional borders was, of course, the television. But this venue, too, was limited in its offerings, and, unless a network made the extraordinary decision to preempt its regular programming, not all that immediate. In big cities, you could watch the local news at six and then choose from three nightly newscasts, aired at the same time every night by the same three networks. But if a story unfolding elsewhere in the country hadn't appeared in your morning paper, and if it didn't rate a mention that night by one of the three somber-sounding anchormen who spoke from the pixelated ether like gods from some distant civilization, then it essentially didn't exist, as far as you knew.

Within about a decade or so of Gary Hart's spectacular collapse, new technologies—first the satellite revolution that made twenty-four-hour news possible, and then the advent of the Internet and the rapid spread of broadband technology—would obliterate this old order, creating a new world of instantaneous and borderless information. But the first signs of change, what you might call the advance guard of the communications revolution, were just beginning to arrive on the scene in 1987.

CNN, which was still in its infancy, had burst into the national consciousness when it carried the only live footage of the space shuttle *Challenger* exploding moments after launch in January 1986. Later that same year, Fox audaciously unveiled a fourth American broadcast network to compete with the giants who had monopolized the airways since the golden age of radio: ABC, NBC, and CBS. Fox's first prime-time lineup, built around the sitcom *Married . . . with Children* and a sketch comedy show hosted by the comedienne Tracey Ullman (and featuring a recurring cartoon called *The Simpsons*) debuted about a week before Hart gave his announcement speech at Red Rocks. Within a few years, both of these ventures—the offspring of two visionary media moguls, Ted Turner and Rupert Murdoch—would lead the way toward a more diversified media landscape, and one that often blurred the boundaries between news and entertainment.

The first technological innovation to erode the dominance of institutional media, however, and the one that made its impact felt almost immediately during that tumultuous first week of May 1987, had nothing to do with television. It was the series of clicks, whirs, and beeps known as the fax machine.

Faxes had been proliferating, commercially, since the early 1980s, but it had only been in recent years—since the 1984 campaign, in fact—that Japanese manufacturers had managed to make them small and inexpensive enough for your average office, and even for some homes. "From office workers to rock stars, more and more people are answering yes to the question, Do you have a fax?" *Time* reported in August 1987. "Once considered too bulky and costly to be practical, fax machines have shrunk to half the size of personal computers and dropped sharply in price, to less than $1,000 for one model." According to *Time,* it cost $14 to send a one-page letter through an overnight carrier but only 50 cents to fax it instantly through your phone line. Sharp had even introduced a model that could double as an ordinary phone.

The implications of this, for news and politics, were enormous. In 1987, a Republican operative named Doug Bailey teamed up with a Democratic strategist, Roger Craver, to create something called *The Hotline*—a nonideological compendium of political news from the various papers around the country, plus some polling and late-night political jokes, faxed directly to subscribers every morning. (During that first year, according to an obituary of Bailey that appeared in *The New York Times* after his death in 2013, prospective customers always asked him three questions: "You're going to do what?," "You want me to pay how much?," and "What's a fax?") In a few years, *The Hotline* would become as much required reading in Washington as any of the big newspapers or magazines, and virtually every news bureau and political office in town would pay thousands of dollars to get it. Purchased by the *National Journal* in 1996, it formed the template for all the web-based aggregators that would later come along to replace it, from blogs and newsletters to *The Huffington Post* and *Politico*'s "Playbook."

Hart's lead advance man in 1987, Michael Stratton, had taken to carrying around what was known in those days as a portable tele-copier machine—essentially a bulky, primitive version of the all-in-one machines that would later be commonplace in home offices. The machine enabled him, if everything worked just right, to send revised schedules or local news clippings to Denver and Washington instantaneously, rather than relying on overnight mail that might show up after the campaign had already left town. Press aides used a fax machine to do what campaigns had never been able to do with telephones—blast their statements out to a hundred media organizations at once, simply by programming a list of newsroom phone numbers into the machine and walking away.

In effect, fax technology did in a limited and rudimentary way what blogs and social media would do twenty years later. It enabled large numbers of people outside the elite media to get and exchange information, and it vastly reduced the amount of time it took for that information to get around. This is how Hart's staff at the Denver headquarters got their copy of the *Herald*'s exposé on that first Sunday morning in May, with aides standing around in suspended dread as the machine slowly spat out the instrument of their fate. And it's how they sent Dixon the typed statement he would read on the steps of Broadhurst's townhouse that morning, after he and his team in Denver had gone over what he should say. When we met in Madison, Dixon gave me the yellowed, crinkly fax sheet he had saved in a box for a quarter century, with a time stamp of 9:19 a.m. and a name he had scribbled underneath the typed, four-paragraph statement: "Miss Donna Rice."

The fax was also how the *Herald*'s story found its way into newsrooms around the country well before the wire services that served most local papers even had a chance to assess it. When the *Herald*'s Jim McGee went to Broadhurst's townhouse late Sunday morning after the story had been published, to try to interview the woman he had spied in Hart's home the night before, he was surprised to find a reporter from *The Denver Post*'s Washington bureau knocking on the door. (No one answered.) Reporters weren't accustomed to news ricocheting across time zones that fast. In retrospect, this sighting was the first visible drop of rain in a violent storm system that was just at that moment beginning to coalesce in newsrooms around the country.

Nowhere, probably, was that drop in air pressure more acutely felt than at the legendary headquarters of *The Washington Post*, a few blocks north of McPherson Square. Ten years after the cinematic adaptation of *All the President's Men*, the *Post* was now widely considered the premier political paper in the country, and the only one ever to force a president from office. The *Post* and its celebrated editor, Ben Bradlee, now immortalized in the public mind by Jason Robards in the film, did not like to get beat on major, breaking stories involving presidential candidates. They especially didn't like to get beat on stories unfolding in their own city, in this case a ten-minute subway ride from the newsroom, by some beachfront paper whose readers probably thought the Watergate was a swim-up bar.

Paul Taylor, the *Post*'s man on Hart, got the call at his home in Bethesda, Maryland, early Sunday afternoon. An editor proceeded to read him the *Herald* story in its entirety. Any reporter who has ever worked a competitive beat knows the sinking sensation Taylor had to feel as another journalist's breathless prose tumbled out at him like accusations over the phone line—the embarrassment of being blindsided by a rival, the instinct to rationalize it away, the desolation as you realize that the next twenty-four hours, at least, are going to be spent slogging through the muddy tracks left by some other intrepid reporter. And then, in Taylor's case, the question that had vexed him for months and that must have occurred to him again the minute he hung up the phone and regained his equilibrium: Was this really the kind of story you wanted to own?

There was nothing fortuitous or stealthy about Taylor's rise to the top of the political journalism establishment, nothing that even hinted at a lucky break. He seemed destined for it. If the new generation of idealistic, highly educated, *professional* journalists had needed a standard-bearer, Taylor could easily have filled the role.

Although he still talked a little like the Brooklyn native that he was (fast and lyrical, as if litigating a dispute over cab fare), Taylor had spent much of his early childhood in Japan and Vietnam, where his dad worked as an American diplomat. He went to Yale and ran the *Yale Daily News,* did his prerequisite couple of years of training at the highly regarded *Winston-Salem Journal* in the early 1970s, and then latched on with *The Philadelphia Inquirer,* where by

1980 he was the paper's top campaign reporter, wooed by both the *Times* and the *Post*. Most reporters who joined the *Post* from other papers had to punch their tickets on metro or some other less than glamorous section, where the paper stockpiled a warehouse worth of younger reporters whose life's ambition was to ride the campaign bus. Taylor, at thirty-two, walked in the door—cool and confident, looking like a young Elliott Gould—as a roving national political reporter. By the end of the '84 campaign, he was the heir apparent to David Broder, the *Post*'s marquee columnist and elder statesman.

And so, naturally, as the next campaign approached, Taylor drew the best assignment in the newsroom. Hart was his guy.

Initially, at least, Taylor thought he and the front-runner had, in his words, "hit it off." This is how he put it in the book he would write immediately after the 1988 campaign, titled *See How They Run*. In that little remembered but thoughtful and highly readable account, Taylor offered this cringingly honest description of his own report-ing style: "I'm a 'good cop' interviewer. I try to ease, tease, coax and wheedle information from sources. With body language, facial expression, tone of voice and other verbal and nonverbal cues, I hope to let them know that I see the same world they see; that I empathize with them; that, beneath my aloof reporter's exterior, I may even secretly admire them." It's doubtful that a politician as experienced and perceptive as Hart was taken in by the "I'm your biggest fan" routine (most politicians are, if nothing else, better instantaneous readers of people than we often give them credit for), but he always appreciated a well-read journalist who seemed actually to be listen-ing, and he liked Taylor enough to sit through several interviews and a long dinner in 1986.

However calculated his approach might have been, Taylor found himself drawn to Hart for much the same reason E. J. Dionne found him compelling: there was a part of Hart that was journalistic in temperament. He had an ability—an inclination, even—to take himself out of the action and see the entire political process as an observer, to appreciate the absurdity of the political spectacle in a way that a sophisticated reporter could appreciate.

But then something shifted. In early March, six weeks or so before his official announcement, Hart gave a speech at the Maryland statehouse, and afterward Taylor rode with him and Billy Shore in the back of a car to the private airstrip nearby. Notebook flipped open, Taylor started asking him why people perceived Hart to be a loner, and why he didn't have the support of his colleagues in the Senate, and why he wasn't having much success lining up endorsements. And you can imagine how this played with Hart, who divided the political world into two camps: those few who got that he was running a nontraditional, idea-driven, antiestablishment campaign, and all the rest, who could only see the narrower political reality. As Hart would have seen it, Taylor had been talking to him for a year, and yet somehow he *still* didn't get it! He thought Hart needed to line up the establishment behind him, as if this were 1960, when that was precisely the thing that would make him most vulnerable to an insurgent campaign.

Taylor slid into the role of political counselor, in the way that some journalists will; he suggested that Hart should be forcibly extracting endorsements by telling party leaders that the proverbial train was leaving the station and demanding that they get on board. Hart couldn't contain his contempt. "That's so ridiculous!" Hart blurted, according to Taylor's account of the conversation. "Nobody does it. Nobody does it anymore! If they do, they're either going to get a punch in the nose or a horse laugh."

"I wondered," Taylor later wrote, "Do I know him well enough to tell him, 'Cut the crap'? Or is it possible he's serious?" Of course, Hart couldn't have been more serious if he'd been ordering a nuclear strike, and Taylor wisely chose discretion.

Taylor walked away from that encounter feeling that his relationship with Hart had been poisoned. Hart now saw him, he concluded, as "a prisoner of the Washington mind-set—a small-bore, nearsighted, all-tactics political junkie." Taylor, who not surprisingly considered himself a creative and complex thinker, found the implication deeply insulting. It would probably be too much to say that this one moment, in which Hart allowed his resentment of the pack mentality to undo his budding relationship with an important reporter, changed the course of events that were about to unfold. But certainly Hart had squandered a reservoir of goodwill that, looking back on it later, might have been crucial.

The other thing Taylor took away from the conversation was that the normally placid Hart was clearly anxious now—that all the background chatter about his character, this business about the weirdness and the "womanizing," was pulling his internal strings ever tighter as the actual campaign approached. Like the other reporters who followed Hart closely, Taylor had long heard the rumors about, say, Hart having women in his hotel rooms on the road, and he accepted them as largely, if not entirely, true. Only recently, he'd heard a story from a trusted source in Texas who said that Hart had invited the hostess of a fundraiser to his hotel room for a thank-you lunch the next day, and that the hostess in question had since been telling anyone who would listen that she had enjoyed a fling with the next president.

Taylor wasn't quite sure what to do with such leads. He was, by his own self-reckoning, an explainer of the larger political and policy debates, rather than someone who spent a lot of time digging for hidden fragments of truth. There was no context, really, in which Taylor could imagine himself staking out a candidate's house the way Fiedler later did. At the same time, if Hart's character was going to become a central issue in the primary campaign, then could the *Post* simply clap its hands over its ears and pretend the campaign was about something else?

In early April, about a month before the *Herald*'s exposé, Taylor and a group of senior editors and reporters sat down in Ben Bradlee's office to discuss this dilemma. That Bradlee ended up the man to preside over such a meeting was ironic, to put it mildly. In his youth, as *Newsweek*'s dashing Washington bureau chief, Bradlee had lived next door to then senator John Kennedy, and their children had played together. Later, when Kennedy occupied the White House, Bradlee and his wife were frequent dinner guests, and when Kennedy was fatally shot in 1963, Bradlee comforted his shocked widow at Bethesda Naval Hospital, where they brought the president's body to be autopsied. Bradlee would always maintain that he hadn't known about any of Kennedy's extramarital activities (even though rumors had been rampant, and it was later revealed that Bradlee's own sister-in-law, who was mysteriously murdered in 1964, had been one of Kennedy's liaisons). But probably no journalist alive better embodied the last era of political coverage, where politicians trusted journalists to observe certain boundaries, and where journalists expected politicians to be both human and accessible.

The journalists assembled around Bradlee's desk wrestled with a series of questions that would have been imponderable in Kennedy's day, and which could have consumed an entire yearlong course in any journalism school. In his post-campaign book, Taylor summarized them this way:

> If a candidate for president is believed to be a womanizer, but there's no suggestion that his sexual activities have ever interfered with his public duties, is it even worth investigating, much less publishing? Is there a statute of limitations, or is screwing around in the past tense just as newsworthy as in the present? Is a series of one-night stands more reportable than a single long-term extramarital affair? Does it matter if a candidate has an open-marriage understanding with his spouse? Is Hart a special case, or if we begin looking into his mating habits, must we do the same with everyone else running for president?

Taylor recalled that he and his colleagues also spent some time discussing the extreme difficulty of even reporting such a story. The two people having the affair wouldn't talk, and corroborating witnesses would be almost impossible to come by, and "most reporters don't want to be Peeping Toms." (As it turned out, of course, the operative word there was "most.")

And then there was the Woodward issue to consider. The way Woodward always told the story, yes, Hart had crashed at his place during his first separation from Lee, but it's not like they were acting out the Odd Couple or something; Hart was over at a girlfriend's most of the time and basically used Woodward's place as a forwarding address. After some weeks of this, Woodward grew uneasy and asked his buddy Gary to camp elsewhere, and that was the extent of it. Still, if everyone in Bradlee's office knew this story, that meant that half of Capitol Hill did, too. And if the *Post* ignored the constant gossip about Hart, and it later came to light that he was still fooling around, then the paper might face allegations that it essentially took a pass in order to spare Woodward's buddy—and perhaps even Woodward himself—any embarrassment.

It was Broder, the voice of experience and wisdom, who formulated a compromise. The *Post* would shortly be in the process of compiling its in-depth profiles of all the candidates, which by that time was a quadrennial rite. There was no need, Broder suggested, for the *Post* to start hunting around in every candidate's sex life just because the issue was swirling around Hart. What they needed to do was commence their exhaustive reporting on Hart's profile and see what came up. If the reporter assigned to the piece decided there was any troubling pattern of behavior when it came to women, something that called Hart's judgment or stability into question, they could figure out how to deal with it then.

"In ways that I thought were very inappropriate, the fact that he had a womanizing problem was becoming part of who he was as a candidate and now the front-runner coming into this next presidential campaign," Taylor reflected when we talked many years later. "I was very uncomfortable with that. And at the *Post,* we said, You know, we're not going to go there, and it's irresponsible to present it that way. It's rumormongering. But we can't close our eyes to the fact that that's part of the world we know very well—the journalists, the candidates, the consultants, the opponents, Hart's own staff. It's all part of their world. It's real, in that sense. It may well make its way into becoming part of this thing. So let's see what there is."

As it happened, the reporter assigned to do the Hart profile, the talented David Maraniss, was at that point wrapping up another assignment. He was just turning his sights on Hart when the *Herald* story hit.

There was an assumption inherent in the *Post*'s deliberations, which was that the *Post,* along with a handful of other elite news organizations, would be the ones who got to decide whether Hart's personal life should be an issue of national prominence or not. That's pretty much how it had worked, to that point, in political journalism. If the *Post* or the *Times* or *The Wall Street Journal*—or, to a lesser extent, the three broadcast networks, who tended to follow the lead of the major print outlets—didn't think a story rose to the level of serious news, then it remained a regional story or an unreported rumor. Bradlee had every reason to be deliberate before reaching a determination on Hart's "pattern of behavior," because he and a small group of other editors ultimately set the agenda for everyone else, no matter what a less influential paper like the *Herald* had to say about it.

That's also why it was possible to think, if you woke up in Washington that Monday morning, May 4, that the story about Hart and Donna Rice, which was now twenty-four hours old, might be short-lived. Taylor had coauthored a piece about the allegations on the *Post*'s Monday front page, but it didn't do much to legitimize the *Herald* piece as important news. NEWSPAPER STAKEOUT INFURI-ATES HART, the headline declared, followed by the subhead: "Report on Female House Guest Called Character Assassination." The *Times*, meanwhile, included a small item inside the national section, the tone of which suggested that editors had placed it there with a pair of tongs so as not to sully themselves. Dixon still found himself surrounded, at Billy Broadhurst's place, by reporters and camera crews, but this was an assemblage of political reporters, most of whom still felt uneasy about the story and who readily observed the traditional rules of decorum.

By that point, however, it was becoming clear that outside Washington something else was happening—something entirely unfamiliar in the political media. Until that moment, you have to remember, Hollywood and its attendant paparazzi had existed in a separate universe from the coverage of American campaigns. No tabloid photographer bothered stalking some boring politician or trying to snap a photo of him in a bathing suit—who would have paid for such a pathetic picture, anyway? But now, as Neil Postman had so brilliantly predicted in *Amusing Ourselves to Death*, the lines between entertainment and politics had become harder to discern. The more political coverage focused on the personalities of candidates, and the more those candidates tried to broaden their own celebrity by showing up on the sets of TV shows, the more *People* and the *National Enquirer* started to think of them as stars in a national drama, just like Jim and Tammy Faye Bakker. As Warren Beatty had understood and tried to explain to Hart, the same paparazzi who had already made privacy obsolete in Hollywood were readying for an incursion onto political turf. All they needed was a reason.

The first sign came Sunday, sometime around noon, at the cabin in Troublesome Gulch. That's when the wave of newfangled satellite trucks lumbered up the gravel drive like a line of tanks rumbling through the desert, disturbing the quiet hum of spring. Lee had taken the weekend off from the campaign trail, because she had a sinus infection that had swollen half her face, and she couldn't fly. Hart had called her Saturday night from Washington to say that there was an ugly story coming, but that he'd done nothing wrong, and Lee told him she believed in him and didn't need the details. But nobody was going to believe that if they saw her puffy face on TV, as if she'd been up all night bawling.

And so, surrounded by her daughter and a bevy of girlfriends who arrived to see her through, Lee hid in the kitchen as these TV trucks barricaded her inside her own home, the telephone on the kitchen wall her only means of reaching her husband or the outside world. (Among the few outsiders who called the cabin to check on her during this time was Hart's rival Jesse Jackson—an act of compassion Lee would never forget.) The words "crowd control" and "perimeter" weren't part of the standard political lexicon in 1987; Lee simply watched through the kitchen window, like some heroine in a zombie movie, as each new photographer to arrive tried to scale her fence or climb a tree just fifty yards from where she stood.

Alarmed by Lee's panicked calls to headquarters, John Emerson grabbed Joe Trippi, the deputy political director, and gave him an instant (if dubious) promotion: chief of staff to the candidate's wife. Trippi's job was to secure the premises and, ultimately, to get Lee out of Troublesome Gulch without her being chased down the mountain by careening camera trucks. Thus it's fair to say that Trippi, who was thirty at the time, became the first campaign operative in American history to personally confront the collision of politics and tabloid media and the sudden mobilization of a satellite-wielding army.

Trippi would forever remember being accosted by a guy, as he tried to get through the front gate, who identified himself as a reporter for *A Current Affair*. The syndicated show, hosted by the gossipy Maury Povich, had started airing a year earlier. Trippi, whose mind was on his candidate's alleged adultery—and who, like most political operatives, had never heard of anything called *A Current Affair*—was incredulous. "You mean they have an entire *show* for that now?" he stammered.

If anybody swept up in this whole fiasco should have understood how to navigate the rabid, explosive culture of celebrity media, you would think it would have been Donna Rice. She had dated Don Henley and Prince Albert of Monaco, had appeared on numerous soap operas and TV dramas, including *Miami Vice* and the outrageously popular *Dallas*. She was represented by agents in New York and Miami. If you were writing the purely fictional account of the Hart scandal, you might imagine Rice in the mold of Nicole Kidman's character in the movie *To Die For*—gorgeous and manipulative, lusting for stardom, indifferent to how she got there or who got trampled in the process.

In reality, Rice was, as she described herself, a "typical Southern girl"—a former Miss South Carolina and head cheerleader, yes, but also a magna cum laude and Phi Beta Kappa graduate of the University of South Carolina, with a major in biology and a minor in business, and her district's top saleswoman of Wyeth products. She felt swept away by Hart, despite only having known him for a few weeks, and the last thing she wanted was to hurt his campaign, about which she knew almost nothing. When the reporters started congregating at Broadhurst's townhouse, Rice repeatedly begged to talk to Hart, who was the only one in the bunch she trusted. She wanted to tell him that she hadn't had anything to do with tipping off the *Herald,* and then she wanted to go home.

So did Armandt. Unlike Rice, she knew exactly how the *Herald* guys had come to be at Hart's townhouse, and you can only imagine how uncomfortable she must have been holed up in Broadhurst's place, like a mob informant at the moment when the cops show up. Before she managed to make her escape, however, Armandt had a private chat with Broadhurst, and then Broadhurst sat Rice down for a serious talk. He told her the campaign had a sensitive question for her: Was there anything embarrassing in her past, anything at all that might surface in the hours ahead?

Rice steeled herself. She really did want to help Hart. So she offered up two deeply personal and painful facts about her life that not even her parents or most of her closest friends knew. First, she had an ex-boyfriend who was in jail for drug charges. And second, a fashion photographer in Miami had once taken photos of her wrapped in an American flag, with a half of one breast exposed. And there it was—the seamy lining of her life, turned inside out. Broadhurst prevailed on her to repeat her admissions for Dixon and a few other campaign aides. From that moment on, Rice felt that, as far as the Hart people were concerned, she was the one on trial, the one whose character was suspect.

In exchange for these tidbits about herself, Rice wanted only one thing. She pleaded with Broadhurst not to let the campaign release her name to the media. All she wanted was to escape this thing without anybody knowing who she was or trying to ask her questions about it. She was devastated when, on the phone a few hours later, her mother asked her why she was all over the TV news and what was going on; in the interest of getting all the facts out at once, the campaign had released her name. By that time, the paparazzi were already arriving at Rice's condo in Miami, waiting to ambush her. Her parents' house in South Carolina would soon be surrounded, too. The Hart team pressed her for the name of someone who could "run interference" for her—meaning a family lawyer or an agent. Rice had no idea what that meant. She had no one like that. Most normal people didn't.

There was no page in the political manual—at least not yet—for what to do with a woman in Rice's position. So there, too, the Hart team had to improvise. They flew in Sue Casey, Hart's scheduler and longtime aide, who was around Rice's age, and had Casey stay with her Sunday night in a hotel at Dulles Airport, then fly with her back to Miami. Dixon had enlisted the help of Tom McAliley, a cigar-chomping trial lawyer and raconteur who was Hart's point man in Florida, and McAliley met the two women at the airport Monday morning and spirited Rice directly to his office. McAliley's plan was first to assemble about a half dozen handpicked reporters and let them question Rice in his conference room. Rice pleaded with him to spare her this ordeal and let her go home, but she was like a captive now; she had promised to do whatever they needed her to do if it would make all of this go away. McAliley had to sequester her in his office, because the photographers and reporters had started to besiege the building. When Rice made the mistake of trying to use the women's room by herself, they descended on her like a pack of wolves, right there in the hallway.

It stung Rice, then and for all the many years after, to find that the reporters gathered in McAliley's conference room already knew both of the embarrassing, intimate details of her life she had shared, privately, with the campaign. Clearly, Hart's people had decided to get out in front of any further disclosures. But outwardly, Rice never seemed rattled. Rather, she was eerily disarming, sweet, relaxed. "I was a professional," she told me many years later, by which she meant that she had learned, as an actress, to set aside her fear and read her lines.

Right up front, according to notes from the session that later ended up in the AP archives, Rice said she was nervous, and she tried to impress upon the reporters that she was a serious person, someone who once "had the opportunity to go to any graduate school I wanted to." She said she hadn't spent the night at Hart's place, but rather had left by the back door, just as Dixon had been saying. She said they were "pals," nothing more, that she preferred younger men, and that "if I had felt there were anything more in his intentions I would have been very upset." (This last bit was, to put it nicely, a complete lie.) "If there had been something fishy," she cannily assured the reporters, "we would have been sneaking around."

When they asked her outright if she'd had "sexual relations" with Hart, Rice was as direct and final as she could be. "No" was her answer—three separate times. As if to call this answer further into question, however, Rice did confirm for the reporters a rumor that had been circulating ever since the *Herald* had heard from its tipster about photographs taken on a private yacht. At McAliley's urging, Rice told the media contingent about the chartered boat and the overnight stay in Bimini, which she described as innocent, but which guaranteed another daily news cycle of salacious headlines.

Twenty-six years later, Rice still wouldn't say how much of her performance that day had been just that—mere performance, rather than the truth. But she allowed that she had been eager to prove that she wasn't the one who had betrayed Hart. "I did what I felt like I had to do based on a difficult situation that I was put in, that I never should have been in," she told me. "I shared the information that I was expected to share and that was in the best interests of the campaign."

Afterward, Rice returned at last to her dockside condo in North Bay Village and was stunned by what she returned *to*. Cameramen blocked the entrance and shot through her windows from rented boats in the waterway. A helicopter hovered overhead. Neighbors had rented their apartments to reporters. Unable to go out, she tried to order pizza, but the delivery guy was practically mugged at the entrance and didn't make it upstairs. McAliley had scheduled a larger news conference for the next day; he said the only way for Rice to get her normal life back was to meet the full force of the media head-on and exhaust their curiosity. But sitting in her condo, where she sought advice from a friend who worked in Hollywood public relations, Rice understood all too clearly that her normal life wasn't coming back. She called McAliley and told him to cancel Tuesday's news conference. She wasn't talking to anyone else.

Later, when all of this was a distant memory, Donna Rice would say that she was lucky to have been thrown into the hands of Tom McAliley, a man who, despite his obvious interest in Hart's political success, came to be a kind of father figure to her in the months and years after the scandal. (McAliley died from an aneurysm in 1994.) He told Rice it was fine if she didn't want to hold a news conference, but she couldn't stay in Miami, barricaded in her building with only a doorman for protection. The next morning, he had a staff member shepherd her through the media crush and drive her to the airport, chased at high speed by a TV crew. McAliley had a private plane waiting, and Rice got on board and anxiously strapped herself in. She had no idea where she was bound.

Whenever Hart came through New York, he preferred to stay with his *Times* pal Sydney Gruson on the Upper East Side. As it happened, Gruson was holding a dinner party for some other elite Manhattanites Monday night. So it came as quite a jolt to his guests when the front door opened, midway through dinner, and in walked the most talked about man in America at the moment, who was said to be in seclusion and not making any public comment. (Hart had his own key to the place.) Hart called out a hello to Gruson and waved mischievously to the dinner guests, taking a moment to savor the stunned expressions on their faces, before heading to the back bedroom where he could work in peace. It was the last bit of tranquillity Hart would know for some time.

After all, Hart wasn't in Washington anymore; this was New York, center of the media world and the hub of tabloid journalism in particular. And what was waiting for him in New York made the chaotic scenes in Troublesome Gulch and Miami look like bingo night at the rest home. Stratton, the lead advance man on the campaign, had worked for Hart, on and off, since 1974 and was now embarking on his third presidential campaign, but he had never seen anything like what he encountered Tuesday morning when he tried to deliver Hart to the Waldorf-Astoria, where the newspaper publishers were meeting. Camera crews blocked his car's path, while paparazzi photographers literally hurled themselves onto the windshield. It was more like a perp walk than a grand entrance.

Inside, Hart sat on the dais next to his fellow senator and presidential hopeful on the Republican side, Bob Dole, staring out at hundreds of newspaper executives and almost as many reporters who had overwhelmed the ballroom and were standing in a crush at the back. Dole had accepted that there was going to be little focus on economics at the lunch, and even less on himself. "Hell of a deal, Gary, hell of a deal," Dole said, shaking his head.

As Hart sat there, squinting into the overhead lights and waiting for his turn to speak, he noticed a familiar, carefully coiffed figure enter the balcony, where a lot of the broadcast crews had claimed their turf. He stared harder in disbelief. Could that really be *Tom*— Tom Brokaw, that is—getting ready to do a stand-up? The same Brokaw who, along with his wife, had dined, in happier times, with the Harts in Washington? Who was enough of a personal friend to have exchanged Christmas presents with Hart? Tuesday, coincidentally, was the first day of the long anticipated congressional hearings on the Iran-contra scandal back in Washington, and yet here was a serious man like Tom Brokaw, the sole anchor of *NBC Nightly News,* choosing instead to cover a banquet in New York where Hart might or might not make his first public comments about an alleged sexual encounter with a small-time actress. Hart's gloom deepened.

His plan at the luncheon, aside from delivering the economics lecture he had come there to deliver, was to drive a wedge between the serious media and the outliers—to appeal to the sense of idealism and decency he had long known to be lurking under the tough hides of men like Sydney Gruson and Jack Germond and Tom Brokaw, too. That Hart had been handed this opportunity—that he found himself, by quirk of the calendar, appearing before an assemblage from the very industry that now controlled his fate—seemed a stroke of providence too precious to waste. Arrayed before him were the leading executives of what was still at that time the dominant source of news in America, and surely they could be made to see the folly of letting a single, midsize newspaper change all the rules of political journalism, of allowing any sense of privacy to be obliterated by an impossibly narrow definition of "character." Surely, if he laid out his case succinctly and persuasively, as he knew how to do better than anyone in politics, the publishers—and even the reporters hovering in the shadows behind them—would swing his way.

The public, Hart felt sure, already had. Polling in the first days after the story broke showed that Hart was still the overwhelming favorite among Democratic voters. In a Gallup poll commissioned by *Newsweek* that week and published the following weekend, a majority of Democrats (55 percent) thought he was telling the truth about what happened, and a plurality (44 percent) described themselves as unconcerned about it. Fifty-three percent of voters overall said marital infidelity had nothing to do with a candidate's ability to handle the presidency; 64 percent thought the media was being unfair to Hart; and 70 percent said they disapproved of the media using covert surveillance. If Hart thought he was winning, it's because, at that point, he surely was.

"Last weekend, a newspaper published a misleading and false story that hurt my family and other innocent people and reflected badly on my character," Hart told the publishers when he at last took center stage. "This story was written by reporters who, by their own admission, undertook a spotty surveillance, who reached inaccurate conclusions based on incomplete facts, who, after publishing a false story, now concede they may have gotten it wrong. And who, most outrageously, refused to interview the very people who could have given them the facts before filing their story, which we asked and urged them to do."

Hart blasted the *Herald* reporters for going to press before even interviewing the woman involved, even though he said they were offered the chance. And then he waded ever so tentatively into the filmy waters of his personal life, which he still believed should be walled off from intrusion. He noted his twenty-eight-year marriage to Lee, whom he described as "a woman with an inexhaustible reservoir of affection, caring and patience," and said they had come through their separations with a stronger marriage. Then he turned the harsh interrogation light, again, on his listeners.

"You, ladies and gentlemen, have the honor of leading the only industry singled out for protection under the Constitution of the

United States," Hart said, his granite chin held high in defiance. "That signifies enormous power. But it also places upon each of you a very heavy responsibility. What is right and truthful? In that spirit, I hope you'll ask yourselves some searching questions: about what is right and what is truthful; about the propriety of a newspaper conducting a questionable and inadequate surveillance of one presidential candidate; about whether the urgency of meeting a deadline is subordinate to hearing the truth; and about whether it's right or good journalism to draw an extraordinary conclusion before hearing some rather ordinary facts."

Hart warned that the time was coming when the voters would demand fairness from their media. "As I struggle to retain my integrity and my honor—and believe me, I will—I hope you will also struggle to save our political system from all of its worst instincts," he said. "For that is the real issue. Not one person's public career, but a nation's public life."

Near the end of this hastily written preamble, Hart tried to strike a delicate balance—between showing some grudging contrition for his own behavior, on one hand, and making clear he had no intention of being derailed by it, on the other. At that time, the public apology was not yet the staple of political discourse and scandal recovery it would become in ensuing years. And while Hart intended to take his share of the responsibility, he was hardly the guy to set some new standard in groveling before his inquisitors.

He concluded:

Since the very first day I entered public life, I have always held myself to a high standard of public and private conduct, and I always will. But the events of the past few days have also taught me that, for some of us in public life, even the most commonplace, appropriate behavior can be misconstrued by some to be improper. This just means that I have to raise my own personal standard even higher.

Did I make a mistake by putting myself in circumstances that could be misconstrued? Of course I did. That goes without saying. Did I do anything immoral? I absolutely did not.

Those who seek national leadership submit themselves to many tests of personal character and fortitude, of integrity and substance, but also of determination and will, of commitment to the nation's interest. I'm here today to restate my intention to insist that whatever may be delivered by the more brutal side of politics, this contest must and will focus on this nation's future. For that and that alone is what's at stake in 1988.

Satisfied with his argument, Hart plunged forcefully into his economics plan. He and his staff had worked on the speech for weeks, and it was one of the rare occasions where the uneasy speechwriters and policy aides were the ones who kept wanting to revise it, while the candidate reassured them that they had gotten it right; usually, it was the other way around.

Hart began by making the case that the nation's problems were not cyclical, as they seemed, but rather "fundamental and structural in nature"—that the country had yet to come to terms with the winding down of its industrial dominance, the decay of its infrastructure and public education systems, the accumulation of public and private debt. He went on to reject both the liberal vision of limitless public spending and the conservative vision of limited government, calling instead for deficit reduction balanced with new investment. He offered some innovative ideas, like the "individual training accounts" for workers who wanted to learn skills for the new economy and the military reforms he had championed for a decade, which he argued would reduce spending while also making the country safer and more prepared for the post–Cold War era. It was a speech—a platform of policies—years ahead of its time, an agenda that neatly presaged the two decades of political debate that followed.

But of course, by that point, no one in the room was listening; Hart might as well have been reading aloud from *The Chronicles of Narnia,* for all anyone cared. Twenty-five years later, you could Google Hart's preamble about his sex life in about six seconds, but there was no record anywhere of the actual speech he gave that day. Even Hart's closest aides—hell, even Hart himself—couldn't say with any certainty later whether he had actually gone through with the economics part of his program or just scrapped it altogether. I was able to read it only after Mark Steitz, a policy aide at the time, went to the trouble of tracking down an ancient version written in WordPerfect and preserved on a hard drive.

Instead, when at last he finished to polite applause, and it came time for the question-and-answer portion of the program, Hart found himself drawn inexorably into a debate with the nation's leading publishers about the calls he had made to Donna Rice (they were about fundraising, Hart lied), and about Bimini (Hart, like Rice, said they slept on separate boats). His answers satisfied no one. They sounded small and evasive.

Somehow, even as he lectured them on their responsibilities, Hart had assumed that the largely conservative, older businessmen who ran America's papers, these pillars of civic life in their communities, would see the reason in his appeal, that they would not want their money used by a new breed of reporter to snoop around in front hedges and alleyways, trying to expose private behavior that most of these men themselves would be in no position to vilify. What he hadn't counted on, though, was the tribalism of the media, especially after Watergate, when an American president had effectively declared war on the entire Fourth Estate. Hart had gone after one of their own, publicly and pointedly, and the publishers were now scrambling to honor their unspoken mutual defense pact. You couldn't hope to make this about the behavior of a single newspaper or a couple of reporters; an attack on the *Herald* was an attack on all of them.

In short order, the *Herald*'s fifty-one-year-old publisher, Dick Capen, rose from the audience to speak. (Capen, a staunch Republican and social conservative, would later be made ambassador to Spain by George H. W. Bush, which did little to quiet the conspiracy theories among Hart loyalists.) "The issue is not the *Miami Herald*," Capen said. "It's Gary Hart's judgment." The utter disrespect in this one line was hard to miss. Capen was talking about "Gary Hart"— not "Senator Hart"—as if he weren't even in the room. He meant not to counter Hart's speech so much as to hijack it altogether.

"He's an announced candidate for president of the United States, and he's a man who knows full well that womanizing had been an issue in his past," Capen went on. "We stand by the essential correctness of our story. It's possible that, at some point along the way, someone could have moved out of the alley door of his house. But the fact of the matter remains that our story reported on Donna Rice, who he met in Aspen, who he subsequently met in Dade County—he acknowledged that he telephoned her on a number of occasions. It is a fact that two married men whose spouses were out of town spent a considerable amount of time with these people. It is also true that our reporters saw him and Donna Rice leaving his townhouse on at least three separate occasions."

Capen's soliloquy was remarkable for a couple of reasons. He had now plainly admitted what Fiedler had written, obliquely, the day before—that Bill Dixon was right, and that the *Herald*'s reporters actually had no way of knowing whether Rice had stayed in the townhouse Friday night or not, because they hadn't watched the back door. But Capen had also asserted, for the first time, that it didn't actually matter, because what mattered was precisely the reverse of what the *Herald* had written—that, in fact, Rice had been seen *leaving* the house on several occasions, and it was this, and not her having stayed inside the house with him, that constituted the truly damning evidence. And Hart must have understood, at that point, that he had chosen a field of play on which he couldn't possibly win. Whether Rice had stayed in his townhouse or hadn't, the conclusion was apparently going to be the same.

Hart couldn't get out of that hotel fast enough. And if he didn't know by then that political journalism was changing in ways he couldn't begin to comprehend, he probably got the point when the photographers chased his car from the Waldorf, like something out of the new *Beverly Hills Cop* movie. This time, Stratton was ready; he had set up drivers in two follow cars to obstruct and mislead the cameramen. When the follow cars swerved across Park Avenue to block the route, one of the pursuing vans actually hurdled the median divider in an effort to catch up. Hart was genuinely perplexed, and afraid. As Richard Ben Cramer later relayed it, Hart, in the lead car with Stratton, muttered a question that was probably more philosophical than literal.

"Why do they have to chase me?" he wondered aloud.

Back in the ballroom at the Waldorf, meanwhile, a different kind of chase was on. It was always a matter of time before the press found out what even Hart's aides didn't know—that the name of Don Soffer's chartered yacht was *Monkey Business*. Broadhurst apparently hadn't thought it essential to disclose earlier, and Hart hadn't even remembered. "I didn't look at the name of the boat," Hart would tell me years later, despite having been photographed in a *Monkey Business* T-shirt. "In this whole business of judgment, it was, Didn't this stupid guy know what the name of the boat was? Well, the answer was, No, I didn't. Should I have? Yes. Would I have gotten off it if I'd known what the name was?" He shrugged. "I didn't think about stuff like that. I just didn't think about it."

As luck would have it, this little tidbit had just surfaced in Miami, and thanks to reporters talking to their editors on the hotel pay phones, it was just then ricocheting through the assembled press corps. Whatever solemnity Hart had hoped to inject into the discussion over his personal life had now been cleared from the ballroom as thoroughly as the overcooked chicken and half-empty coffee mugs.

A scene was now unfolding unlike any that had ever been witnessed in the coverage of a presidential campaign. On one side of the cavernous ballroom, Kevin Sweeney was trying to hold off a press pack that Cramer later described as "feral," answering questions about the unfortunately named boat and how Hart had ended up on it. Among the reporters pressing in with tape recorders and shouting inquiries was the *Post*'s Paul Taylor, who demanded to know how it was that Hart had managed a trip to Bimini when he maintained that he hadn't had time to visit his wife.

Simultaneously, about ten yards away, Tom Fiedler found himself surrounded by his own shifting amoeba of cameras and recorders and boom mikes, holding what amounted to a dueling press conference. He had come there, like any other campaign reporter, to cover the story, but by the time Hart finished attacking the *Herald* from the podium, Fiedler had become a central part of it. Later it would seem obvious to Fiedler that he really shouldn't have been there if he didn't want to get personally caught up in the controversy, but like everything else related to the Hart saga, this was only clear in hindsight. Before 1987, no campaign reporter had ever imagined finding himself at the center of the scrum.

In fact, from that moment on, Fiedler was a national star, pictured in the pages of newsweeklies and beamed into millions of living rooms. That night, his name made all the evening news shows and then he appeared live, along with his *Herald* colleague Jim McGee, on ABC's *Nightline,* hosted by Ted Koppel. (The Hart story led the half hour program, followed by a segment on the opening of the Iran-contra hearings.) As he had in the ballroom, Fiedler nervously presented himself as a disinterested reporter who was simply following the story where it led, doing what any reporter would do when tasked with the responsibility of vetting candidates and their character. But Koppel, one of the toughest and most respected newsmen in America, showed little patience for this routine. In fact, he seemed rather disgusted by the entire story.

When Fiedler flippantly tried to dismiss a question about the back door of the townhouse—"If we are conceding that we are not as good as the F.B.I. in conducting a surveillance, I don't think we have any problem agreeing to that," Fiedler joked—Koppel abruptly cut him off.

"Well, hold on," the anchor huffed. "That's kind of cute, but that's not the point. The point is, did she spend the night with him or didn't she spend the night with him? And if, in fact, she left, let's say a half hour after she got there, which is what she claims, then she would not have spent the night with him." Koppel wasn't finished—he also hammered Fiedler about his casual and repeated reference to the supposed "relationship" between Hart and Rice. Decades later, Fiedler would describe this first appearance on national television as one of the worst moments of his life.

As Fiedler was bumbling through his appearance on *Night-*

line, Doug Wilson was waiting at the China Air terminal at Kennedy Airport in New York. Hart's trusted foreign policy advisor, who had negotiated and attended Hart's remarkable meeting in Mikhail Gorbachev's office at the Kremlin five months earlier, had been depressed and expecting the worst from the moment he heard about the *Herald* story Sunday morning. Now, after some hesitation, he was waiting to board a flight for Taiwan, for the start of a long scheduled visit with political leaders in the Far East who were eager to know more about Reagan's likely successor. Lee Hart had been scheduled to go with him, but her sinus infection had made that impossible. So Wilson was leading the small delegation, and he was waiting to be joined at the terminal by one of the campaign's top fundraisers, Weston Frank.

Just before 11:30, Frank burst into the terminal, beaming. He explained breathlessly that Hart, having recovered from his car chase earlier in the day, had just rallied hundreds of supporters with another defiant speech at a fundraiser held by Ted Sorensen, the former Kennedy aide. ("The cause goes on!" Hart had assured them, echoing Ted Kennedy's famous speech at the 1980 convention. "The crusade continues!") Frank was gushing about what a great night it was, about how Hart had turned a corner.

What do you know? Wilson thought to himself, his mood suddenly brightening. Maybe he had been wrong to think that a scandal this tawdry could overtake the candidate's lofty appeal to ideas.

Then Wilson looked up at the mounted TV in the terminal, which wasn't tuned to ABC and Koppel, but rather to NBC and *The Tonight Show Starring Johnny Carson.* Just as the power of a single advertising line—"Where's the beef?"—would probably elude modern media consumers, so, too, might today's fans of Conan O'Brien or Jon Stewart have a hard time understanding the cultural power Carson still possessed in 1987, almost twenty-five years after he took over the show from Jack Paar. In the age of three networks, before ubiquitous cable or the Internet, Carson effectively owned America's last waking moments, after the local newscasts at eleven. Koppel, whose show had quickly become one of the most successful news programs in American history, couldn't begin to compete with Carson when it came to the number of viewers or the sheer power to shape public perception.

So there was Carson, coming out to do the monologue everyone would be talking about tomorrow in the office, before moving on to the night's interviews with George C. Scott and a gymnast named Kristie Phillips. And this is how he started: "By the way, before the monologue begins, if Gary Hart is watching, you might want to hit the 'mute' button on your remote control.

"I really don't need a monologue tonight," Carson said. "I think I'll just bring out and read the front pages of the newspapers around the country. It is getting so wild that people standing in supermarkets are rushing out to buy regular newspapers.

"Now, we have a lot of people here in the studio. Can I ask a favor of you? I am going to ask you tonight to leave by the front entrance because I don't want anyone saying we've spent the night together."

On it went like that, for several minutes, while the studio audience roared. And then Doug Wilson knew with certainty that he hadn't been wrong, after all.

By this time, Bill Dixon was back in Denver. He might have been watching either Koppel or Carson, had he not consciously decided to check out completely from anything that mattered.

In his book, Paul Taylor would write that Dixon had grown despondent when he heard about the Bimini cruise from Rice's news conference, rather than from his own candidate, and that he had fled town in a funk, having concluded that his friend and client had betrayed everything they believed in. This was partly true, but only partly. Dixon had, in fact, heard about the Bimini piece of the story earlier Monday, when he sat Broadhurst down and made him go through the entire story again. "Jesus Christ, Billy," he said, when Broadhurst finally came clean about the pleasure cruise. As a skilled lawyer, Dixon instinctively understood that he needed to get all the facts out, and get them out fast. He had made real progress in the first twenty-four hours after the story broke, identifying the weakness in the *Herald*'s investigation and forcing the paper to take a step back, and now all of that would be lost in another news cycle focused on sex.

But it was a gross oversimplification to assume that Dixon was just angry at Hart when he decided to leave Washington that Monday. He felt then and later that he had no actual evidence that Hart was lying to him, no reason to assume that his friend of fifteen years had made a patsy of him in the press. Dixon wasn't the type to think the worst of someone he admired, and Hart was someone he admired very much.

It was guilt, as much as anything, that knocked the air out of Dixon's lungs. In the months leading up to the announcement, he had gone out and personally recruited a team of brilliant and devoted aides, many of whom had left jobs and sold houses, taken their kids out of school and signed long-term leases—all because Bill Dixon assured them that Hart intended to go all the way, or at least that's how Dixon saw it. And now it was clear that while Dixon was vouching for Hart's seriousness of purpose, Hart was drinking margaritas in Bimini with a model twenty years his junior. It crushed Dixon, the thought that all of the promises he had made might evaporate, because of *this*.

And he was disgusted, too, with a media that seemed to him, just in the last twenty-four hours, to have somehow gone insane. Like Hart, Dixon had known reporters his entire adult life, and felt well served by them. He'd proudly played a key role in the greatest political story of all time, the exposing and punishing of a corrupt president. Were these the same reporters, the ones who were stalking a candidate in the alley behind his home, who were writing speculative stories about what he did in his private time and following his children around to school? Had the world turned completely upside down?

Now he was fielding a rumor every five minutes, it seemed, some fresh call from headquarters or a state supporter who had heard something damning. Hart had been seen hitting on coeds in Florida. Or he had been spotted hounding in Georgia, or with another woman in Washington. For even a fraction of it to be true, Hart would have had to do nothing with his time but hop from one city to the next, bedding any woman he could find, and even then he would probably have had to be cloned. What about the looming threat of nuclear war, Dixon wanted to know? What about the rising number of homeless on America's streets?

It was all of this, Dixon would say many years later, when he finally talked about it at all, that shook the faith from deep in his bones that Monday, left him feeling exhausted and melancholy. There was simply nothing more to be done, nothing more to give. After twenty years in politics, he felt suddenly and shockingly adrift. And so when Dixon landed in Denver Tuesday afternoon, at around the same time Hart was indicting the media at the Waldorf, he didn't go to headquarters to reassure his troops on the front line, who badly needed some reassurance. Instead, he went to his apartment and instructed his twenty-three-year-old son, who was staying with him, to take the phone off the hook. He popped open some beers, turned on a baseball game. He told no one at the campaign where he was or when he might return. For the next two days, while the political universe as he had known it spun apart, Dixon did something utterly unthinkable for a political operative in his position. He disappeared.

And in those first hours of his self-imposed isolation, Dixon made a promise to himself—that he would never again set foot in Washington, a city where a man of Gary Hart's integrity could be effectively executed for nothing but the most trivial transgressions, just for sport. And in all the years that followed, despite the steady flow of invitations to weddings and funerals and even the inauguration of his friend and legal associate Barack Obama, Bill Dixon never broke that vow.

While Fiedler sparred with Koppel on one channel and Carson bitingly ridiculed Hart on the other, the phone rang in Paul Taylor's Manhattan hotel room. The *Post's* political editor, Ann Devroy, was on the line, and filled in her star reporter on the strange things that had been transpiring back in Washington.

In the days after the *Herald* broke its story, the *Post*, like other major papers, had been deluged with anonymous tips of all kinds. One stood out. It was an envelope that contained a private investigator's report. Someone had hired the investigator to tail Hart. And so, on a Saturday in December 1986, days after Hart and Doug Wilson returned from Moscow, the private eye had followed Hart as he gave the Democratic response to Reagan's weekly radio address in a Virginia studio, then to his townhouse and a bookstore, and then finally to the home of a woman who was a well-known lobbyist in town. Hart had apparently spent the night with this woman, who was rumored to have been involved with him on and off for many years, going back to his separations from Lee.

Who sent the envelope, or why, wasn't known. (Bizarrely, Dixon had heard, and campaign aides always believed, that one of Hart's former colleagues in the Senate, Maryland's Joe Tydings, had hired the investigator because he feared that Hart was sleeping with his then wife, who was a close friend of Lee's and worked for her on the campaign. Tydings denied it at the time.) But it was exactly what editors at the *Post* needed in order to reestablish the rightful order of things—the break that might transfer ownership of the entire story over to the nation's most storied political paper. Of course Bradlee knew the woman in the photos personally (or at least he knew someone who knew her), and he even volunteered to confront her and get the truth. The *Post* was waiting on Bradlee's confirmation, and in the meantime Devroy wanted to make sure that Taylor was staying close to Hart, in case he needed to get a quick response from the candidate.

As it happened, Hart had decided to finally confront the press at a news conference the following afternoon, Wednesday, at a hotel in New Hampshire, on the Dartmouth campus—an event he hoped might put the whole affair to rest and allow him to go on campaigning. Taylor arrived in New Hampshire, as he later put it, in an "uncharitable frame of mind" toward the candidate, having overcome whatever qualms he had once had about delving into Hart's personal life. Taylor had been "brooding" on Hart's speech in New York, and he was angry about it. Here Hart might have explained himself, been contrite, shown some humility and candor. But instead, he had chastised the media like you might a kindergarten class, and he had claimed the moral high ground despite the obvious fact—at least it was obvious to Taylor and the other reporters—that he had lied about having sex with Rice. As far as Taylor was concerned, he would later recount in his book, "Hart's protestations that the relationship was strictly platonic were instantly rendered laughable" once the news about Bimini and *Monkey Business* had come out. "The only question was how long it would take him to realize it."

You can imagine that some of Taylor's irritation at the speech was probably residual, too. Even in his moment of disgrace, Hart had somehow managed to affect exactly the condescending tone that had so stung Taylor when he had pressed Hart about endorsements on the tarmac in Maryland months earlier. Once again, Hart's manner suggested that he alone saw the bigger picture but was being forced to endure the smallness of shallow minds.

But it's also not hard for a fellow reporter, looking back through the lens of time, to discern another motive, aside from his own irritation, that Taylor might have had for confronting Hart that Wednesday afternoon at Dartmouth. After talking to Devroy, Taylor had to have sensed that he was on the cusp of a huge story—one that would redeem his paper and might, at the same time, make him more famous than Fiedler had suddenly become. But as it stood, Taylor's impending scoop (if the private investigator's finding could be verified) amounted to little more than a crass story about illicit sex, which was exactly the kind of thing for which he did not imagine himself becoming known. All it would prove was that Hart had been involved with a woman who was not his wife. Hart had never actually claimed unwavering fidelity to Lee—all he had said was that they had been separated and that he wouldn't respond to rumors—and, this being 1987, no one had even considered asking him directly whether he had ever been a disloyal husband.

If Hart could be cornered into denying publicly that he had *ever* stepped out on his wife, however, then the issue of the investigator's report would become much weightier than mere sex. Then Hart would be exposed as a liar and a hypocrite, someone who claimed to hold himself to a "high moral standard" even as he blatantly deceived the press and the public about his "womanizing." That would make him a man of shoddy character whose presidency could imperil the country, just as Nixon's had. If you were already writing that story in your head, as Taylor surely was when he arrived in New Hampshire that afternoon, the difference was clear. A story about Hart having an affair was little more than titillating. But a story that proved he had baldly lied about that same affair could be construed as serious journalism. It was, arguably, a public service.

And so that is precisely what Paul Taylor set out to do, in a way that would shock the political world and forever shift the boundaries of campaign journalism, every bit as much as the *Herald* had.

If the scene in New York had disoriented Hart, then New Hampshire was like some planet with zero gravity, where nothing behaved according to the natural and immutable laws of politics. Actually, the insanity had begun at the airport in Newark, New Jersey, Wednesday morning, even before they got off the ground, when Mike Stratton, who had now hired a group of Pinkerton guards to protect the candidate, had to drive out onto the tarmac to avoid the bevy of photographers and reporters in the terminal; somehow they had learned of the flight Hart was taking and were preparing to board it, like raging barbarians brandishing cardboard tickets instead of swords. Upon boarding the plane with Hart, Stratton, dressed in a suit and tie and possessed of an air of authority, suggested to a flight attendant, with some urgency, that it might be about time to depart. The agent assumed, reasonably enough, that Stratton and his rented security retinue were Secret Service agents (in fact, it was too early in the campaign for Hart to have received federal protection, and he would have resisted it in any event), and she immediately relayed Stratton's message to the pilot, who abruptly took the plane up while the stranded reporters watched with horror from the gate.

By the time they landed in Manchester an hour later, the FBI was waiting to question Stratton, who stood accused of having impersonated a federal agent. The investigation, in fact, would linger on for many months, tormenting Stratton, until federal authorities finally decided not to charge him. (Among those who spoke to FBI agents on his behalf was Richard Ben Cramer, who was along for the ride and witnessed the incident. Cramer kept the entire episode out of his book, for fear that, even years later, the government might not be finished with Stratton and would use the account against him.)

Up to then, in the seventy-two hours since the *Herald* story had first come spilling out of fax machines all over the country, there had been, in effect, two distinct press corps following the story: the campaign reporters, who were now consumed with all aspects of Hart's character but who otherwise observed the general rules of decency, and the tabloid press, who cared not a whit about politics but whose photographers flung themselves onto windshields, heedless in their pursuit of the salable shot. Idyllic little New Hampshire was the place where the two media strains finally merged into a single organism. The paparazzi and the *Current Affair* types would do anything to get near Hart—leap over bushes, hop in front of oncoming cars, elbow and claw their way into the center of the swarm. But this time the stunned political reporters and network crews weren't about to get shoved aside; this was *their* story, and New Hampshire was their turf.

Adding to the mayhem was the fact that, for the first time, all these TV guys had brand-new handheld cameras that carried videotape instead of film, and didn't have to be plugged into a portable deck or require constant tape changing, which meant the cameramen could sprint or leap or hunker down in pursuit of their target. A press horde twice the size of what anyone in politics expected was now completely out of control, laying siege to ordinary voters and to each other, trampling any patch of land that lay between them and the candidate.

In subsequent years, the advance staff on a major political campaign would be trained to behave almost like a mobile security force, similar to the entourage that envelops a rapper or sports hero in public. They would learn to enforce the kind of distance once reserved only for presidents and Hollywood starlets. But in New Hampshire in 1987, at the moment when political media became subsumed into some larger cultural phenomenon, it was just Stratton and Shore and Sweeney, all uncommonly peaceful souls, trying in vain to hold off a human crush that seemed indifferent to their desperate pleas for calm. Hart wanted to shake hands and hold conversations with the voters who came out to see him; his strategy, as he would later describe it, was to "keep going, keep going, keep going." But it was like trying to read a book while the plane you were on was crash-landing. He couldn't hear, or move, or think.

The pack only got more frenzied after word spread that Lee had arrived. Trippi had smuggled her out of Troublesome Gulch under cover of darkness Tuesday night, by driving his wife and baby daughter down the gravel drive and past the waiting horde at the gate—with Lee lying on the floor, under the little girl's feet. That's how the wife of the nation's leading presidential candidate came to be at the Denver airport the next morning, boarding a plane to New Hampshire, where she finally gave a statement to a local reporter. "I know Gary better than anyone else, and when Gary said nothing happened, nothing happened," Lee said. "If it doesn't bother me, I don't think it ought to bother anyone else." She added a broadside against the *Herald* for its "tremendous breach of journalistic ethics."

This was about as unambiguous a statement of support as any wife could have given, short of vowing to avenge her husband by killing his enemies with her bare hands, but the media wasn't about to take it at face value. As Taylor wrote after the fact: "The words were brave, but Lee's face, still swollen from the infection, was a picture of pain and betrayal."

The Harts reunited upstairs at the Hanover Inn on the Dartmouth campus, not long before the news conference that was to be held downstairs. Trippi, who had made the trip east with the candidate's wife, would recall that Lee arrived to find her husband inside a suite, sullen and wearied. "Hi, babe," he sighed, before she closed the door behind her, shutting the staff outside. Lee wanted to take the stage with Hart, even make a joke of the whole controversy by painting a fake black eye on him with a marker, but Hart insisted on facing the press alone. He was adamant that Lee shouldn't act as some stage prop, planted at his side to vouch for his rectitude.

The plan for the news conference, like everything else about the New Hampshire trip, was hopelessly quaint, further demonstrating that Hart's campaign aides, the best in the business, hadn't even begun to acclimate to the allegorical rabbit hole they'd fallen into. Rather than put Hart on some kind of ballroom dais, above the assembled press and removed from them, Stratton and Sweeney had situated him on the floor of a small event space with no protective zone at all, so that the reporters were almost literally on top of him. (At one point, Stratton, in desperation, got down on all fours and tried to make himself a human buffer, so Hart could stand his ground.) With more than a hundred reporters and photographers packed into the room, and more than a dozen cameras rolling under white-hot klieg lights, the temperature soared to an almost unbearable level. Hart was on his heels, dripping sweat, penned in on all sides. He looked less like a statesman than a Roman prisoner in flight from the lions.

Nonetheless, for twenty minutes or so, Hart was masterful. He opened his remarks by calling Lee "the most extraordinary human being I have ever had the pleasure of knowing." Then he parried question after question deftly. When the reporters demanded to know whether Hart's judgment had been called into question by all of this, Hart allowed that it had, but he told them that a man's judgment had to be measured over fifteen years in public life, not by a single weekend. When they wanted to know why these stories about his womanizing persisted and were believed, Hart—rather than advising the reporters to look in the mirror, which he might fairly have done—calmly explained, instead, that he had friends who were women, and that he and Lee had been up-front about their separations. He'd written spy novels, Hart noted wryly, eyebrows dancing, and if he were going to have a secret affair, he'd have done a better job of it.

Would Hart take a lie detector test? one reporter asked. No, Hart replied easily and quickly—he thought the voters were a pretty good lie detector test. As Cramer later described Hart in this moment, "his mind was working on every level" and with "shocking clarity."

Hart saw what he took to be the rage in his inquisitors' faces, their determination to punish him for this character flaw he had exhibited, but even with their breath and the odor of sweat in his face, he retained his evenness. He knew what they were going to ask before they asked it. He could see around the corner once again.

And that's when Paul Taylor hit him with The Question. He spoke hoarsely but intensely, almost in a whisper, his voice quavering with the gravity of what he was about to do. He spoke at unusual length for a reporter in such a setting, as if he and Hart were having another philosophical conversation in the back of a car, rather than a terse exchange in a packed and sweat-soaked banquet room.

"Senator, in your remarks yesterday you raised the issue of morality, and you raised the issue of truthfulness," Taylor began. "Let me ask you what you mean when you talk about morality, and let me be very specific. I have a series of questions about it."

If this prelude alarmed Hart, he didn't object.

"When you said you did nothing immoral," Taylor went on, "did you mean that you had no sexual relationship with Donna Rice last weekend or at any other time that you were with her?"

"That is correct," Hart replied, unflinching. "That's correct."

Taylor took his time, with lawyerly skill. "Do you believe that adultery is immoral?" he asked next.

"Yes," Hart said immediately. He must have been sensing the danger at that point, aware that he was being outflanked but unsure of how to head it off. And then Taylor just came out with it.

"Have you ever committed adultery?" he rasped, while reporters gaped, and while the campaign aides standing off to the side looked at each other in amazement.

Almost three decades later, it sounds like a plausible political inquiry, if not a routine one. Have you ever committed adultery? What would you do if your wife was raped? How did it feel when your child was killed? But in the context of 1987, to Hart and his aides and to the older reporters in the room who would always remember it as a watershed moment, Taylor might as well have asked him to disrobe right there and submit to a cavity search. No reporter had ever asked a presidential candidate that kind of personal, sexual, broad question. Campaign aides had guessed that someone might, but hearing it was still a surreal experience.

Hart froze. You could see it in his eyes, the sudden loss of focus. You could hear it in the room—a long silence that sounded like the end of something, several blank seconds that lingered like a month, during which all his life's ambitions and grand ideas seemed to flutter away. Sweeney had actually warned him, aboard the plane to New Hampshire, when they were rehearsing an exchange the way candidates and aides often do, that someone might ask him the question. Hart's reply then had been a terse and outraged, "I don't have to answer that!" That was perfect, as far as Sweeney was concerned—that was exactly the right response. But somehow, in the moment, Hart's self-righteousness and fluency deserted him. He retreated, instead, into the recesses of his mind.

In those several seconds, Hart, the former divinity student, began to mull the biblical definition of adultery. Was it, as the Old Testament said, limited to intercourse when one party was married? Or could it be, as Jesus taught, a lusting in the heart? Did it count if you were separated? Or if it didn't amount to intercourse at all? Could there be a simple answer to this question?

"Ahh," Hart finally stammered. "I do not think that's a fair question."

"Well," Taylor retorted, "it seems to me the question of morality—"

"You can get into some very fine distinctions," Hart said.

"—was introduced by *you*."

"That's right, that's right," Hart said, stalling.

"And it's incumbent upon us to know what your definition of morality is," Taylor pressed.

"Well, it includes adultery."

"So that you believe adultery is immoral."

"Yes, I do," Hart said again. And so Taylor returned to his original question.

"Have you ever committed adultery?"

Here's what Hart would always remember: looking up at the faces of reporters, twisted with disdain and sanctimony, and seeing in his

The scene at the Hanover Inn on May 6, 1987 with Paul Taylor (circled) attending. He asked the question that would change politics forever. CREDIT: JIM COLE, ASSOCIATED PRESS

mind a flash of images from the 1984 campaign. He happened to know, thanks to the inevitable gossip among campaign aides, who in this crowd had hooked up with whom. Even decades later, Hart still wouldn't say which of the journalists he had in mind—their sex lives, he still believed, should remain private, just like his. But casual, ill-advised "campaign sex" was rampant in those days (even more so than in the still boozy campaigns I covered later), and some of the reporters involved were, inevitably, married. Hart saw some of them now, awaiting his response to Taylor's question, these reporters who dared to call *him* a hypocrite.

"I do not know—I'm not going to get into a theological definition of what constitutes adultery," he said. "In some people's minds it's people being married and having relationships with other people, so . . ."

Taylor wasn't through. He had the floor, having jolted most of his colleagues into silence, and he had Hart on the defensive. They weren't in the back of Hart's limo anymore.

"Can I ask you," Taylor said, "whether you and your wife have an understanding about whether or not you can have relationships, you can have sexual encounters with—"

"My inclination is to say no, you can't ask me that question," Hart said. It was too late for that, however, and he knew it. "But the answer is no, we don't have any such understanding. We have an understanding of faithfulness, fidelity, and loyalty."

The press horde was waiting for Hart after the news conference so they could stalk him all the way to Littleton for his final event of the day—the kind of Q&A with voters that would later be known as a "town hall." But Hart wasn't waiting for *them*. Instead, he somehow got himself behind the wheel of a supporter's white Jeep and came barreling out of the Hanover Inn and past the assembled press as if reenacting a scene from *The A-Team,* one arm on the wheel and the other holding his wife. (Hart had been campaigning in New Hampshire since 1972—he didn't need a map.) In Littleton, the campaign closed the doors before the cameras could catch up, and Hart answered questions about Gorbachev and the proposed oil import tax—but, notably, not a single one about Donna Rice. Then he went out to dinner with Lee and the staff, where they kicked around a bunch of ever-narrowing strategic options, and where Hart learned for the first time, from Lee, that reporters had staked out his daughter at her college lecture hall in Denver.

Taylor, meanwhile, hung back in Hanover to write. For the first time in a campaign, the *Post* had given him and other reporters these new laptop computers—heavy, briefcase-size things that you could use for basic word processing and then, if you had the right cable and access number and everything worked just right, send your copy remotely across a telephone line. He pulled off this minor miracle in the filing center at the Hanover Inn early Wednesday evening, transmitting his story for Thursday without having to call the political desk and dictate it to a clerk.

"The extraordinary intimacy of the questions made Hart and the more than 150 journalists crowded into a small lounge at the

Hanover Inn on the Dartmouth campus palpably uncomfortable," Taylor wrote near the top of his story, as if he were a mere observer of the process. "For better or worse, new ground was broken in the nature of questions put to a presidential candidate." The use of the passive voice here ("new ground was broken") should have conjured Reagan's infamous phrase about the Iran-contra affair four months earlier: "Mistakes were made." In keeping with the journalistic convention of the time, Taylor didn't dare note for his readers that he was the one who had wielded the groundbreaking shovel.

As this story was making its way across the cables, Taylor learned from his editors, on another line, that Bradlee had spoken with his buddy who was also close to Hart's mystery woman. And, sure enough, she had confirmed the affair. She was desperate to keep her name out of the paper—which Bradlee was glad to do, but he wasn't going to tell Hart that. Instead, he wanted Taylor to get his ass to Littleton and get a comment from the candidate.

Quoting the journalist James "Scotty" Reston, Taylor later described himself as being caught up in an "exhilarating chase" as he drove the seventy-plus miles to Littleton in the dark, through a series of rustic towns that had already retired for the night. Amped up and nervous, he talked to himself in the car, running through Hart's likely responses and his best rebuttals to those responses. When at last he arrived at the hotel where the campaign and press were staying, he saw Sweeney sitting at the bar with three other reporters, one of whom was Bill Peterson, a colleague of Taylor's from the *Post*. Taylor described himself as "delighted" to see Peterson. He wasn't thrilled with the prospect of confronting Hart in his hotel room alone, and instantly hatched a plan for them to double-team the candidate.

The problem was that Peterson, about five years older than Taylor and one of the best liked and most admired journalists on the trail, wanted nothing to do with this escapade. As Taylor summed up Peterson's objections, "He thought the hour was late, the tip was weak and the story was sleazy." Taylor and Peterson argued a bit in the lobby and "agreed to disagree." Taylor, who was by this point nearly hyperventilating with nerves, headed back into the bar, alone, to grab Sweeney and tell him that he needed to see the candidate immediately.

In his own retelling of the event, Taylor didn't mention his colleague again. But according to Cramer's account in *What It Takes*, Peterson and Taylor had one more significant exchange. Taylor had just sat down with Sweeney, and was trying to marshal his breathing so he could explain the situation to the press secretary, when Peterson burst back into the lobby and tried once more to stop him. "We're not doing this," Peterson said, according to Cramer's account. "Paul, you don't have to do this. You don't . . . have . . . to *do* this."

"Bill," Taylor replied with finality, "there's just a lot of pressure." (Peterson died of cancer three years later, at forty-seven. His own recollection of this event was never written.)

At last, Taylor told Sweeney that the *Post* had evidence of another affair and he needed to see Hart. After hearing the details, Sweeney deflated; he had been with Hart on the day that was the subject of the investigator's report, but he'd had no idea where Hart had gone after dropping him off at home. Sweeney repaired to his room, ostensibly to see what he could do about arranging an interview for Taylor. It wasn't until hours later, around midnight, when Taylor confronted him again, that Sweeney finally revealed to Taylor that Hart wasn't actually in the hotel. The Harts, it turned out, wanted to be nowhere near the press and had been quietly rerouted to a hotel across the border in Vermont. Taylor would have to wait until morning, at least.

What Taylor didn't yet know was that, in those intervening hours, a crestfallen Sweeney had called John Emerson in Denver, and Emerson had called (of course) Billy Shore in Vermont, and Shore had taken the long walk down to Hart's door at the hotel—it was one of those two-tiered, motor-inn type structures. Shore apologized and told Hart he really needed to call Sweeney right away, and once they were on the phone, Sweeney told Hart the details of what the *Post* had.

"This isn't going to end, is it?" Hart asked.

"You would know better than I would," Sweeney said coldly.

"Let's go home" was all Hart could say. He had concluded that he would never be able to survive another revelation, would never be able to keep campaigning or raise the money he needed. But almost as much as this, both Hart and his aides would later say, he was increasingly distraught by the idea that all the women he had known, some romantically but most not, would soon find their own private lives exposed in the pages of papers as notable as the *Post*. Hart told me that he had already gotten a note from a woman he had seen during his separation from Lee; she wanted him to know that if the reporters came knocking at her door, she would kill herself.

Early Thursday morning, they boarded Hart secretly onto the same private plane that had taken Lee to New Hampshire, while Sweeney and Trippi announced to the press, after considerable misdirection, that Hart had left the state and was suspending his campaign. (Many years later, the draft of that statement, with Hart's handwritten notes, hung framed in Trippi's office on Maryland's Eastern Shore—a reminder of what might have been.) Hart read Tolstoy's *Resurrection* on the plane, which had to be rerouted away from Stapleton Airport in Denver because of all the media camped out there, and which ended up landing at a smaller airport that was besieged by yet more media. Hart wasn't sure what to expect when they landed, but the NBC helicopter that hovered above his car as he raced through Bear Creek Canyon, pursued by cameramen, pretty much answered the question. He could barely get through the front gate at Troublesome Gulch with all the lenses swarming around the car and banging up against the windows, like giant, predatory insects that literally rocked the car.

When he and Lee were back in the cabin, an empathetic photographer slipped a note under the door. It said the cameramen had telephoto lenses and could see through the windows into the kitchen. They were surreptitiously shooting the family. So the Harts pinned sheets and blankets over the windows and sat by themselves in the dark.

· · ·

Hart's official withdrawal the next day, an astonishing five days after the *Herald* story hit and before he could even lose his perch atop the national polls, robbed the *Post* of its opportunity to take down another would-be president—at least as far as the public knew. Once it was clear that Hart would step aside, there was no rationale for publishing the story about his affair, and Bradlee assured an emissary from the campaign that the *Post* would drop it. It was time to call the dogs off Hart because, as Cramer memorably quoted Bradlee as saying: "The coon's up a tree!"

This outcome didn't seem to bother either Bradlee or Taylor much, though. Taylor described himself as "relieved, then triumphant" when he heard that Hart was bowing to reality, adding, "The interview I never got had worked out fine. Just fine." The way Taylor saw it, he and his colleagues had managed to protect the nation from another rogue and liar who aspired to the presidency, and he had acquitted himself well in the competitive chase for the story. But he hadn't come to *The Washington Post* so he could make a career of trafficking in sex lives and marital disputes. And when the adrenaline of the fast-breaking story started to subside, Taylor didn't do much boasting about it. Like E. J. Dionne and Tom Fiedler, Taylor would say that he had done what he'd had to do in the modern political environment, but he had done so joylessly, the same way a veterinarian might get paid to euthanize an injured horse.

Upon his retirement from the *Post,* about four years after the Hart episode, Bradlee granted a lengthy interview to the British journalist David Frost. (Like Bradlee, Frost had become famous in America for his connection to Watergate; he managed to force an apology out of Nixon during a series of sit-downs with the disgraced former president in 1977, which later became the basis for the play and movie titled *Frost/Nixon*.) The hour-long, edited interview with Bradlee, conducted in stateroom-type armchairs at the editor's home in Georgetown, was part of a public television series called *Talking with David Frost,* and like a lot of taped shows that didn't cry out for digital conversion, it's long since disappeared from most archives. I was able to view it one day in a back room of the Library of Congress, wearing bulbous earphones attached to a suitcase-size, push-button videotape-editing machine that looked as if it hadn't been manufactured since 1984. Lines of horizontal static buzzed across the screen, bringing back distant memories of Betamax and rabbit-ear antennas.

Several minutes into the interview, Frost asked the silver-haired Bradlee to name his most significant failures in a quarter century of running the *Post*. "There were plenty of mistakes," Bradlee shrugged. Frost tried the question another way.

"Is there anybody," he asked, "you feel is right to have a grudge against the *Post* in the last twenty-six years? A rightful grudge?"

"That we have really ruined without cause?" Bradlee asked. Frost nodded. Bradlee seemed to hesitate.

"Well. Gary Hart thinks that. He really is sore at us." He then added, quickly, "I don't think with reason," although the mere fact that he had chosen to bring up Hart, with no prodding and with twenty-six years of material from which to choose, suggests that Bradlee had some conflicting thoughts about this. Having raised the subject, Bradlee then seemed eager to move on, but Frost was intrigued and wouldn't let it drop.

"Do you think the lines you drew on a politician's personal life, that you drew them about right over Gary Hart? And since?"

"Yeah, I don't think we made a mistake in that," Bradlee said. He allowed that a politician's private life might not, by itself, have much to do with the public business, "but if you lie about it, I think it's public domain."

"So the crime is getting found out?" Frost asked dubiously.

"Yeah," Bradlee replied.

Frost was an excellent interviewer, and he let this answer echo for a moment, in all its hollowness. And then at last Bradlee seemed to open up a bit. In doing so, he offered what was probably the clearest window into what he and his colleagues at the *Post* had come to accept during that frenzied week in 1987.

"I'll tell you what makes this argument hard," he said. "It's that *someone*'s gonna do it. You can get on your ethical perch and make Solomonic judgments, and then some little paper's gonna run it. And then the AP's gonna run it. And then you don't run it, because you made the original decision not to run it. Then someone will write a story about how you refused to do it, even though the AP has done it. And then it's on television that the *Post* yesterday refused to name . . ."

Bradlee's voice trailed off, and he waved his arm in disgust. "It takes it out of your hands," he said finally, "and you end up looking silly."

In other words, Bradlee, the most influential and recognized editor of his generation, had been forced to accept that a behemoth like *The Washington Post* could no longer decide what was and wasn't a story for the rest of the media world. Now those decisions were made for him, and all the *Post* or anyone else could do was try to keep up.

Not five minutes after this exchange, Frost, whose mind was clearly still on Hart, brought up John Kennedy and the revelations about *his* personal life that had surfaced since 1963. Bradlee admitted that the stories about Kennedy's myriad affairs—including one with a prominent mobster's girlfriend who may or may not have passed messages between the president and the mob boss—were certainly troubling, and he said Kennedy had concealed them from him, as he had from most everyone else.

Then Frost reminded Bradlee of what he had written at the time of Kennedy's death—that America was "a lesser land for the loss of JFK." How long, Frost wanted to know, had Bradlee gone on believing that?

"I still believe that," Bradlee said.

6

ALL THE TRUTH IS OUT

HART WROTE HIS FIERY WITHDRAWAL SPEECH, the one where he talked about the hunters and the hunted and warned that America might "get the kind of leaders we deserve," after a late-night consultation with Warren Beatty, and it reflected the same vision of political integrity Beatty would later explore in his movie *Bulworth*—the impulse of the caged politician to come out and say exactly what he's thinking, consequences be damned. (Hart's staff had given him a version of the withdrawal speech that was more of an abject apology, and it made him want to vomit.) Among the media who were its target, Hart's tirade immediately met with a collective howl of mockery and contempt. In one much discussed column, the man who had until recently been Ben Bradlee's counterpart atop *The New York Times*, Abe Rosenthal, attacked Fiedler and the other *Herald* reporters, whom he said had "damaged journalistic self-respect by skulking around Mr. Hart's house all night." But Rosenthal reserved the bulk of his criticism for Hart's ungracious withdrawal.

"Instead of saying goodbye with a measure of dignity, regret and introspection, Gary Hart told us he had decided that Gary Hart was a wonderful man after all and that everybody was responsible for Gary Hart's political demise except Gary Hart," Rosenthal wrote in that Sunday's *Times*. "He almost managed to make the *Miami Herald* look good and it is not his fault he didn't succeed."

As if this kind of criticism from a journalistic paragon he admired wasn't enough to make Hart despair, he received some positive reinforcement from someone he could hardly have admired less. "This is just a line to tell you how I thought you handled a very difficult situation uncommonly well," began the note from Richard Nixon, whose supposedly last political press conference in 1962 ("You won't have Nixon to kick around anymore") had been considered, to that point anyway, the most petulant on record. "What you said about the media needed to be said. They demand the right to ruthlessly question the ethics of everyone else. But when anyone else dares to question their ethics, they hide behind the shield of freedom of speech."

If Hart thought he'd weathered the worst of what the media could rain down on him, though, he was wrong. Because now that the Hart-Rice liaison had become the biggest story in the country, Lynn Armandt saw no reason why she shouldn't cash in on her supposed friendship with Rice. Armandt sold her story, which differed in significant and sensational ways from Rice's, to *People* for $150,000, and she sold some of the pictures Rice had lent her to the *National Enquirer* for about half that much. From the minute the photo of Rice sitting on Hart's lap appeared in the *Enquirer* at the end of May—she wearing a short white dress, and he the MONKEY BUSINESS CREW T-shirt and a crooked, startled grin—it became the defining image of Hart in the public mind, then and forever.

Years later, most Americans who lived through the scandal would recall, erroneously, that the iconic photo had ended Hart's candidacy. The truth was that it didn't appear until weeks after the fact and had nothing to do with Hart's aborted campaign. At that moment of shared experience, just before the technological Big Bang that would shatter America's media into thousands of fragments and audiences, a single photograph still had that kind of power—to become so deeply embedded in the culture that it actually transformed our memory of the event.

Hart, meanwhile, found himself preoccupied, for the first time in his life, with making money. Whatever aspersions people wanted to cast now on his character, Hart hadn't managed to get in on any land deals or stock sales during a career in public service. His only job now, outside of running for president, was at the Denver-based law firm of Davis Graham & Stubbs, from which he had taken a leave that just about everyone had assumed to be permanent. So at 8 a.m. that Monday after his withdrawal speech, Hart strolled through the doors of his firm without so much as a heads-up call to the partners, and settled in behind his desk as if he'd never left. For that whole week, he sat there half petrified, ears alert to the shuffle of feet in the hall, fearing the moment when the managing partner would poke his head into the office and tell Hart that his presence was a distraction, that maybe it was time to go their separate ways. In fact, no one knew quite what to say to Hart, and they mostly left him alone. He opened mail and took the occasional call from a well-wisher. Most times the phone rang, it was some reporter wanting an interview. Hart wouldn't grant them.

There were small kindnesses he would always remember, notes and advice from old friends and some of the world leaders he had met in his travels. None were more unexpected, or more important, then the signals of support from Mikhail Gorbachev, who watched all of this unfold from the Kremlin, and who would have been within his rights to jettison altogether this failed American candidate he had befriended.

When Hart had shown up at the Kremlin at the end of 1986, he brought along his daughter, Andrea, who was then a college student. Hart just wanted her to see the place in all its shimmering, Easter-egg brilliance, since she was majoring in international relations, and few Westerners had ever set foot inside. He intended for Andrea to wait outside while the two leaders and their aides met. But Gorbachev had insisted she join them during their hours-long meeting, asking questions about her education and her plans, and then he had invited her to return after graduation so she could study in the Soviet Union as his personal guest—an opportunity that seemed almost as inconceivable in 1987 as it would have been, twenty-five years later, to study in North Korea at the invitation of Kim Jong-un. Hart was practically kicking Andrea under the table in a way that said: "For God's sake, say yes." Which of course she did.

Now, in his shock and despair, Hart was preoccupied with what would happen to Andrea's dream. Had he ruined that, too? Clearly Gorbachev had made an offhand gesture of political goodwill when he offered to personally lift the Iron Curtain for an American college student, and it was a gesture that could no longer advance any cause. So, with a sick feeling that any father could appreciate, Hart called a Soviet emissary in Washington and told him that he understood if the arrangement was no longer possible, that he just needed to confirm as much for Andrea's sake. A call soon came back relaying a message from Gorbachev himself: By all means, Andrea was to come as his guest, just as they had planned. Gorbachev was a father, too.

In fact, Gorbachev had developed an affinity for Hart that would make a concrete difference in Hart's post-campaign life. The Soviet premier helped rescue Hart financially, by personally steering to him the legal business involved in getting American telecommunications companies to string up wires across the newly liberated Soviet republics. Those contracts not only made Hart a viable contributor to his law firm, but they kept him traveling and engaged firsthand in Russian affairs for years after his withdrawal from public life—a gift that had value well beyond what could ever be listed on a legal bill.

At home in those first weeks, after a long day of not much work, it was just Hart and Lee and the unendurable quiet that descended after Hart's official withdrawal sent the paparazzi home. Hart told his wife that she could have one day to interrogate him, to ask any questions, to talk through the anger and then return to their seminormal lives. He wasn't going to spend the rest of his days feeling ashamed and accused by the silence. It sounds pretty self-absorbed now; here Lee had been humiliated on a national scale unlike any political spouse before her, and *he* was going to set a time limit on how long *she* would be allowed to resent him for it. But Lee understood. He couldn't take any more judgment. They had to move on.

Some of Hart's aides moved on, too. The political director, Paul Tully, wound up with the eventual nominee, Mike Dukakis, while Joe Trippi, who had been Tully's deputy before rescuing Lee, wandered over to Dick Gephardt's camp. Others, like Bill Dixon and Kevin Sweeney, withdrew from politics altogether; for a while, Sweeney went back to waiting tables in San Francisco. But a small cadre of longtime loyalists—Billy Shore, Sue Casey, Mike Stratton—became accustomed to getting periodic calls from Troublesome Gulch, where Hart was watching his former rivals in the Democratic race vie for legitimacy. It was obvious to Hart's confidants that while he might have departed the race corporeally, his spirit remained very much engaged. Quietly, they put out the word to their most devoted organizers in Iowa and New Hampshire: Stay neutral and wait. Hart still had time to change his mind, or so he thought.

Later, Hart would say that he had been unable to walk away from the race once and for all because of his children, who believed he had given up too soon. He wanted to prove to them, as any father would, that he wasn't a quitter. But as touching a sentiment as that is, Hart's aides knew he was still paying attention to the polls. And really, it would have been hard for him not to. At the end of June, almost two months after Hart's withdrawal, Gallup found that Jesse Jackson, fueled by strong African American support, was leading the Democratic field with 18 percent. You couldn't have found a political insider anywhere who thought any black candidate had a realistic chance of becoming president in 1988, much less a reverend with a history of controversial statements. And yet the only other Democrat who even broke into double digits was Dukakis, the unknown governor of Massachusetts, with 11 percent.

A month after that, at the end of July, Gallup tested Hart as part of the Democratic field. Even disgraced and out of sight, Hart finished first, with 25 percent of the vote. Among the so-called Seven Dwarfs, only Jackson broke the 10 percent barrier. And by now it was clear that there would be no savior—no Mario Cuomo or Lee Iacocca or Ted Kennedy—to swoop in and spare the party a fragmented and uninspiring primary season.

Hart wanted to believe that the numbers told a story about a disconnect between the media and Democratic voters. He wanted to believe that the polling, in a sense, ratified everything he had been saying for years about the power of insurgency and antiestablishmentarianism in the modern era of picking a president. The elite media, along with party insiders and campaign funders, had written him off as tainted and irrelevant, and this had only legitimized his standing as a true outsider. In fact, Hart convinced himself that the inverse was true, as well—that it had been his challenge to the status quo, the power of his ideas, that had prompted the media and political establishments to try to discredit his character and drive him from the race. And for all their efforts to kill him, the polling was telling him, they had failed.

In reality, as it would turn out, the polling did tell a story—but it wasn't the one to which Hart clung. Because Hart had been the front-runner going back to the closing days of 1984, and because his rivals, with the exception of Jackson, remained so obscure in the public mind, Hart's was the only politician's name that primary voters recognized. What they were telling the pollsters is that they hadn't yet warmed to any of these faceless or flawed candidates, and they still wanted an alternative who excited them as much as Hart had before the scandal. But it wasn't really him they were looking for.

Nonetheless, Hart spent the fall testing the climate for a comeback, while the media eagerly awaited the spectacle of his return. In September, still sore from the beating he got for his withdrawal speech three and a half months earlier, Hart decided to go on *Nightline* and show his softer, more contrite side. (He agreed to the interview only after ABC agreed to let him sit alongside Koppel on the set, as a peer, rather than appearing from a remote studio.) After "Mr. Koppel," as Hart still insisted on calling him, offered him the chance to make an opening statement, Hart assured the audience he was sorry for his own behavior.

"I will always bear a burden of responsibility—and I assume total responsibility—for those actions and for what transpired that led to the end of that campaign," he said. "I do not blame anyone else and I have never tried to shift blame away from myself. I am totally and fully responsible for my own actions and I want to say to all of you how sorry I am and apologize to you for those actions." Then, in characteristic fashion, he closed his preamble by quoting the his-

torian John Buchan from a biography of the Scottish patriot Mont-
rose, on the necessity of infusing old ideologies with new passion.
One can only imagine what Koppel's audience, the largest since he
had interviewed Jim and Tammy Faye Bakker months earlier, made
of this.

It didn't take long for Hart's highbrow literary references to
devolve into sensational admissions. Picking up where Taylor had
left off months earlier, Koppel confronted Hart about whether he
had committed adultery. "It was a terribly awkward question," Koppel later said in an ABC retrospective about his years as a host, "but
there was no way of doing that particular interview without asking
it, because it had become the central issue of his candidacy." And so
Hart became the first politician on national television to say, yes, he
had cheated on his wife. But he refused to say whether this applied
in the case of Donna Rice. There had to be a line somewhere.

"I don't care what questions are asked tonight or anytime in the
future," Hart told Koppel. "I'm not going to answer them on any
specific incidents. Now, I've been made, forced—I have been made
to make a declaration here that I think is unprecedented in American political history, and I regret it. That question should have never
been asked, and I shouldn't have to answer it." (Hart left unclear
whether he regretted the adultery, or whether he regretted answering Koppel's question.) Whether he did or didn't sleep with Rice,
Hart said, "was nobody's business"—which, of course, was the
answer he wished he'd given Taylor months earlier.

Hart finally got back into the race, officially, on a glacier-cold
December day in New Hampshire, standing in front of the statehouse in Concord. "When I suspended my campaign last spring, I
believed other national leaders would enter this race, and I hoped
that my ideas for strategic investment economics, for military
reform, and for enlightened engagement would be adopted and put
forward by others," Hart, hatless and coatless as always, told the
assembled camera crews. "After more than six months, neither of
these things has happened." Submitting his $1,000 registration fee
as a candidate in the February primary, he said he had no headquarters, no staff, and no consultants to tell him what to do—as if he ever

would have listened to them, anyway. "I have the power of ideas, and I can govern this country," he declared. "Let's let the people decide!"

They decided, and rather quickly—that Hart was just too damaged, too much of a traveling freak show, too "unelectable." If they had any doubts, all they had to do was turn on the TV. "In, out, in, out—isn't that what got him in trouble in the first place?" David Letterman asked on his late-night show. Carson joked that the nomination would fall into Hart's lap—if there was any room left there. On the highly rated sitcom *Golden Girls,* one of the little old ladies commented of another character: "She's Gary Hart's campaign manager. It doesn't pay much, but you don't have to get out of bed to do it." Tom Paxton, the folk singer, was breaking up his audiences that fall with a song he'd just written called "Ballad of Gary Hart," which featured lyrics like: "Who's that running down the alley in the dead of Friday night, as he zippers up his trousers in the inky, slinky light."

The sudden collision of sex and presidential politics had unleashed something latent in the popular culture, some powerful impulse toward gossip and ridicule that couldn't be restrained. When it came to Gary Hart, the entire country seemed to be engaged in a game of free association. No mention of his name could fail to elicit something base and whimsical.

"I don't know how to ask this, except to ask it," Chris Wallace, hosting NBC's *Meet the Press,* told Hart in New Hampshire just before the primary. "Aren't you concerned at all that you may become an embarrassing figure?"

In the end, Hart couldn't wrest even half a percentage point of the vote in Iowa. In New Hampshire, the state where Hart had blindsided Mondale four years earlier, he finished dead last with only 4 percent. After that, Hart told his aides and loyal supporters that they were released from their obligations and should probably go do something else. Hart intended to stay in the race through Super Tuesday, to fulfill his pledge to let the voters have their say, but he was through with the trappings of an actual campaign. He was just going to ride around and talk to people, instead.

And that's what he did. He found voters, mostly on college campuses, who didn't really care so much about sex and scandal, who just wanted to hear the man talk and debate, and he regaled them with a kind of traveling seminar about the emerging digital economy and the outmoded military, about the detailed, alternative federal budget that he had, at last, released. It was pilgrimage and penance sewn into one—a lonely conversation with whichever voters were left, because he had promised to give them the substance they deserved, and he wouldn't relent now. Then he'd go out to dinner and drink with whoever was on that particular leg of his journey—Lee or one of the kids, local supporters who had been with him forever, the stalwart aide whose job it was to advance the trip and drive, although now there were no cameras left to chase Hart and no crush of outstretched hands to navigate.

Among these few unpaid, lingering loyalists was Martin O'Malley. A twenty-five-year-old law student who had first gotten to know Hart as a volunteer on the 1984 campaign, O'Malley had become ever more integral to the Hart operation as everyone more senior deserted. He had lived an itinerant life since Hart reentered the campaign, having been handed the formidable task of making sure that Hart got on the ballot in every primary state, starting with Illinois and Pennsylvania. Then O'Malley took charge of the calamitous campaign in Iowa. (When he apologized to Hart for officially registering zero percent on the night of the caucuses, Hart told him dryly: "Martin, this was not an organizational problem.")

After New Hampshire, O'Malley hung around, driving his mentor through long nights on stretches of blackened highway. They shared a bond that bridged the difference in years and that would endure for decades. O'Malley, a serious-minded graduate of Jesuit schools and Catholic University, shared Hart's deep appreciation for history, poetry, and theology. And, of course, for politics.

They were driving in Virginia one night, just the two of them, in O'Malley's yellow 1972 Pontiac Catalina, on their way from a debate in Williamsburg to Richmond. O'Malley worked up his courage and told Hart that a lot of his supporters were frustrated, that they believed in him still and wanted to go through the motions of running an actual campaign, if nothing else. Couldn't they at least put up lawn signs, or knock on some doors?

Hart shook his head. It would be his name on those signs, he reminded O'Malley, and he had already made his decision about the way he would play out this final stage of his candidacy. He was going to make his argument to as many people as would show up and listen, and if O'Malley wanted to stay by his side and be a part of that, Hart was happy for the company. But Hart had no use for advice or pep talks. If volunteers needed to unleash their creative energy, he said, let them find some other outlet.

Chastened, O'Malley nodded and kept driving. Silence swallowed the air in the cavernous car. And then, after a few minutes, Hart turned and looked at O'Malley again.

"Have you ever read the William Butler Yeats poem 'To a Friend Whose Work Has Come to Nothing'?" Hart asked.

O'Malley said no. Hart proceeded to recite it, slowly.

By the time O'Malley told me this story, more than twenty-five years later, he was in his second term as Maryland's governor, frequently talked about as a presidential contender in his own right. In the basement of the governor's mansion, next to the pool table, he had hung a Hart campaign poster from 1984, and taped to the back, where no one could see it, was a copy of Yeats's poem, which he had long ago committed to memory himself.

> Now all the truth is out,
> Be secret and take defeat
> From any brazen throat,
> For how can you compete,
> Being honor bred, with one
> Who were it proved he lies
> Were neither shamed in his own
> Nor in his neighbors' eyes;
> Bred to a harder thing
> Than Triumph, turn away

And like a laughing string
Whereon mad fingers play
Amid a place of stone,
Be secret and exult,
Because of all things known
That is most difficult.

When Hart had spoken the last line, he peered over at O'Malley in the driver's seat, eyebrows pirouetting.

"It is a very, very good poem" was all he said.

To the editor:
I'm the Washington Post *reporter who put the question to Gary Hart that offended so many* New York Times *columnists. I suspect it offended other folks, too. It's not hard to see why. The question—"Have you ever committed adultery"—seemed to turn me, and by extension my profession, into some kind of morals police. That's not a comfortable role for anyone.*

So began the letter from Paul Taylor that appeared in the *Times* at the end of May 1987, the same week the photo of Rice sitting in Hart's lap made its way onto every newsstand in America. This was an extraordinary thing—a reporter from one nationally renowned paper defending himself in the pages of its chief competitor. But Taylor couldn't stomach being pilloried by colleagues who portrayed him as sleazy and superficial. He pointed out, as so many others had by now, that Hart had promised to hold himself to a high standard of moral conduct.

"Your columnists raise questions about proportionality, civility and privacy," he wrote. "It is not the job of a journalist to win plaudits for civility (though it's certainly nicer when we do). Nor is it our job to pry into the most private matters—except when public figures, in conducting and discussing their private affairs publicly, force our hand. Sometimes this job demands that we raise questions we'd rather not ask. Your columnists suggest I broke some kind of gentleman's code in this instance. I say, poppycock. What I did was ask Gary Hart the question he asked for."

If the scandal had reduced Hart to a "farcical figure," as Taylor would later write in *See How They Run*, then Taylor hadn't understood how profoundly it would affect his own life. The first inkling came on the day after he asked the adultery question, when he returned to the *Post* newsroom and talked to Bradlee, whom he assumed had paid close attention to the news conference in New Hampshire. "*You* were the one who asked that question?" Bradlee asked, astonished. "Sheee-yit!" Then Koppel called Taylor at home, while he was playing with his kids, and personally asked him to come on *Nightline*, as Fiedler had done a few days earlier. Taylor demurred. He told Koppel he was a reporter and wasn't comfortable being in the middle of the story.

Comfortable or not, Taylor would soon come to understand that he was no longer Paul Taylor, hottest young political reporter in Washington. He was now Paul Taylor, the Guy Who Asked The Question.

Hart's undoing—and the role that both the *Herald* and *Post* had played in it—touched off an anguished debate in American journalism. Newsrooms were deeply conflicted, and nowhere was this conflict more apparent (or more confusing, perhaps) than in the pages of *The New York Times*. The editorial page, which carried a tremendous amount of influence in 1987, called the *Herald*'s stakeout "eminently justified." The paper's Washington bureau chief, Craig Whitney, sent a reporter to the other campaigns to find out how the rest of the candidates would handle inevitable questions about adultery. "I'm not offended by any question," Whitney told a reporter for the *Post*. "There's no question that should be regarded as out-of-bounds."

On the op-ed page, however, the liberal Anthony Lewis said he felt "degraded in my profession" by the *Herald* stakeout and that Taylor's big moment marked a "low point" for political coverage. The conservative columnist William Safire slammed Taylor as one of the "titillaters" who was "demeaning" journalism. Abe Rosenthal, the *Times*'s former executive editor, called Taylor's question "nause- ating." Years later, Tom Fiedler would tell me what he had heard from higher-ups at the *Herald* that year—that a disgusted Rosenthal had made clear to them that if the *Herald* so much as nominated its Hart story for a Pulitzer Prize, he would use his influence to block the paper from receiving any Pulitzers at all. Whether or not this was the reason, the *Herald* chose not to nominate its scandal cover- age. (It did win two Pulitzers for other stories.)

Perhaps the most cogent critique of the media came from Hen- drik Hertzberg, the former speechwriter for President Carter who was now writing for *The New Republic*. "Gary Hart has now become the first American victim of Islamic justice" is how Hertzberg began his essay, titled "Sluicegate," a few weeks after Hart's first with- drawal. He went on:

He has been politically stoned to death for adultery. The differ- ence is that in Iran, the mullahs do not insult the condemned prisoner by telling him that he is being executed not for adultery but because of "concerns about his character," "questions about his judgment," or "doubts about his candor."

As far as I can determine, Gary Hart is the first presidential candidate, president, prime minister, Cabinet member, congres- sional committee chairman, party leader, or television evangelist, American or foreign, ever to be destroyed solely because of what David S. Broder, the dean of American political reporters, calls "screwing."

Hertzberg didn't bother trying to defend Hart against the allega- tions at hand, which he assumed to be true. But almost alone among the commentators in that moment, he intuited that the casualty of all this character appraisal would be the broader concept of char- acter itself—that everything else a politician had done or been in his life would now be swept away, routinely, by a single, sensational revelation. "The fact that a person will lie in the context of adul- tery proves nothing about his general propensity to lie," Hertzberg wrote. "The point is that if Hart is a liar there must be one or two more lies among the millions of words he has spoken as a public man. Let them be produced." None were, then or later.

Eventually, as the media moved on, and as issues of "character" became the recurrent and dominant theme in our elections, there emerged an uneasy consensus among most influential senior columnists and editors about what had transpired in 1987. While they were reluctant to criticize colleagues, they didn't really approve of the decisions that reporters for the *Herald* and the *Post* made that week. They didn't think sex mattered, or that reporters should spend time delving into who spent the night where. And yet, at the same time, they basically decided that Hart had deserved what he'd gotten, because while sex didn't matter, judgment certainly did. And what the events of 1987 had proven was that Hart didn't have the stability or steadiness to be president. He was a loner who didn't take anyone's counsel or care what anyone thought, a ladies' man who couldn't control his impulses—or who was, worse yet, drawn to avoidable peril. And this was something the public needed to know about him.

It was a confounding issue for American journalism, and it remained so. A quarter century later, when I interviewed some of the reporters from that time, I found that they would often struggle and contradict themselves in an effort to make sense of the rules they had constructed.

"I hated that week," E. J. Dionne told me. "I hated everything about this story. The stakeout bothered me. I really respect Fiedler, and I don't want to get into the business of criticizing somebody else. But the stakeout is something I just could not have done. I knew in my gut that we journalists were opening up a can of worms, that we were sort of sexualizing politics in a way we hadn't before. And given that I'm basically much more of a policy and ideas guy, I felt like we were just pulling politics away from what I think politics ought to be about.

"And yet I was also mad at Hart," Dionne said, reflecting on the "follow me around" quote that ended up stalking Hart through the years. "Because I thought that, A, he should have listened to the folks who were telling him that you can't get away with it this time.

And B, why in the world did he say that to me? Why did he choose to put it that way to me?"

I found Jack Germond, who once counted Hart a personal friend, but who hadn't spoken to him in years, to be similarly conflicted when I visited his home in West Virginia, on the banks of the Shenandoah River. This was three months before his death in August 2013, at the age of eighty-five.

"I don't think I would have done the reporting Tom Fiedler did," Germond told me. Nor could he envision himself asking the question Taylor asked. "He's asking what you did on that boat, or in the bedroom, or in the apartment," he told me. "And we don't need to know that. I thought that was an unfair question, in the sense that it did not advance the story in any serious way. Paul Taylor was a very good reporter, but I did not agree with that question." Germond told me that as a younger reporter he used to know a lot about which candidates were sleeping around, and with whom, but he never considered it anyone's business.

None of that, however, kept him from believing that the scandal that forced Hart from politics had revealed something essential about the man he'd known since 1972. "If Gary Hart's going to fuck every woman he sees when he walks down the street, then he doesn't deserve to be president," Germond said bluntly. "It's good to know this stuff."

Most Americans probably would have agreed. And yet if you think about it for more than a minute, you can see that the argument that became the norm in political journalism after 1987—"we care about a candidate's judgment, not his sex life"—required an acrobatic contortion of logic. After all, if the media didn't care about the sex lives of candidates, and in fact had never written about them before, then how could it have been such abhorrent judgment for a candidate to engage in extramarital sex? If reporters didn't actually find adultery by itself newsworthy, then what was so stupid and self-destructive about carrying on with a woman in the privacy of your own home? As Hertzberg put it: "If judgment, not sex, were truly 'the issue,' as we have been told over and over, then Hart's campaign would still be alive. And the headline in the *New York Post* would have been HART'S JUDGMENT REVEALED AS FAULTY, not GARY'S LOVE BOAT FOLLIES."

The truth was that all of this business about judgment and character was a rationalization, and not a very persuasive one. The political media may not actually have cared much about sex, but it was clear now that the popular culture did, and this exerted a powerful force of gravity. What really happened in 1987 was that the finest political journalists of a generation surrendered all at once to the idea that politics had become another form of celebrity-driven entertainment, while simultaneously disdaining the kind of reporting that such a thirst for entertainment made necessary.

Where the journalism establishment ultimately netted out on the decisions made in 1987 is probably best illustrated by the career arcs of those who found themselves caught up in the moment. Tom Fiedler wasn't immediately feted the way Woodward and Bernstein were by his sanctimonious colleagues, and after he read Rosenthal's comments, he knew he wasn't going to be able to make the jump to *The New York Times*—something he had been seriously discussing with the paper's Miami bureau chief. But Fiedler did get his Pulitzer a few years later, for his part in an impressive investigation into an extremist cult. He went on to become both editorial page editor and executive editor of the *Herald* and then, after his retirement, a leading academic, oft quoted on journalistic ethics and integrity, well liked and well respected.

Among Fiedler's colleagues on the stakeout, Jim McGee moved on to become a top investigative reporter for *The Washington Post* (and later a senior investigator for a congressional committee on homeland security), while Doug Clifton later became the top editor at the Cleveland *Plain Dealer*. E. J. Dionne ended up an op-ed columnist for the *Post* and one of the most admired liberal theorists in Washington. Howard Fineman, who set the whole thing in motion by reporting rumors of Hart's affairs, became not just the last of *Newsweek*'s great political writers (before moving on to *The Huffington Post*) but one of the most ubiquitous pundits on cable TV. Just about everyone who had any role, integral or passing, in taking

Hart down went on to scale the heights of national and political journalism.

Everyone, that is, except Paul Taylor. He emerged from the Hart scandal and the 1988 election as a famous and sought-after correspondent, clear heir to the *Post*'s storied political franchise. He would never cover a campaign again.

Taylor was gracious but notably unenthusiastic when I emailed him in the spring of 2013 and asked if I could come by and talk about the ancient history of 1987. Now sixty-four, Taylor still lived in Washington and had spent the last decade at the Pew Research Center, where his title was executive vice president for special projects. This meant that he spent a lot of his time studying polls and putting together reports on social and demographic trends in the electorate—writing incisively and substantively about the larger undercurrent of politics, in other words, without having to interrogate any more politicians.

Taylor seemed uncomfortable revisiting the events of that week, and he told me more than once, after I sat down and started asking him about it, that he didn't remember much other than what he wrote at the time. But he did take me through the months and years after the scandal. He told me that after the 1988 campaign he had gone off to Princeton for a year to teach journalism and work on his book. But by the time he finished reliving that campaign, he found he simply had no stomach for another one. One day he walked back into the *Post* and told his editors he didn't want to write about politics anymore. He was taking himself off the fast track to political preeminence.

It wasn't that Taylor was driven from political reporting by his guilt about Hart or his embarrassment about the crucial role he had played in the scandal, as Hart's former aides always believed (or wanted to believe). Nor was it that he felt too scalded by the criticism he had endured after the scandal, although that clearly left a mark.

What motivated Taylor, really, was that he could sense a change coming in the atmosphere of political journalism. Taylor was a down-the-middle reporter who prided himself on being an observer of history, rather than a shaper of it. He had never envisioned himself sitting in judgment of politicians or becoming the kind of columnist who wrote about their moral failings, as his father sometimes urged him to do. But now colleagues were talking about Hart's demise and how Taylor had "put a notch in his belt," which was nothing like the way he looked at it, and suddenly the whole focus seemed to be on what was wrong with candidates, what was flawed or indecent about them as people, rather than on what they believed or what they could accomplish, which is what mattered to Taylor.

"More and more, it was all just, these guys are a bunch of . . . *you know* . . . and it's our job to expose their follies," Taylor told me. "And you know, if you're a clever writer you can build a following around that. And I didn't want to go there." The day hadn't quite arrived when reporters would spend chunks of their days on cable TV, tossing out glib and knowing insights into the character of candidates, but it wasn't so far off that Taylor couldn't glimpse it on the horizon.

"I could see that that would be a way to get ahead," he told me. "To have that sort of snarky, contemptuous, clever way. If you're good enough and you've established a good enough relationship and you get deep into their world, then you can kind of give them a little elbow now and then, and be clever about it, and live to fight another day. You know, I didn't want to go there. I think much of political coverage *has* gone there, to the detriment of politics and political journalism."

By the time Bill Clinton was running to unseat George H. W. Bush in 1992, Taylor had gotten as far away from American politics as you could physically get. He chose an assignment as the *Post*'s correspondent in South Africa, where apartheid was unraveling, and where no one could question the seriousness of the work he was doing. If there was any doubt about that, it was pretty much settled in his first week on the job, when he was shot near the collarbone and very nearly killed. (Fortunately, he made a full recovery.) When he returned to the States four years later, Taylor left the *Post* and journalism altogether and founded an organization dedicated to electoral reform, mainly by changing the laws around campaign spending and TV advertising.

You could have seen that as a kind of atonement for sins past, but Taylor told me he was at peace with the decisions he had made in 1987 and didn't regret having asked The Question. He had done what he had to do as a reporter covering a story, and he was satisfied that he had acquitted himself as well as anyone could have, and there was nothing more to it than that. "You get to cover the three-alarm fire, you go cover the three-alarm fire," is how Taylor put it, with obvious ambivalence.

"Every circumstance, every story kind of develops its own logic and its own momentum, and it seemed to me that that's where we were in that story," Taylor told me. "It was the right question to ask, and it was the right topic to raise. But if it never gets asked again, no one will be happier about that than me."

I pointed out that it did get asked—or at least some version of it—all the time. Taylor nodded.

"Many people made this point that we're sort of debasing the political process if we use this as a lens to judge character," Taylor said. "And I get that as a problem. So my response to that would be, 'Agreed.' Let's not go there. Let's *do* respect people's privacy. And let's *do* understand that private morality and public morality, they may influence each other, but they are separate entities. I think that's the right starting point.

"But rules have exceptions," Taylor said with a shrug. "And shit happens. And there we were."

I asked Taylor if he had ever talked to Hart after the moment in New Hampshire when they faced one another twenty-six years ago, and he shook his head. He said he had written Hart a letter in the months after, asking to talk, and had received a polite reply from Hart saying he wasn't interested.

"You know, there's a time where I thought it would be nice, just on a human level, to bring some quote-unquote closure to it," Taylor said. "But I don't know what I would say. I have no burning desire to say anything to him. I expect he doesn't think too highly of me. That's the nature of the beast, and I'm okay with that."

What Taylor seemed not to be okay with, what clearly still gnawed at him after all these years, was the idea that this one question, among the thousands he had asked of politicians in more than a decade of political reporting, was still the thing that defined his career. Not infrequently, if you mentioned the Hart scandal to political insiders who lived through it, one of the first people they mentioned, with a knowing smile, was Paul Taylor. Like Hart himself, Taylor had become stuck in an inglorious moment, and for a guy who considered himself intellectual and idealistic about politics, this was understandably hard to stomach.

"This is my life and career, and I take it pretty seriously," Taylor told me. "If everybody gets to choose their fifteen minutes, this wouldn't have been mine."

In the 1980s, at the height of what Neil Postman called the Age of Show Business, the old adage about life imitating art was almost literally true. Virtually every aspect of the culture was informed by entertainment. Michael Jackson debuted his "Billie Jean" video in 1983, and thanks to MTV and NBC's *Friday Night Videos,* every American under thirty was soon moonwalking his way to the bathroom. After the movie *Top Gun,* starring Tom Cruise as a renegade fighter pilot, exploded into the American consciousness in 1986 (along with aviator glasses and bomber jackets), the Navy reported a sharp increase in the enlistment of aspiring pilots. So naturally the first televised sex scandal in American politics, the five-day miniseries starring Hart and a sexy model that gripped the nation in 1987, had immediate repercussions in politics and journalism, and not just on the presidential level. In congressional districts and statehouses across the country, reporters were suddenly looking to stage their own versions of this new morality play, and politicians were desperately seeking ways to avoid a starring role.

Within a few weeks of Hart's withdrawal speech in Denver, a Democratic congressman from Massachusetts, Barney Frank, announced that he was gay. Frank said he took a look around and guessed he wouldn't be able to keep it a secret for long. He was probably right. "The more the discussion is trivialized and sensation-alized, the less you'll get serious, substantive discussion," Frank warned. "At the rate we're going, the *National Enquirer* will be up for the Pulitzer Prize." (In fact, that wouldn't happen until 2008, when the *Enquirer* won plaudits and serious Pulitzer consideration for nailing John Edwards.)

A few weeks after Frank's admission, Richard Celeste, the Dem-ocratic governor of Ohio and one of the party's more promising national talents, had to give up any hope of a presidential run after the *Plain Dealer* wrote about his extramarital affairs. Celeste had been asked at a routine news conference about rumors of his "Gary Hart–type problem," and he had denied them. The *Plain Dealer*'s editors—who, of course, knew, along with half of Columbus, that Celeste wasn't being entirely forthcoming—considered this his ver-sion of "follow me around," and promptly set out to prove him a man of faulty character. Celeste was finished in national politics, although he later served as ambassador to India.

By that time, as Taylor would later write, reporters on the cam-paign trail were already delving into the sex lives of Jesse Jackson and George H. W. Bush, following up on a bevy of rumors. Jack-son was now alleged to be sleeping with the actress Margot Kidder, although that bit of gossip never actually became a story. (Nineteen years later, Jackson was forced to admit having fathered an illegiti-mate daughter by another woman.) In Bush's case, the rumors were persistent enough that his oldest son, George W., felt the need to call Fineman at *Newsweek* to set the record straight—a move that served only to intensify speculation, which lasted right up until Election Day.

Meanwhile, a rumor that Kitty Dukakis had once separated from her husband, Michael, just as Lee and Gary Hart had, forced the soon-to-be-nominee's wife to publicly disclose her treatment for addiction to diet pills. She figured it was better to admit she had been treated at a Minnesota clinic for a month, thus explaining her prolonged absence from Massachusetts, than to let gossip about marital problems overshadow her husband's campaign.

The Dukakis story prompted E. J. Dionne to write in the *Times* that Hart's downfall seemed to have triggered a new era of "confessional politics," in which "candidates and their spouses are being pushed, by their advisors or their own apprehensions, to disclose aspects of their lives that in another era would have remained private." Eddie Mahe, a Republican consultant, told Dionne, "The press has collectively made a decision that when any information is presented to them and documented, they will publish it. So the new rule on these things is: you'd better talk about it, and you'd better talk about it first." The impact of this reached even beyond national borders. By 1989, Paul Taylor noted, heads of state in Greece and Japan were being forced from office at least partly because of sex scandals.

On a rainy day near the end of March 2013, I sat in the back of a shabby Capitol Hill bar with Joe Trippi, discussing this period in the late 1980s. After smuggling Lee Hart out of Troublesome Gulch on the floorboards of his car, Trippi had gone on to become a leading adman and strategist in Democratic campaigns, although usually in the role of a renegade assaulting the party establishment. He masterminded the tech-savvy presidential campaign of Howard Dean in 2004 (at least until a very public breakup late in the campaign, after Dean ran out of money), and then advised Edwards in his 2008 run.

Trippi told me that almost exactly a year after Hart left the race the first time, he got a frantic call from one of his closest friends, Tom Pappas, with whom he had worked as a kid on Ted Kennedy's 1980 campaign. Pappas was now chief of staff to Roy Dyson, a Maryland congressman, who was being investigated by the Federal Election Commission for campaign spending violations. Pappas, it turned out, had received a six-figure consulting fee from Dyson's campaign and failed to disclose it. But what had Pappas so distraught, the reason he had called Trippi for help, had nothing to do with money. He said *The Washington Post* was preparing to run a story that Sunday saying he was gay. Trippi had been dealing with reporters for years and was known to have good, mutually respectful relationships with them. He called one of the reporters working on the story and tried to talk him out of running it.

"Sunday morning, I'm shooting commercials in West Virginia for a gubernatorial candidate, when the front page of *The Washington Post* . . ." At this, Trippi's voice suddenly caught, and to my surprise, he started to weep right there in the bar. ". . . When the front page of *The Washington Post* says he's gay. . . ."

That story, which I later retrieved, was actually more complicated than Trippi remembered. The piece was ostensibly about Pappas's strange and demanding behavior toward male aides, like one he had allegedly fired just for leaving a party. The reporters never actually came out and said Pappas was gay, but the subtext was clear. They mentioned, for instance, that Pappas was divorced and that his boss was single, and that Pappas often stayed with the congressman at his house.

"Killed himself," Trippi told me then, choking on those two words after all these years. "Jumped out of a twenty-four-floor building. He jumped. He was in New York." In fact, I would later learn, Pappas had hurled himself from a window at the Helmsley Palace Hotel near Grand Central Station minutes after hearing about the story. Trippi got the news from one of the *Post* reporters, who tracked him down that Sunday morning. "The question was not, How did I like the story or you know, something like that," Trippi said. "It was: I need to ask you some questions for a story we're doing for Monday. Today Tom Pappas threw himself out of a building and killed himself. What do you have to say?" He shook his head in disbelief. "That was the press."

Trippi swigged from his Miller Lite and rubbed his eyes clear. "It just kills me, every time I even remember that guy," he said. "I just don't understand it. Even if it was true, it wasn't fucking front-page news. We were just going through this whole thing where the personal stuff just wasn't out of bounds anymore. The Hart thing just unleashed this really crazy period."

Then and forever after, Hart's name would be linked with every sex scandal in politics, no matter how tenuous the connection. And yet the Hart Effect, if you can call it that, wasn't solely, or even chiefly, about sex. In fact, the very purpose of political journalism—the prime directive, as any *Star Trek* fan might put it—had now been redefined. As Hart himself had predicted, and as Taylor had astutely observed, political journalism was now concerned almost entirely with exposing lies and unearthing character flaws, sexual or not. Coverage had been trending this way, of course, ever since Watergate, and the bookish generation now ascending into the highest ranks of journalism had always taken a less trusting, more adversarial approach than the hard-drinking old guys. But Hart's downfall was the thing that tipped the scales completely, the catalyst that made it okay—even necessary—for all aspiring political reporters to cast themselves as amateur PI's and psychotherapists. If post-Hart political journalism had a motto, it would have been: We know you're a fraud somehow. Our job is to prove it.

Often, it must be said, the stories this new culture spawned had genuine value. A senior congressional aide who routinely harassed staffers clearly had something to answer for, and the fact that these stories might have gone unreported in years past didn't make them any less relevant. The media had good reason to be more skeptical in a society that had already felt the cost of trusting its leaders too much and where carefully choreographed, patriotic TV images could obscure a lot that mattered about a candidate.

The problem, as Hendrik Hertzberg understood, was that along with discretion, the media had discarded any sense of context, too. Once the public heard about your misstep, that was *all* the public would hear about you—or about anything else, if the story were big enough—until you did your duty and disappeared, or until the mob simply exhausted itself and left you lying in the dust. As with Hart, even the intimation of scandal could displace anything else you'd ever done as a measure of character. It was reasonable to argue that Tom Pappas's profiting illegally from political campaigns—or even his sexuality, if in fact it pertained to repeated mistreatment of the men who worked for him—were newsworthy facts. But looking down from the twenty-fourth floor of the Helmsley Palace that Sunday morning, it must have seemed to Pappas that this was all anyone would ever know of him again, the totality of his career in public service reduced to a single headline he might never outlive.

And, of course, it didn't take long for political operatives to grasp both the peril and the opportunity of this new order. If reporters were ever in search of the single embarrassing fact, however personal or trivial, that could destroy the hard-won reputation of your candidate overnight, then those same reporters could destroy your opponent just as quickly—if you could find his vulnerability first and slyly maneuver it into the right hands. Once politicians and operatives understood the destructive force that had been unleashed, like some sorcerer's elixir, by this obsession with character, there was no containing it.

The second casualty of the 1988 campaign, after Hart, was Joe Biden, who was perhaps the most promising of the New Garys vying to fill the vacuum in the field. Biden prided himself on hailing from a kind of loquacious, freewheeling tradition of Irish storytelling, and in Iowa he had warmed to a riff from Neil Kinnock, the Labour Party leader in England, about being the "first in a thousand generations" of his family to graduate college. Normally, Biden would credit Kinnock when he got to this part of his shtick, but on at least one occasion, during a debate in Iowa, he carelessly neglected to source the citation. And so, less than four months after the Hart scandal, John Sasso, who was Dukakis's chief strategist, quietly slipped a videotape of that debate to Maureen Dowd at *The New York Times*.

It took all of eleven days for the frenzy that followed this small story to claim Biden's candidacy, during which it was revealed that he had also lifted isolated passages from the Kennedys in the past—which hardly differentiated him from any other Democrat of his generation—and that once, in law school, twenty-odd years earlier, he had been accused of plagiarism. (Sasso, too, would be forced to resign from the campaign after his role in the scandal came to light, although he later returned to help Dukakis during the general election.) In Biden's case, as in Hart's, all the truth was out. It just wasn't clear that *all* the truth was actually illuminating.

In early 1989, after Bush survived rumors of his own infidelity and won the White House, he nominated John Tower, the former senator from Texas, to be his defense secretary. Confirmation hearings in the Senate were thought to be a formality—until the conservative activists who had long disdained Tower (mainly because he had supported Gerald Ford against Ronald Reagan in 1976) accused him of drinking and "womanizing" and turned the hearings into a referendum on his "moral character." After weeks of debate and breathless coverage, Tower's former colleagues, by a narrow margin, made him the first cabinet pick of any newly elected president to be rejected by the Senate.

In *See How They Run*, Paul Taylor pointed to the Tower episode as an example of admirable restraint on the media's part, because reporters "let the Senate take the lead role" in investigating Tower's personal proclivities. But this was probably beside the point. Senators and their ideological allies understood now, in the wake of the Hart scandal, that if they could manage to instigate a debate about someone's character, whether having to do with sex or some other private lapse, the media would lock on to it like a laser beam, and nothing more substantive would ever be discussed. Reporters had "let the Senate take the lead" only in the sense that the guy who pins your arms down is letting another thug take the lead in beating the tar out of you. The relationship between personally ruinous politics and scandal-obsessed journalism was symbiotic.

If Tower's implosion marked the start of a more personally perilous chapter in the life of the Senate, it was downright genteel next to what was transpiring down the hall in the House of Representatives. By end of 1989, as Taylor noted, "no fewer than four members of the U.S. House of Representatives were being investigated by the House ethics committee for alleged sexual misconduct." (One of these was Barney Frank, who, it was revealed, had been allowing an escort he had hired and befriended to operate a male prostitution ring in his home.) Meanwhile, the Democratic House speaker, Jim Wright of Texas, was fending off a separate investigation into his own lapse in integrity, which centered on a charge that he had conspired to accept more money in royalties from his memoir than he was allowed to accept under House rules. Wright resigned in June 1989, making him the only speaker in history to be forced from office by scandal. (It would be less than a decade before another man who was about to become speaker, Robert Livingston, would have to bow out over allegations of adultery.)

Historically speaking, the Wright scandal was as significant for the career it most elevated as it was for the man whose ambitions were dashed. It was a conservative and combative congressman from Georgia named Newt Gingrich who brought the initial charges against Wright and used the case as a platform. In some ways, Gingrich, while seven years younger, was Hart's generational opposite. Erudite and reflective, with a doctoral degree in history, Gingrich embraced Hart's concept for military reform early on, and like the Atari Democrats, he was enamored of the new digital technologies that were about to transform the American economy. Like Hart, he was a prolific writer who prided himself on being able to peer around corners—although Gingrich would long be ridiculed for some of the wackier predictions he floated, like the idea that American factories would soon be making metal alloys in space.

But where Hart studied military history and literature for insights into how he might win campaigns (he was fond, during the McGovern campaign in 1972, of citing the insurgent General Kutuzov from *War and Peace*, whose strategy was to "attack and retreat, attack and retreat"), Gingrich studied them mainly for the purpose of destroying his enemies. If Hart was Kutuzov, then Gingrich more closely resembled Napoleon. And after 1987, Gingrich clearly understood that the evolving political culture could work to his advantage.

Republicans had been a minority in the House for more than thirty years. But what Gingrich saw immediately in the post-Hart moment was that it would now be far easier to take your adversaries down in a surge of scandal—or, more precisely, multiple scandals— than it would be to unseat them at the polls. You were never going to get rid of a giant like Jim Wright by out-campaigning him, but you might succeed by finding the moral transgression that could be used to taint his character and tantalize the media. After Wright, Gingrich went after the entire Democratic majority this way, exposing their personal venality when it came to writing bad checks off the House bank or using the Congressional Post Office for campaign mail. (In fact, about 320 members and former members of Congress from both parties had written checks that required overdraft protection on their account—including Gingrich himself.)

Eventually, Newt, as he was universally known, would lead a Republican takeover of the House and become the party's first speaker since 1955. And history would cast him as the principal adversary of the first president of the boomer generation, a man whose own faulty character would obliterate all other political discussion in the waning years of the American century.

Among Democratic insiders of the period, it's often been said that Bill Clinton could not have existed without Gary Hart. This is true in more than one sense. Hart's essential argument to Democrats in the 1980s—that a party grounded in New Deal industrial policies and Vietnam-era pacifism had to modernize and rethink if it wanted to remain relevant—formed the basis of the electoral and governing philosophy that would come to be known as Clintonism. But just as important, Hart's shocking ruination meant that the new culture of political journalism was no longer a shock to anyone else. Had Clinton, a notoriously flawed husband, been the first to encounter tabloid-style journalism and satellite-driven coverage of his private life, he almost certainly would have been consumed by the same kind of media inferno that claimed Hart. As it was, coming four years after the *Monkey Business* blowup, Clinton knew exactly what to expect, and he had a better sense of how to navigate it—or, more precisely, how not to.

In fact, Clinton was thinking hard about this issue in the run-up to his own presidential campaign. Sometime around 1990, Tom Fiedler spoke about media ethics at a panel in Little Rock, where state legislators happened to be meeting. Afterward, an aide to Governor Clinton approached and asked Fiedler to spend some time with the governor. In a suite at the Excelsior Hotel (the same hotel where Clinton would later be accused of having sexually harassed a woman named Paula Jones), Clinton questioned Fiedler about where he and his fellow reporters would draw the line on extramarital affairs. Was it news, he wanted to know, if a presidential candidate had cheated on his wife in the past, but wasn't doing it currently? (Fiedler thought not.) What was the media's statute of limitations likely to be? Fiedler found himself in the uncomfortable position of being consulted as an expert on the new category of sex scandal—which, of course, he was.

Later, Fiedler, like many others, would consider Clinton's career in national politics proof that the Hart episode had not, in fact, led to an era where imperfections of character would overwhelm everything else. Fiedler had maintained all along that it wasn't the reporter's job to decide which aspects of a candidate's life or persona were relevant to his abilities and which weren't; those decisions were best left to the voters, who would ultimately be able to work through these disclosures and put them in context. As Fiedler saw it, in the case of marital infidelity, the voters had taken four years to process what had happened with Hart, and by 1992 they had decided that simply having cheated on your wife (and even having lied about it) was not, by itself, a disqualifying factor for a presidential candidate. Hart was the first, and perhaps he was treated more harshly because of it, but America had not become the place he warned of in his acid farewell, where politics existed only as treacherous sport. Rather, we had quickly evolved into a more forgiving society with a more complex notion of character.

There was a lot of validity in this. In the years after Clinton won not one but two terms in the White House, the list of politicians who would manage to rebound from sex scandals that made Hart's look quaint grew almost as long as the list of those who hadn't. Americans became desensitized to scandalous revelation, whether it involved sex or drug use or cheating on a college exam. You could disappoint us, certainly, but we were now a very hard country to shock.

And when politicians didn't rebound, you could generally make a pretty good case that their moral transgressions were worth our knowing about. Did Eliot Spitzer deserve to be New York's governor—and a moralizing one, at that—after it was revealed that he had routinely rendezvoused with hookers while traveling on the taxpayers' bill? Should we not have cared that Anthony Weiner, the brash candidate for mayor of New York, was "sexting" young women, even after he had been drummed out of Congress for it and had promised to get the habit under control? It was reasonable to suggest that this hinted at some deeper compulsion or insecurity that was not unrelated to—and, in fact, was probably central to—his craving for public validation.

Perhaps, in the years after 1987, the electorate had become worldlier and more discerning, as Fielder suggested. At the same time, though, when it came to the presidency, mere survival had replaced any actual record as the central test of success. Sure, Clinton managed in 1992 to avoid the calamitous judgment that had befallen Hart an election cycle earlier. But despite presiding over a surging high-tech economy, his presidency would mostly be remembered as a series of personal scandals and evasive maneuvers that would have been unthinkable in another era—things like "Troopergate" and "Whitewater" and some silly affair involving the White House Travel Office that no one even remembers now, not to mention a blue dress with semen stains and the first actual impeachment in 130 years.

In the age of what Clinton himself termed, with notable clarity, "the politics of personal destruction," independent prosecutors were far more numerous than significant triumphs of legislation. More than one Clinton aide would tell me, after the fact, that Clinton would have pushed hard to reform industrial age entitlement programs in his second term had it not been for the impeachment saga that sapped his presidency. Whether or not that was true, by that point Clinton could only hope to last out his second term and nothing more. It's telling that the most authoritative book about Clinton's presidency, written by the journalist John Harris, was called not "The Reformer" or "The Progressive," as Clinton might have hoped back in 1992, but rather *The Survivor*.

Just as important, Clinton embodied a profound change in the nature of candidacies after Hart and how they were evaluated.

Clinton didn't succeed where Hart had failed so miserably simply because a few years had passed and no one really cared anymore, as Fiedler suggested. He succeeded because he was an entirely different genre of politician, with an entirely different skill set. Hart was cerebral and certain of himself, prone to trust his own counsel, someone who clung stubbornly to his own idea of principle, even when it did him no good. He held himself at a certain emotional remove. These were qualities that, for most of the life of the republic, were considered the traits of strong leadership. This is why being called a loner in the media never alarmed Hart as much as it did his younger aides; to him, it conjured images of Lincoln and Kennedy and perhaps even Reagan—men of resolve, self-reliance, and at times a certain inscrutability.

Clinton was a whole other type. Like Hart, Clinton made a point of saying he didn't think any candidate should have to discuss the cracks in his marital life, but then he did exactly that—at length, expertly and disarmingly, with his wife pointedly by his side. Clinton was all too willing to emote about the "pain in his marriage" on *60 Minutes,* to play the saxophone like some street-corner hustler on *The Arsenio Hall Show,* to share the intimate details of his underwear choices on MTV. Clinton openly yearned for approval and acceptance, for any kind of physical contact, any hand outstretched. He was famous for telling whoever was in the room last whatever he wanted to hear. As the country would find out later, Clinton was also willing to lie, outright, when it came to behavior he considered irrelevant or couldn't face in himself. Clinton was a brilliant and complex thinker, a magnetic personality, but also frustratingly needy and malleable.

These were exactly the attributes it took to get hit in the face with roiling wave after roiling wave, revelations and innuendo and attacks on your integrity, and then pop back up in the surf, fully expecting to get hit again. But they were not necessarily the qualities one needed to lead the country steadily through an economic and global transformation unlike any in a century. This was not the psychological makeup of a president who would tell people the hard truths they didn't want to know, or who would forge ahead with modernizing old systems even when popular sentiment turned the other way.

To be clear, the events of 1987 weren't the only thing that caused Americans to redefine the essential qualities we looked for in a national leader. Other equally large and ominous trends were just then emerging in politics, too, and have been written about at great length: the proliferation of cable news, the professionalization of polling, the surge of big money in political campaigns. But beginning with Hart's demise, we in the media made this shift explicit.

There had been plenty of "horse race" journalism before the 1980s, stories about who was likely to win which primaries and all of that, but the candidates themselves were discussed mostly for their arguments and strategies, rather than for their skills as evaders and salesmen. In the Age of Show Business, however, the measure of a leader became his hunger for the game, his talent for dazzling crowds, his deftness at surviving an unreasonably brutal and small-minded process. We openly admired roguish candidates who could dexterously deflect assaults on their character—from their adversaries, and from us—and disdained those who thought themselves above it. We set traps and then marveled at those who could escape them with Houdini-like grace, which is why Clinton came to be known, almost universally, as the most talented statesman of the age, despite having achieved relatively little of his governing agenda. In short, we came to confuse actual leadership with the capacity to endure, and to entertain.

The first presidential candidate I covered was the former senator Bill Bradley, who ran for the Democratic nomination in 2000 and lost badly. Because Al Gore, the sitting vice president, was assumed to be the inevitable Democratic nominee that year (an assumption that seemed very much in peril by late 1999, when for a few pivotal months Gore lagged behind in fundraising and polling and started to look a lot like Mondale in 1984), Bradley's campaign drew a cadre of young, eager reporters, many of whom were new to the campaign trail and eager to imitate our older colleagues.

Bradley was, by any contemporary standard, a remarkably accessible candidate; he granted me several long sit-down interviews, including one on the day he withdrew. And yet, much like Hart, Bradley, who had been a basketball legend long before he ever entered politics, exuded the sense that there were things he valued more in the world than becoming president—namely his privacy and his notion of dignity. This baffled us. Though we thought the candidate a nice enough guy, we couldn't help fixating on his refusal to talk about his religious beliefs or his medical history, his general aloofness and obvious aversion to political theater. Writing for *Newsweek*, I wasted few words on Bradley's actual proposals (I barely remember them now), but I wrote disdainful stories about his stubborn refusal to "go negative" on Al Gore, who smeared Bradley as hostile to Iowa farmers. The consensus among reporters on the bus was that Bradley lacked the showmanship and utter desperation necessary to run a modern presidential campaign. We were right.

It wasn't until several years later, after I met a long-retired politician in the foothills of Denver, that I began to reconsider my own notions of what constituted political genius, and to wonder whether we might be getting the leaders we deserved, after all.

7

EXILE

ON EASTER SUNDAY 1995, Gary Hart had something of a religious experience. He found himself standing on a windswept mountain, staring into the awful eyes of God.

Hart awoke that morning in the cabin, piled his two chows, the black Samson and the silver Delilah, into the truck, and drove into town for his Sunday *New York Times,* as he had on most mornings since returning to his home for good seven years earlier. But when Hart arrived back at the cabin a few minutes later and popped open the back of the truck, Samson, as peaceful a dog as you will ever meet, leaped out and took off down the gravel road at a dead run, heading east. Then, as Samson scaled the almost sheer wall of dirt and rock that loomed just behind the cabin and the road, and as his confused owner squinted into the morning sun, the dog let go a piercing howl of alarm, which bounced off the opposite hill and rattled around in the still morning air like some primeval roar.

This isn't about a deer or a rabbit, Hart thought to himself.

Hart, who had hiked just about every inch of this land, and who at fifty-eight still possessed the ruggedness he'd honed driving railroad spikes in the summer as a teenager, walked down the road 150 yards or so, just to the first bend, and started ascending. He didn't hear howling or barking above him now. He didn't hear anything but his own breath. He began to feel a sickly fear for his four-year-old companion. He steeled himself for what he might see when at last he came to level ground, near the trees and shrubs under which a wounded animal might crawl to die.

About forty yards up the hill, he found himself standing before the base of a large tree. Under it he saw Samson, unhurt but agitated, crawling and sniffing and pawing at the dirt. Then Hart heard a long, slow rumble, a growl that was more like the coming of a distant train.

Slowly Hart looked up, and there, perched on a branch maybe ten feet above and directly in front of him, was a full-grown, magnificently muscular, tawny brown mountain lion. Hart wasn't a hunter (who could ever shoot a thing like that?), but his father had taught him to track game as a boy in Kansas, and he estimated the beast's weight at about 150 pounds, maybe 175. It was prone, as if to leap. And it had taken note of his arrival.

Hart knew exactly what to do in such a situation. Make yourself large. Don't run. Whatever you do, don't make eye contact. He knew how the cat would kill him—not by mauling, but by snapping his neck cleanly, as a boot heel snaps a twig. Not six miles away, a mountain lion—maybe *this* mountain lion—had not long before broken into a house, killed the owner's dogs and dragged them into the cold. Hart had always had a premonition, as a child, that he would die young, like his favorite uncle, who succumbed to brain cancer at forty-four. He was no longer so young, but maybe it was the suddenness of his death he had sensed, the violent end to an unsettled life.

But Hart couldn't look away, didn't want to. Instead, he stared directly, mesmerized, into the yellow eyes, which seemed to regard him thoughtfully. They were like-minded creatures, the two of them, intense and brooding, bound by their natures to do what they must. Hart was resigned to his fate. Let it be, he thought. Just do what you came here to do.

For those five seconds, which felt to the frozen Hart like many minutes, it was as if the lion were trying to decide whether this tormented man had ambled over the ridge with a wish to meet his judgment, or whether he was simply too bone tired to turn around and leave.

At long last, the lion turned his head away. Then he soared—that was the only word that described it. He soared through the thin, mile-high air and landed, maybe twenty-five or thirty feet from Hart. And then he bounded away. Hart breathed deeply, but it wasn't relief he felt. Rather, it was a sense of awe and privilege, or maybe transformation. He felt, for that moment, as if he had stepped backward into Eden, to an untamed wilderness and a time before sin.

Hart had broken with the Nazarenes almost forty years earlier, after he left his Bible college on the Plains for the worldlier confines of New Haven. He had essentially abandoned religion, at least in an organized sense, when he made the switch from Yale Divinity to the law school—and the pursuit of politics—a few years later. He remained a believer, but he had never quite found a church in the foothills that made him entirely comfortable, a minister who could manage to fuse his dueling impulses toward the spiritual and the political. And so he spent his Sundays communing with Lee and his dogs and the *Times,* instead.

But he wondered, in the hours and days after he stumbled back down the hill and took stock of his life, whether God was trying to tell him something now, about his present circumstances and the road ahead. He could have died on that ridge, but he didn't, and the awareness of that unexpected mercy filled Hart with an emotion he had almost relinquished: hope. What if the creator wasn't finished with him, after all? What if the journey didn't just end here, at this place of bottomless regret, but there were turns still to be revealed?

Several times over the years, Hart would remind me of that story, as if wanting to relive it. Each time, his eyes would get moist and pink, his voice thinner. He would look to that ridge and remember. He would see that lion soar and feel redeemed.

"Accept your death and become dangerous."

A supporter sent Hart that note, one of hundreds he received and cherished during those first few months after the scandal, when there was little to do but open mail in the law office. The writer said it was a Native American proverb, which made Hart like it all the more; he had always had a deep affinity for the tribes he represented as a senator. And it resonated with him, this idea that the establishment he had always challenged still might be made to regret marginalizing and lampooning him. Hart had little, really, left to lose, and history was replete with great men—his idol Robert Kennedy among them—who had found in their depression and isolation the resolve they needed to confront the system.

The problem for Hart, it turned out, was that he just couldn't seem to accept his political death. He may have disdained the Democratic establishment in Washington, but he valued what only the establishment could offer—the chance to serve in some kind of formal capacity, to be inside the room when vital decisions were made. Hart was a dissenter, yes, but not a bomb-thrower, and he respected the institutions of government and media too much to jettison any hope of the legitimacy they conferred. He had already given up any thought of ever again running for office by the time he bowed out finally in 1988; if he couldn't be president, there was no point in enduring the tedium of more campaigns. But having just passed fifty-one at that time, Hart was far from ready to relinquish his status as a visionary in his own party, and especially on the global stage. He wanted badly to serve, once the cloud of disgrace had dissipated.

What Hart couldn't know—what no one could know—was exactly how long that might take. After all, no politician of Hart's stature had ever endured this particular kind of national humiliation. The closest analogue was probably Nixon, who retreated to San Clemente after his resignation and set about writing a memoir and plotting his rehabilitation (yet again) as a kind of policy sage. But Hart could never have identified with Nixon, and anyway he had committed no high crimes or misdemeanors, nothing he felt required him to be rehabilitated.

Instead, typically, Hart drew his inspiration from history and philosophy. He reached through the ages and found a kindred spirit in Niccolò Machiavelli, the sixteenth-century Italian diplomat and public official who was arrested and subsequently exiled by the Medici who conquered Florence. Yearning to be of service to the new regime, Machiavelli wrote a series of essays about the exercise of power and governance to a young member of the Medici clan, a collection of which was later published as *The Prince*—the work that made him immortal.

Although Hart would never come out and make the comparison explicitly, clearly he felt that he, too, had been banished, and that he, too, might best prove his value to the political class by issuing grand thoughts on paper from his own remote estate. Ensconced in his book-lined, cedar-paneled study upstairs, overlooking the living room and picture windows, Hart wrote no fewer than five books in the decade after the 1988 campaign (including the first of two novels published under a pseudonym, "John Blackthorn," so that they might be taken seriously). The third of these books, *The Patriot*, published in 1996, was Hart's explicit homage to *The Prince*, except that his version was addressed to a young American leader. It featured a rather pretentious subtitle—*An Exhortation to Liberate America from the Barbarians*—and opened with a quote from Machiavelli himself: "Fortune has decided that I must speak about the state."

Hart's real-life prince, however, the contemporary to whom he addressed his most important correspondence on issues of the state, was Bill Clinton. In theory, at least, it was a stroke of good fortune for Hart that Clinton, rather than some other Democrat, rose to fill the vacuum in the party that Hart's disappearance had created. The two had known one another since 1972, when Hart, as McGovern's campaign manager, gave Clinton, then a twenty-five-year-old law student, his first job in politics, as McGovern's Texas coordinator. They had remained in touch over the years, and both had gravitated to the anti-orthodox, more reformist movement inside the party. The centrist Democratic Leadership Council, which served as Clinton's platform in the late 1980s and early 1990s, had taken a lot of its economic and foreign policy ideas directly from Hart's campaigns. What Clinton called the "New Democrats" in 1992 were indistinguishable from the "neoliberals" for whom Hart had spoken in the 1980s.

Plus, there was a good deal of continuity between Hart's inner circle and the team that Clinton put together. One of the loyal Hart acolytes who ended up close to Clinton was John Emerson, the Californian who had been Dixon's number two at the top of the Hart command. In September 1992, after Clinton had accepted the party's nomination and appeared weeks away from unseating the incumbent president, George H. W. Bush, Hart sent Emerson a three-page memorandum recommending policies and strategies to deal with the pressing challenges of recession, energy dependence, and defense spending. The greatest challenge facing the country, Hart wrote, was to fundamentally restructure the society before it faced "a depression or economic catastrophe."

After Clinton took office, Emerson, who now had a senior job in the West Wing, brought Hart in for a private and warm talk with the new president. Hart was too proud to come out and ask the president to return the favor of twenty years before, and the subject of a specific job never came up. But it was clear that Hart still had value, both for his expertise on policy and for his connections in both parties and across several continents. And clearly he coveted some role in public life that would help erase the stain of what had become a comic scandal beyond any reasonable proportion. All he needed to do, Hart figured, was to keep the lines of communication open.

Thus began a trail of occasional letters, usually policy-laden but at times more personal, that would last, on and off, for many years. (Hart shared both sides of this correspondence with me only after Clinton, who was by then out of office, assented.) Hart's immediate thoughts were on Russia, where he'd spent a good deal of time doing legal work since 1989; the first of his post-scandal books, written in 1991, was *Russia Shakes the World: The Second Russian Revolution and Its Impact on the West.* Twice in 1993, Hart sent Clinton his thoughts on dealing with Russia—and offering his services in any way they might be needed. Clinton responded politely both times and invited Hart to join the board of a new government fund for investment in Russia. This wasn't exactly the kind of senior posting Hart had in mind, although he accepted.

Hart decided, apparently, to try a different tack. In July 1994, when Clinton was taking a pounding over allegations of sexual harassment and of a shady land deal while he was governor, Hart sat down at his desk and wrote him a personal letter of support—in longhand and all capital letters, just like the memos he used to send his Senate staff. "Dear Mr. President," he began. "The tallest nail gets hit the hardest and longest. The issue is whether it will be driven flat like all the others. This is the true character issue." Hart continued:

> You are right to believe you are being criticized more harshly and unfairly than your modern predecessors. Franklin Roosevelt and John Kennedy were hated by much of the business community, but over philosophical differences. It requires a return to Lincoln and Jefferson to find precedent for the meanness of your vilification.
>
> It is partly a decline of civility in our age. But it is also ad hominem, a result of your critics' failure to have the wit or grace to debate the merits of your reforms. You are the victim of your own exceptionalism which inexplicably draws irrational fire. . . . My conviction is that, some years from now, you will be judged a very great president. Your continued perseverance is the only response this note requires.

Clinton responded in kind, days later. "Dear Gary," he scrawled in longhand, "Your letter was generous, thoughtful, and a boost for me, beyond the call—thanks." He asked Hart to send him more ideas for "how I might better articulate and communicate what I'm trying to do."

Hart didn't need a second invitation. The next month, he sent Clinton a dense, three-page memo on the negotiations over Britain's control of Northern Ireland. Referring to himself, characteristically, in the third person, so as not to appear presumptuous, Hart wrote that "the author" had several initiatives in mind, the first of which went like this: "After consultation with all parties, you should appoint a 'personal representative' to observe, monitor, and report to you on the progress of further peace negotiations, with an emphasis on seeking new formulas to facilitate progress." Hart didn't spell out who might fill this role of presidential envoy, but he noted his "long-term personal friendship" with one of the British prime minister's most trusted advisors on the issue. Contrary to the long-standing British policy of opposing such a mediator, Hart expressed confidence that the British might secretly welcome his intervention.

Clinton replied about three weeks later and shot down the idea. "For the moment," the president wrote, "and especially in light of recent developments, I believe the U.S. can be most helpful by supporting the process through existing channels with strong White House involvement." Underneath the official letter, as was his custom, Clinton penned a more personal note, as if to soften the blow. "Some of your specific recommendations may yet be needed," he wrote, "but at least we have a breakthrough we're working toward."

In fact, less than a year later, Clinton did take Hart's suggestion to name a personal representative in the talks, but the man he named was George Mitchell, Hart's former colleague in the Senate. (Mitchell would be awarded the Presidential Medal of Freedom, the nation's highest honor, for his work on the issue and would thereafter be considered a kind of roving senior statesman—precisely the dream Hart fostered for himself.) Hart's determination to get back in the game never flagged, but his ambitions grew more modest and his attempts a bit more desperate. Having been rebuffed on Russia and Northern Ireland, Hart proposed to Clinton—more than once during Clinton's second term—that he be engaged to work out a formal peace agreement between Russia and Japan. (Apparently, the two countries hadn't reconciled in the fifty years since World War II and were technically still at war.)

"I urge you to give serious consideration to this proposal and, as always, wish you the very best success," Hart wrote the president in April 1998, upon renewing this request. A month later, he received another awkward, staff-written reply from Clinton rejecting his proposal, along with another handwritten note under the signature. "I agree that you could help resolve this if they were willing to have outside help," Clinton scribbled, a bit more brusquely than in previous letters. "For different domestic reasons, they don't appear to be at this time."

Emerson and others who had been close to Hart, and who now worked for Clinton, continued to push his case inside the West Wing and at some cabinet agencies—namely Defense—during the nineties. At times, his former aides despaired at what they saw as Hart's impossible pride and self-regard, the fact that he considered most open jobs beneath him, and that he refused to lobby administration officials on his own behalf. But as the exchange of letters shows, Hart *was* willing to lobby, at least directly with the man whose opinion mattered most.

The more salient problem, as one of Hart's allies finally told him, was that whenever his name would surface in any high-level discussion, someone on the political side of the White House would dismiss the idea immediately. ("That's hard to know," Hart said of this bit of intelligence.) The last thing Clinton needed was to invite a raft of new cartoons and late-night jokes about the world's most famous adulterer taking on the world's second most famous adulterer as a running buddy. In the public mind, Hart stood for one thing, and it happened to be the one thing Clinton spent most of his presidency trying frantically to transcend.

For Hart, it was a decade of profound disappointment. He had to watch, from his cabin in the hills, as Clinton got credit for modernizing and moderating liberalism, which is what Hart had been proposing to do since the 1970s. And although Al From, who had founded the Democratic Leadership Council and recruited Clinton to be its spokesman, would always credit Hart with having inspired the New Democrat movement, Hart himself rejected the comparison; he developed contempt for Clinton's "third way," which he saw increasingly as a cynical strategy, a way of simply stealing the conservative argument that liberalism was dead, rather than breathing life back into the liberal ideal. Hart admired Clinton's political skill, but if he had ever really believed what he wrote in 1994, that Clinton would be remembered as a great president, he did not believe it for long.

You can imagine, though, that what really anguished Hart had less to do with Clinton's policies than with the universal injustice his endurance as a politician seemed to represent. After all, it wasn't as if Clinton had succeeded, becoming the first Democrat since Franklin Roosevelt to win two terms, because he had avoided making the same mistakes Hart had made—far from it. By 1998, it was clear that Clinton's personal transgressions made Hart look like a eunuch by comparison. The creepiest thing any woman had ever said about Hart was that he had once answered his hotel door in a bathrobe when a reporter knocked on it during the 1984 campaign, which was a long way from groping random women or enjoying fellatio from an intern while talking on the phone with world leaders—all of which were part of Clinton's legend by the end of his presidency.

And yet, somehow, Clinton's hubris and his sexual personality disorder (there was really no other way to look at it) came to be seen as proving his immense political talent, rather than negating it. He emerged in the public mind as roguish and irrepressible, in the way made famous by leading men on TV dramas—a man too dynamic and insatiable for his own good, but not necessarily for ours. As the decade came to a close, Gary Hart remained the political equivalent of Hester Prynne, cast out and humiliated because of a single lingering photo. Bill Clinton, who endured impeachment for wagging his finger and lying to the country about his long dalliance with Monica Lewinsky, a twenty-three-year-old woman in his charge, left office with an approval rating of 68 percent.

In September 1998, when Clinton was finally forced to give a speech confessing to his sins and his months-long deception about them, he publicly apologized to Lewinsky and her family for the ordeal he had put them through. (*The Washington Post* had broken news of the president's sex-capade, more than a decade after Paul Taylor's question and more than six years after Ben Bradlee's retirement.) Weeks later, although he would later say the two things weren't connected, Hart sat at his oak desk in the study and stared at a phone number on a sheet of paper. Then he picked up the phone, listened for a dial tone, and punched in the 703 number a longtime supporter had found for him—a number in Northern Virginia.

After a few rings, during which he probably considered hanging up, Donna Rice answered the phone.

Hart hadn't seen Rice since the confusing night in 1987 when he watched Billy Broadhurst shepherd her and Lynn Armandt toward the back door of the townhouse he had long since sold. For some time, Hart wondered—as Rice guessed he did—if she might have been involved in some plot to derail his campaign. (She had pleaded with McAliley to tell Hart she hadn't known, and she had personally assured Hart of the same thing during a private phone call in McAliley's office a few weeks after the scandal broke, which was the last time the two had talked.) But as years passed, that theory seemed less and less plausible to Hart, and eventually he added her to the list of people he felt deserved his remorse, whose lives would have been different had he made some wiser decisions. Whatever the nature of their bond to that point, Hart and Rice were united ever after by a shared experience that few others, if any, could really understand. They knew what it was to be transformed into tabloid caricatures overnight.

The life of the Donna Rice who was sitting on Hart's lap in the dockside photo had essentially ended on the morning two days after the *Herald* story broke, and twenty-four hours after the campaign had released her name to the media, when she climbed aboard the twin-engine plane that Tom McAliley had secretly chartered, with little more than some hastily packed clothes and a toothbrush. The plane, it turned out, was headed to the Florida Panhandle, where McAliley had a friend whose place was empty. That's where Rice watched TV as Hart withdrew from the race, and as the picture taken with her own camera, by a woman she had thought to be a friend, became ubiquitous. She stayed there, in hiding, for weeks. Eventually, she went back to work for Wyeth, but reporters followed her on her sales calls to doctors' offices, and one doctor even tried to sell her business card, and when it was clear after a few months that her notoriety wasn't going to fade, her bosses made it equally clear that she should probably resign. After that, she had no income, no privacy, and nowhere to go.

She had always talked about moving to L.A., where she had friends. She thought she could have a career as a TV actress, or maybe even a writer. So Rice moved out West and signed on with a talent agency. For the rest of 1987, and especially after Hart reentered the race, the offers flew at her. *Playboy* was willing to start at $1 million—really it was a blank check, she was made to understand—if she would consent to do a simple Q&A, with a tastefully done headshot and nothing more. ABC would pay at least that much for her cooperation with a made-for-TV movie. CBS brought in all of its division heads—news, entertainment, and so on—to meet her, because it was said that the network's president, Laurence Tisch, had decreed he wanted her on the network, and he didn't care how.

What most of the media wanted, though, wasn't Donna Rice; it was her story. Networks and magazines were more than willing to make her wealthier than the daughter of a federal highway engineer had ever dreamed of becoming—if only she would give them the real goods on Gary Hart.

Rice wouldn't go there, not for any amount of money. Her grandmother counseled her that she had already been blamed for ruining this man's ambitions once. She couldn't allow herself to be held responsible for doing it again.

She did give some cautious interviews to Barbara Walters, because the anchor seemed genuinely interested in who she really was, and that was as close as Rice could get to trusting anyone. She did an ad campaign, too, for "No Excuses" jeans—a decision she immediately regretted. The problem was that what Rice yearned for now wasn't money or onscreen fame, however much she had coveted all that in a former life. Rather, she wanted the one thing the world wasn't offering. She wanted to prove she was a good, decent person—not this loose, partying swimsuit model with a smoky look on the cover of *People*. She wanted to believe that all of this had some meaning or purpose, that something redeeming would ultimately come from the shame and ridicule.

And that's when Donna Rice rediscovered Jesus—not in the eyes of a mountain lion, but in the hiss of a cassette tape. Actually, it was her mother and her grandmother who first put the idea in her head, who told her she "needed to get right with God." Then a friend from high school, a girl she hadn't talked to in years, sent her a package through her family. The note said she didn't know if all this stuff she was reading was true, or what had happened to the Donna Rice she knew. But it didn't matter, because it was never too late to ask forgiveness and change your life; she enclosed a tape of herself singing songs they had sung together in a Christian youth group many years earlier. The way Rice would later explain it, the Lord worked his miracle through that tape. He made sure, also, to steer her into the company of other devout Christians who had no agenda, other than to take her in and heal her.

There were no role models for Donna Rice, you have to remember—no women made famous by political scandal who had somehow found their way back to respectability. The closest thing she found during those months, the only example that inspired her to carry on, was a memoir by Chuck Colson, the Watergate figure who had been born again in prison and ultimately became a minister. And so it seemed like God's plan at work when Rice, at the invitation of one of her new Christian friends, came to Washington for the National Prayer Breakfast in early 1989 and found herself in the company of some of the people who had rallied around Colson and who had even offered to serve his prison time for him, had the system allowed it. Not just the *kind* of people who had supported him, mind you, but the very same ones. They wanted to support her, too.

And so Rice ended up falling into the comforting embrace of what was known as "the Fellowship" or sometimes simply "the Family," a group of religious activists who sought to keep national leaders on a righteous path. As she had during those nightmarish days when Hart's coterie of aides had smuggled her from one place to the next and told her what she had to do, Rice trusted her fate to others, people who knew what to do.

She moved to Northern Virginia, lived with a Christian family, and did volunteer work. Eventually, Dee Jepsen, the wife of a retired conservative senator, recruited Rice to work for her new group Enough Is Enough, which was crusading against pornography. In 1994, Rice became the communications director and began a long, noble fight against the emerging world of Internet child porn and sexual predators. Eventually, she rose to become the executive director. She married a conservative businessman named Jack Hughes and lived in tony McLean (epicenter of wealthy, conservative Washington), pinned her blond hair back, and dressed in classic business suits. The congressmen and senators who worked closely with her on the first major Internet porn bill in the mid-1990s didn't even realize that Donna Rice-Hughes was *that* Donna Rice until *The New York Times* profiled her and let everyone know. Donna's mother had begged her to drop the "Rice" when she got married, because of all the baggage it carried, but by then it didn't matter. Donna Rice was, as ever, smart and beautiful and beguiling, and in any way that mattered, she, like Chuck Colson, had been reborn.

Rice wasn't shocked on that fall day in 1998 when the shaky voice on the other end of the phone, ringing with a familiar mountain twang, identified himself as Gary Hart. An intermediary had already contacted Rice to confirm the number and to let her know Hart would be calling. She was curious as to his purpose, but not especially nervous; the truth was she didn't think about him much anymore. She had really liked him back in 1987—trusted him, as she was inclined to do with older, interesting, self-certain men—and he had jettisoned her completely, thrown her to the media wolves with little more than a glance. But Rice had practiced forgiving. She felt sorry for him. She had completely reimagined her life, while Hart had simply disappeared.

But here he was, an oddly familiar voice, saying what he probably should have said a decade ago. Hart said he was sorry for all the bad things that had happened to her back then. He said he had always felt responsible and that she hadn't deserved any of it—he knew that. She thanked him. They talked for a while more, said some things that no one else needed to hear, that would stay between the two of them.

Through all the years of their estrangement, Rice thought she could hear the pain and loneliness in his voice. She thought he sounded lost in regret. So she told him about the Fellowship. They had a place in Northern Virginia where the devout and politically connected, along with the occasional pop star or world leader, came together to eat and pray. Maybe he would think about coming to dinner there with her and her family, Rice said. Maybe they could help him.

Hart thanked her for the invitation. "And that was it," he told me later. He sounded sorrowful, as if he had hoped the conversation might come to some more enlightening end. "I said, 'We'll see.' But that was it."

Clinton actually did do Hart a significant favor before leaving office, although it didn't seem like much at the time. Along with his proposals for intervention in Northern Ireland and in the contested Kuril Islands between Japan and Russia, Hart had been pushing Clinton to establish some kind of commission to rethink America's national security policies for the period after the Cold War. This was in the unstable period just after the fall of the Berlin Wall, when long-simmering ethnic rivalries were boiling over in parts of the world like the former Yugoslavia, and there was much confusion about what role the United States should play. Clinton evidenced no more interest in this suggestion than he had in the others, but it turned out that, once again, Newt Gingrich had been eyeing the same horizon as Hart. In 1998, with Clinton reeling from scandal and desperate for an agreement on anything substantive, Gingrich talked him into creating the U.S. Commission on National Security/21st Century. Among the fourteen commissioners were Gingrich and Hart.

The commission seemed like just another of these shapeless, blue-ribbon panels whose main purpose is to give a few deep thinkers something about which to pontificate. It was to be chaired by two of Hart's former colleagues in the Senate, both recently retired: the Republican Warren Rudman and the Democrat David Boren.

But then Boren, who was by that time president of the University of Oklahoma, realized he was too busy to chair another of these invisible commissions. As luck would have it (and Hart was certainly entitled to some), Clinton's second-term secretary of defense was Bill Cohen, Hart's friend and onetime coauthor. The two had remained close, and so Cohen stepped up where no one else in the administration had. He recommended that Hart be elevated to cochairman, in part because he was better qualified than almost anyone else, but also because he seemed to have a lot more time on his hands than most of the other commissioners. Clinton agreed.

Hart was tentative at first. It had been more than a decade since he had served alongside men and women he respected, and he didn't know how much of their respect he might still command. More than one member of the commission noticed that Hart had trouble finding the voice that had once seemed so compelling to his contemporaries. But as the old confidence returned, so, too, did the trademark sharpness of mind and intensity. Newly energized, Hart traveled more than any commission member and surprised his staff by rewriting much of one report himself.

The final, highly cogent result—a series of three reports, released between September 1999 and January 2001—was collaborative, but it bore more of Hart's signature than it did any other member of the commission. And not surprisingly, the findings were penetrating, in many cases echoing themes Hart had been talking about since the early 1980s. Among the commission's central findings was that the main threat of the twenty-first century would emanate not from any government, but rather from stateless terrorism. "Americans will likely die on American soil, possibly in large numbers," the first report warned in 1999. The commission recommended that Congress create a new federal agency to grapple with "homeland security"—a phrase that had not yet entered the American lexicon.

All of this barely elicited a yawn from the media at the time the reports were released. But that was before the attacks on the World Trade Center towers and the Pentagon in September 2001, when suddenly everyone wanted to know how this could have happened and whether there was any blame to be assigned, and within days it came to light that, yes, there was this report that had all but predicted the attacks, and no one in the Bush administration had wanted to listen. (In fact, Hart had personally lobbied senior officials, Donald Rumsfeld among them, to pay attention to the commission's findings, but Bush had subsequently announced that, instead, Vice President Dick Cheney would be studying the issue of terrorism all over again.) And just like that, in America's darkest hour, Gary Hart was back. This time, there were no late-night monologues, no cameramen hurling themselves onto windshields, no moralizing from the keepers of the op-ed pages. Serious times had returned—and with them, it seemed, a serious man.

Hart was all over TV and quoted in the papers, without a single mention, for once, of Donna Rice. He was on the speaking circuit again, touring the country with a sixteen-minute speech that seemed perfectly calibrated to scare his audiences into a collective cardiac arrest. The next bomb would probably be biological, Hart said, or maybe chemical. It might be shipped from Singapore to Long Beach, put on a train bound for Newark and detonated, remotely, in Chicago. The attack might strike not at New York or even Los Angeles, but at multiple cities at once—maybe Denver or Cleveland or Dallas. Hart warned his newly rapt audiences that an invasion of Iraq, which Bush was readying to undertake, would prove costly in casualties and would achieve little to make the country safer.

When, in the spring of 2002, the former Democratic congressman Steve Solarz asked Hart to sign a letter to Bush from Democratic statesmen who supported a potential invasion, the idea being that pro-war Democrats in Congress needed some political cover from respected voices inside their own party, Hart fired back a note that, read with the benefit of history, now sounds chillingly accurate. "Though I am flattered to have been on the distribution list for your proposed letter to President Bush," Hart began, "the last thing in the world I'm going to do, as a Democrat or as an American, is give this administration a blank check to make war on any country." He concluded:

Once it has been established that Iraq has weapons of mass destruction and the means to deliver them, there will be plenty of time to enact appropriate U.N. resolutions authorizing the international community to act in concert to remove them.

With all due respect, Steve, and there is plenty of that, I think this proposed letter is unwise and ill-conceived. If unqualified, open-ended, mindless support for whatever [Paul] Wolfowitz and [Richard] Perle have on their minds is such a good idea, Democrats in Congress won't need us to make it easier for them. This letter will come back to haunt all who sign it.

Hart had, indeed, found his voice on issues of the day. The question was what to do with it. Even as he had cochaired the presidential commission in hopes of reentering public life in some way, Hart had been pursuing another, long-deferred dream of sorts; in 2001, he earned a doctorate in political science at Oxford. (His thesis, later published as a book, centered on the Jeffersonian ideal in twenty-first-century politics.) While he was there, Hart became something of a hero to a group of American students who were there on Rhodes Scholarships, who were blown away by his intellect and who were too young to remember or care much about the events of 1987. And after the tragedy of 2001, when Hart became, if only briefly, a voice of conscience again, the students hatched a plan. They started pushing Hart to run for president once more. And when he didn't immediately shut down the idea, they managed to get a story written in *The New Republic,* just to float the idea.

That's when I met Hart in Troublesome Gulch, at the end of 2002. At sixty-six, an age when most of his contemporaries were retiring from politics, Hart was enjoying what he hoped might be a resurgence. "Walter Mondale can just go away," Hart explained to me then, or tried to explain, as he and Lee and I stood around the island in his kitchen. "John Glenn can go away. Michael Dukakis can go away. I can't just go away."

It was Lee who asked him why—not for my benefit, but because she genuinely wanted to understand, and it wasn't every day she could get him to reflect on it.

"I don't know," Hart said candidly, shaking his head. He repeated this phrase a few more times. Then he turned to me.

"If I weren't doing this," he asked, meaning publicly entertaining another campaign, "would you be here right now?"

I said probably not.

"Well, there are only two places to be in American life," Hart said. "On the sidelines or on the playing field. I don't need to run for president. But I do want to be heard."

Hart always knew it wasn't a viable idea, this notion of another presidential campaign fifteen years after the last one imploded. He had no money, no real agenda, no staff or base of support beyond a handful of students. He had never loved the business of campaigning, anyway. After he abandoned the pretext, some Colorado Democrats tried to recruit him to run for his old Senate seat, but Hart demurred on that one, too, and more quickly. All he really wanted—really all he had ever wanted, after it became clear that his presidential hopes were shot forever—was to be a Wise Man of the sort the country used to regularly produce, a George Mitchell–type figure on whom presidents and secretaries of state would call for advice and sensitive missions. In truth, as Hart had proven on the national security commission, he was more than qualified for such a role.

He hoped that John Kerry, who had been a colleague and then a personal friend, would at long last help him fulfill this ambition. Perhaps, had Kerry won the presidency in 2004, which he very nearly did, he would have tapped Hart for some senior appointment. Perhaps Hart had every reason to believe that he might get the same consideration four years later, when he jumped in early in the primary season and endorsed Barack Obama on his way to the presidency. But as the decade wore on, it must have occurred to Hart, even if he was too proud to say as much, that he had misjudged the extent of his reclamation, especially in Washington.

Sure, the commission and all the attention it received had for a while reestablished Hart as a brilliant thinker, especially among an elite set of policymakers. But Hart's intellectual firepower had never been in question. It was his character that the media had declared beyond remediation, and nothing about the events of 2001 seemed

At Troublesome Gulch, near Hart's home, 2003 CREDIT: ANDREA MODICA

to have altered that. His Wikipedia page, while it contained a healthy section on the national security commission, still led with the scandal and still featured that infernal photo from the dock at Bimini, and no amount of editing ever managed to erase it for long. Hart confided once that he could feel the stigma, still, when he ran into old friends, journalists or former lawmakers, on the streets of Washington. He could see it in the way they looked at him. It was one of the reasons he came back less and less.

A few months after Obama's victory in 2008, I ran into Hart on my way into the restaurant at the Hay-Adams, across from the White House. Hart always tried to stay at the august old hotel, where he had bargained for a closet-size room in exchange for a reduced rate. He was just leaving a breakfast, and I was meeting a couple of Democratic contributors from New York for coffee.

Hart and I chatted for a moment about the president-elect's transition, and then I headed over to the table where my hosts had already been seated. My mind was still on my previous conversation. "You know, that was Gary Hart I was talking to," I said as I unfolded my napkin.

The older man, who was probably in his eighties, smiled broadly. "You mean from the *Funny Business*?" he asked me, chuckling.

"Actually, it was the *Monkey Business*," I muttered reflexively, almost to myself. I spent the rest of the meeting distracted, staring out absently at Lafayette Park and the majestic columns of the White House. I found myself returning to the three words Hart had once jotted on a memo, to the amusement of his aides, so many years ago:

I despair, profoundly.

Why, in the end, did Hart remain stuck in time? After all, redemption and reinvention were everywhere in twenty-first-century America, as much a part of the modern culture as Starbucks and televised talent shows. Bill Clinton wasn't the only scandalized politician who managed to make people forget his transgressions, or at least not care so much about them. Consider the case of Mark Sanford, who as South Carolina's governor had abandoned both his state and his wife because of a new love. Or Governor Spitzer, who was busted for paying for sex. Both found their way back to public life (if not, in Spitzer's case, to public office), just as ballplayers who used steroids got to keep on playing or coaching, and movie stars who went to jail got to keep playing leading roles. And yet somehow Hart remained trapped on a boat in 1987, which sailed on forever in the public mind.

It's true that, apart from his letters to Clinton, Hart was too proud to plead for jobs that might have restored his legitimacy—he would say he believed in a meritocracy and wanted to be asked. "Averell Harriman would never have said, Me, me, me" is the way Hart put it. Sometimes he seemed, in his brokenness, to fear rejection more than he feared his continuing exile. Obama's election, for example, seemed likely to open a door for him back into public office; one of Obama's closest advisors, David Axelrod, had covered Hart as a reporter in 1984 and still considered him a visionary, and some of Hart's former aides were pushing for him to be considered for a top Defense post or ambassador to Russia.

But then Hart flipped through the nine-page questionnaire that the new administration was handing out to job seekers, and on the last page, under "Miscellaneous," he spotted this question: "Have you had any association with any person, group or business venture that could be used—even unfairly—to impugn or attack your character and qualifications for government service?" Hart actually laughed out loud when he recalled this moment. He said he had considered writing underneath: "Are you kidding me?" Instead, he tossed the papers aside, and that was that.

It was true, too, that Hart resisted the modern ethos of image rehabilitation. He understood, in those first months and years after the scandal, that the quickest path out of exile lay in some kind of public reckoning, maybe an apologetic memoir or a series of cathartic interviews. He might have become the go-to expert on scandal coverage and how it felt to be in the center of it, had he been able to stomach it. "I could have dined out for years and years on privacy, the role of the press," he told me. "You know, any controversy that comes up, I'll get a call. My secretary takes it. She just knows not to even . . ." His voice trailed off and he waved the rest of the sentence away.

"Oh, the theme of the last five or ten years has been, How do you recover from setback?" Hart started laughing convulsively again. To a lot of my contemporaries, rehabilitating oneself by counseling others in this way would have seemed quite natural, but it struck

Hart as terribly funny. "I could have gone out on the lecture circuit and made a fortune on 'recovering from setback'!" He paused, catching his breath. "Can you *imagine*?"

But Hart's old-world sense of decorum, his refusal to beg for work or devise some transparent PR campaign on his own behalf, was something we might just as easily have admired about him, rather than disdained. None of that fully explained the peculiar way in which not just the political establishment, but the culture as a whole, had emphatically, almost maliciously reduced Hart's life's work to an irresistible punch line from the past, as if the very idea of him had been ridiculous from the start. There is a book Stephen King wrote in 2004, the seventh installment in his *Dark Tower* fantasy series, in which a character named Susannah finds herself transported to an alternate version of 1980s New York where Ronald Reagan was never elected president. When she asks her friend Eddie who the president is, he tells her it's Gary Hart. "He almost dropped out of the race in 1980—over that 'Monkey Business' business," Eddie says. "Then he said 'Fuck 'em if they can't take a joke' and hung in there. Ended up winning in a landslide."

The most likely explanation, when you come down to it, is that we ridiculed Hart because he embarrassed us. It wasn't just that Hart belonged to that bleak, hopelessly uncool period in the eighties from which nothing emerged that wasn't ever after referenced with a sense of parody—shoulder pads and parachute pants, A Flock of Seagulls and the sitcom *ALF,* wine coolers and New Coke. It wasn't simply that he had the misfortune of melting down at exactly the moment when just about every cultural hallmark became ossified in time, because we hadn't yet figured out how to embrace modernity without making everything around us seem tacky and synthetic.

No, it was also that Hart served to remind us of the decisions we had collectively made, the moment when the nation and its media took a hard turn toward abject triviality. In some way, it was easier for us to sneer at Hart than to grant him the perspective he kept asking for, easier to proclaim him unfit than to consider the contributions he might have made. On some unconscious level, perhaps, we needed to blame Hart for having come along and created this new obsession with character flaws and tabloid scandals. That way we never had to cringe at the meaningless, destructive brand of politics we had created. We never had to consider all the history that otherwise might have been, or how we had since come to a place where most Americans considered politics to be dysfunctional and debased.

And in our need to dismiss Hart, to consign him to some purgatory for the politically lost, not only had we failed to reckon with the larger forces at work in the culture, but we had also denied ourselves whatever service the man might have rendered. Maybe it was true that Hart's essential temperament was wrong for the modern presidency, and it was entirely possible, whatever the poll numbers suggested in early 1987, that he would ultimately have lost the election for the same reason. Introverts haven't generally fared well in presidential politics since the advent of the primary process in the early 1970s, and by 1988 it was already a cliché among pundits that voters had to be able to envision themselves sharing a beer with a candidate in order for him to succeed. (Although it should be noted that neither of the eventual nominees that year, Michael Dukakis or George H. W. Bush, had a whole lot to brag about in the likability column.)

But whether or not Hart would ultimately have become president—and even if you believed he should have come down off his mountain, literally, and pleaded for his own redemption in the years afterward—it was hard not to conclude that his long exile cost us something. He was widely acknowledged to possess one of the great political minds of his time, had been the first to hold up a torch and illuminate the darkened passage just ahead, the challenges that would confound us in the age after East–West showdowns and factories churning on triple shifts. A quarter century after Hart's exit from politics, neither his party nor the nation had really figured out clear approaches to moving beyond the combustion engine, or modernizing rusted cities, or retooling schools for a different kind of economy. We hadn't simply marginalized a politician; somehow, we had marginalized the things he had tried to make us see.

It seemed a waste that Hart himself hadn't been put to more

meaningful work on any of these issues, beyond serving on some commissions and sending off the occasional op-ed. I made this exact point to Hart during one of our conversations at the cabin. It was a late winter's day, and the light was fading from the study, so that his face was only half illuminated as he leaned forward in his chair, his white mane silhouetted against the darkening sky. He seemed to be disappearing before me.

"It is a waste, but not in a way that others might see it," Hart told me quietly, haltingly. "This is very complicated to talk about. This gets into spirituality for me, and one's purpose for being."

He paused, and for a long moment I thought he might be seeing that lion again.

"I think I mentioned," Hart said, "that of the parables in the New Testament, the one that means the most to me is the one of the master and the three servants." He hadn't mentioned this, but I nodded anyway. "And Jesus tells the story of the master going on a trip. And he gives the three servants talents, a talent being a form of money. And to one he gave ten talents, to one he gave five, and to one he gave one. And he said, 'You are to be the stewards of these talents. And manage them wisely for me.'

"He comes back from the trip and he asks all of the three servants how they managed the money that he'd given them. The ten-talent man had invested it and made some money. The five-talent man had wisely invested. But the one-talent man was afraid to lose it, and he buried it, and he just had the one talent to give back. And the master condemned him and said, 'You are not a faithful servant, because you didn't . . . uh . . .'"

Hart's voice, already trembling a bit, caught momentarily. "'Because you didn't use your talents wisely,'" he managed finally.

"Well, this haunts me," Hart said, looking directly at me in the darkness, his eyes brimming and red. "Because I think you are given certain talents. And you are judged by how you use those talents. And to the degree I believe in some kind of hereafter or transmigration of the soul, I will be judged by how I did or did not use the talents that I was given. And I don't think I've used them very well."

8

A LESSER LAND

THESE DAYS, WHEN I CONSIDER what's happened to political journalism
in the years that I've been doing it, going back to the late 1990s,
I think of my strange experience with John Kerry. At the time he
accepted the Democratic presidential nomination in 2004, after a
plodding but efficient run through the party's raucous primaries,
Kerry seemed like a decent bet to unseat George W. Bush—which
was precisely why Democratic voters had chosen him over more
exciting candidates like John Edwards and Howard Dean. Here
was a decorated Vietnam veteran and an experienced hand at foreign policy, an unobjectionable if uninspiring alternative, running
at a moment of deep anxiety over terrorism and the flagging war
in Iraq. His record of service and patriotism seemed unassailable,
which was exactly the message he sought to underscore in the only
truly memorable line from his acceptance speech in Boston: "I'm
John Kerry, and I'm reporting for duty!"

And yet, to Kerry's great surprise, the coverage of his campaign
focused almost entirely on questions of his character. In Kerry's case,
the issue wasn't sex or recklessness, but rather chronic insecurity
and inconstancy. He had signed up to fight in Vietnam and gotten
himself a plethora of combat medals (which, Republicans asserted
in an unconscionable attack, he hadn't actually earned), but then he
had turned around and thrown those medals over the White House

fence when public opinion shifted. He had, according to his own infamous admission, voted for the war appropriation in Iraq before he voted against it. He was a Massachusetts liberal masquerading as a Clintonian centrist, a wealthy windsurfer with a mansion on Nantucket who pretended to be a regular guy. To the modern media horde, every candidate was a hypocrite waiting to be exposed, and Kerry's brand of hypocrisy was that he claimed to believe in things but never really did.

That summer, my editors at the *Times Magazine* had the idea for a long cover piece about Kerry's philosophy when it came to terrorism and national security generally. Although most Democrats in Washington thought it was enough just to know that Kerry wasn't Bush, and they assumed the electorate could be made to feel the same way, the candidate's specific views on the most pressing topic in American life remained maddeningly opaque. (He resorted mostly to vapid lines like, "The future doesn't belong to fear, it belongs to freedom," and so forth.) And this inability to clarify an argument seemed to be adding to the sense that he was a man without conviction, generally. In a *Washington Post* poll that fall, only 37 percent of voters agreed with the statement that Kerry would make the country safer. A *Times* poll, meanwhile, found that while half the respondents thought Bush would make the right choices to protect the country from terrorists, only 26 percent said the same of Kerry.

After some customary wrangling back and forth, Kerry's campaign ultimately agreed to have him sit with me for three long interviews—the first aboard his campaign plane on a flight from Nantucket to Denver, and the others in hotel suites in Seattle and Santa Monica. I assumed Kerry would welcome the opportunity to elaborate on his actual plan for governing, rather than having to answer yet more questions about the authenticity of his war medals; that I assumed wrongly was evident in our very first meeting, when Kerry delayed our interview for almost the entire flight and then threw me out of his cabin after a few hard questions about Iraq. (An aide apologized, saying he had fallen asleep and woken up irritable.)

Kerry, who was surrounded by layers of media coaches, did his level best to be more civil in our subsequent conversations, but his contempt was unmistakable—and perhaps, given his experience to that point, not unreasonable. He seemed to regard me not as someone who sought to explain his views (which is how I saw myself), but rather as a hired assassin who had just walked through the front door without so much as a struggle. He had no doubt I had been sent there to kill him; what he couldn't understand was why he was being forced to sit there on the couch across from me, making a big, fat target of himself.

At the outset of our second meeting, before asking a single question, I tried to put Kerry at ease with the kind of idle chatter at which politicians excel. He had turned down a bottle of Evian, instructing his aide to go out and find some of "my water." I wondered aloud what he didn't like about the Evian.

"I hate that stuff," he said. "They pack it full of minerals."

So I asked Kerry, without any particular interest in the answer, what kind of water he preferred. This is what you sometimes do as a writer when you're trying to transcend the usual, transactional dynamic that exists in more typical and hurried campaign interviews. I ask you what kind of water you drink, you ask me something in return, and before you know it we're having an actual conversation, like normal people who don't suspect one another of treasonous crimes.

"Plain old American water," he replied gruffly.

This confused me, since I hadn't thought of Evian as being un-American, although technically it is. "You mean like tap water?" I asked.

Kerry froze. It was as if I had laid a series of mines that now had to be carefully, gingerly sidestepped. Was I going to write that he made a show of drinking tap water like a regular person, even though we all knew he could afford to buy Evian's entire spring if he wanted? That he made a point of eschewing French water, so as not to underscore the fact that he speaks fluent French? Did I have a picture of him drinking from an Evian bottle somewhere in my saddlebag? Exactly what kind of "gotcha" game was I running here?

"No," Kerry said carefully. "There are all kinds of waters." He tried to think of some while I sat there waiting, awkwardly. "Saratoga Spring," Kerry said. Then, after a pause: "Sometimes I drink tap water." The rest of our conversations went more or less like this.

As it turned out, Kerry's paralyzing suspicion was well founded, though not because of any subterfuge on my part. My final, eight-thousand-word cover piece, titled "Kerry's Undeclared War," was an exhaustive attempt to find some cohesion in his ideas, using his interviews and his long record in office. About halfway through the piece, I noted a significant difference between Bush and Kerry when they talked about the nature of terrorism: Bush always talked about his "global war on terror" as an unending, almost apocalyptic struggle that probably couldn't be won with any finality, whereas Kerry seemed to regard stateless extremism as containable and controllable, and not necessarily the framework for an entire foreign policy.

"We have to get back to the place we were, where terrorists are not the focus of our lives, but they're a nuisance," I quoted Kerry as saying. "As a former law-enforcement person, I know we're never going to end prostitution. We're never going to end illegal gambling. But we're going to reduce it, organized crime, to a level where it isn't on the rise. It isn't threatening people's lives every day, and fundamentally, it's something that you continue to fight, but it's not threatening the fabric of your life."

By the time that Sunday's *Times* appeared on newsstands, less than a month out from Election Day, the Bush campaign was already running an ad featuring that quote. And for at least the next forty-eight hours, Kerry's "nuisance" quote dominated the coverage on cable TV. All this punditry had virtually nothing to do with any real debate over the nature of terrorism and ideas for combating it; it was about character and hypocrisy. Once again, Kerry had been caught pretending to be something people wanted him to be (in this case, a fervent antiterrorist), when in fact we now had proof that he didn't consider terrorism to be a problem any bigger than an illicit game of Texas Hold-'em. That he hadn't said that, exactly, and that I had offered a more thorough explanation of his point in the piece, was irrelevant. Context required too much explanation, and it was only going to get in the way of the overarching objective, which was to expose the flaw in Kerry's character that everyone already assumed to be there.

When it was over, when Kerry had narrowly lost Ohio and thus the election, Democrats in town were looking to blame just about anybody for his defeat. A few of them even blamed me, at least in some small part. Within a few weeks of the election, I ran into Joe Lockhart, the former White House press secretary and an advisor to Kerry, on a train from New York to Washington. Lockhart and I had always gotten along, but he was still wounded from the election, and he made very clear where he felt that he and his team had failed their candidate. "Our mistake was in talking to you at all," he said angrily, by which, I gathered, he meant not just me specifically, but my entire industry. "We don't need you, and he shouldn't have talked to you."

On one hand, I found it hard to conjure much sympathy for Kerry. He had run, I thought, a timid campaign, premised more on who he wasn't than on who he was. Kerry, the former Swift boater, had made it his goal to simply complete the mission without taking risks that might get him blown up, rather than trying to advance any bolder argument for what he would do as president. If others had succeeded in twisting his words or distorting his character, it was chiefly because he had left such an obvious vacuum in the public mind, waiting to be filled.

And yet I also came to have a certain admiration for Kerry, especially when I compared him to the candidates I wrote about in the next two campaigns. However much he may have disliked spending time with me, Kerry had nonetheless accepted that interviews like these were part of his responsibility to the process, and he had subjected himself to four hours of intense questioning on global affairs from someone who knew a lot less about the topic than he did. In his tortured way, Kerry had actually endeavored at some length to make the nuances of his worldview understood, just as generations of other presidential candidates had done. Looking back at that moment later, I realized how unlikely it was that any nominee of either party would ever feel compelled to do that again.

. . .

Candidates for president—and for most other significant offices, really—don't try to explain their ideas or their theories of the moment anymore. It's hard to know if they really have any. Technology had a lot to do with this, of course. Kerry's controversial quote overwhelmed his campaign, at least for a few days, because of the twenty-four-hour cable news cycle that hadn't even existed when Hart ran back in 1987—a senselessly competitive environment where inexperienced producers fixate on whatever minutiae seems new, to the exclusion of all else, and where reporters and pundits rush into TV studios armed with little more than vague impressions. (It struck me, watching some of the coverage of the Kerry "nuisance" controversy, how few of the commentators seemed to have actually read the piece they were talking about.) But the reverberation of that one comment would have been exponentially louder just four years later, with the sudden popularity of blogs and sites like YouTube and Facebook, and it would have been downright deafening four years after that, after Twitter had taken over the world.

By now, every candidate knows that a single misspoken line, a single emotional or ill-advisedly candid moment, can become a full-blown, existential crisis by the time the bus pulls up at the next rally. And if there's not much room for nuance in a cable TV report, there's none in 140 characters, which means that even a well-articulated argument can (and almost certainly will) be reduced and distorted by the time it reaches the vast majority of voters who will pay attention. Rarely is any candidate willing to risk sudden implosion by actually thinking through the complex issues out loud, as the most talented politicians of Hart's day were accustomed to doing; it's safer to traffic in poll-tested, blandly comforting gibberish about "middle-class jobs" and "ending business as usual," which disturbs no one and does no harm. It's safer to tell yourself, as Joe Lockhart did, that you really don't need to cater to reporters anymore, because you can talk to your own email list directly instead. Candidates routinely complain that reporters never talk to them about the actual substance of governing, but the truth is that with few exceptions, when you ask them to do exactly that, their reflexive response is no.

At the heart of this changed dynamic, though, isn't merely a technological shift in the nation's media, but a cultural one. There was a time when politicians and the journalists who covered them, however adversarial their relationship might become at times, shared a basic sense of common purpose. The candidate's job was to win an argument about the direction of the country, and the media's job was to explain that argument and the tactics with which it was disseminated. Neither could succeed without the basic, if sometimes grudging, cooperation of the other, and often, as in the case of Hart and some of his older colleagues in the media, there existed a genuine trust and camaraderie. Modern media critics might deride these kinds of relationships as coziness or corruption, but there was a very real benefit to it for the voters, which was *context*. Reporters who really knew a politician could tell the difference between, say, a candidate who had misspoken from exhaustion and one who didn't know his facts. They could be expected to discern between a rank hypocrite, on one hand, and a candidate who had actually thought something through and adjusted his views, on the other.

In his engaging book *The Eighteen-Day Running Mate*, about Tom Eagleton's disastrous foray into national politics, Joshua Glasser describes how a bevy of reporters actually camped out in Eagleton's hotel suite so they could be there if McGovern called to offer him the number two spot on the ticket. (He did, and they were.) Later, when Eagleton's candidacy was in peril, a few reporters went down to the tennis courts at the lodge where they and McGovern were staying, because the nominee was playing a match and they wanted to ask him a few questions. McGovern invited them to ride back to the lodge with him so they could talk.

Glasser relays these scenes as if they were commonplace, and yet they jolted me when I read them; to someone who has covered multiple presidential campaigns in the modern era, it couldn't have sounded any more bizarre if he had reported that McGovern had personally murdered a reporter and disposed of the body. In today's political climate, even if I could somehow manage to find out where the candidate was spending his downtime, I wouldn't get within a hundred yards of that tennis court without being turned away, probably with a stern lecture. Today, even a phone call from someone like me requesting a routine interview mobilizes a phalanx of highly paid consultants whose job it is to deflect my questions and then, if they see any merit in having the candidate cooperate, to orchestrate and rehearse his responses.

"You didn't prep for a candidate's meeting with Jack Germond," Joe Trippi told me when we talked. "What you'd want is for a candidate to just have a beer with Germond and answer his questions, you know? And back then, frankly, most of them could." Now, Trippi told me bluntly, "No one would walk into an interview with you unprepped. I wouldn't let it happen."

That's largely because, beginning with Watergate and culminating in Gary Hart's unraveling, the cardinal objective of all political journalism had shifted, from a focus on agendas to a focus on narrow notions of character, from illuminating worldviews to exposing falsehoods. Whatever sense of commonality between candidates and reporters that existed in McGovern's day had, by the time my generation arrived on the scene, been replaced by a kind of entrenched cold war. We aspired chiefly to show politicians for the impossibly flawed human beings they were—a single-minded pursuit that reduced complex careers to isolated transgressions. As the former senator Bob Kerrey, who had been accused of war crimes in Vietnam after a distinguished career in public service, told me once: "We're not the worst thing we've ever done in our lives, and there's a tendency to think that we are." That quote, I thought, should have been posted on the wall of every newsroom in the country, just to remind us that it was true.

Predictably, politicians responded to all this with a determination to give us nothing that might aid in the hunt to expose them, even if it meant obscuring the convictions and contradictions that made them actual human beings. Both sides retreated to our respective camps, where we strategized about how to outwit and outflank the other, occasionally to our own benefit but rarely to the voters'.

Maybe this made our media a sharper guardian of the public

interest against frauds and hypocrites. But it also made it hard for any thoughtful politician to offer arguments that might be considered nuanced or controversial. And, just as consequential, the post-Hart climate made it much easier for candidates who *weren't* especially thoughtful—who didn't have any complex understanding of governance, or even much affinity for it—to gain national prominence. When a politician could duck any real intellectual scrutiny simply by deriding the evident triviality of the media, when the status quo was to never say anything that required more than ten words' worth of explanation, then pretty much anyone could rail against the system and glide through the process without having to establish more than a passing familiarity with the issues. As long as you weren't delinquent on your taxes or having an affair with a stripper or engaged in some other form of rank duplicity, you could run as a "Tea Partier" or a "populist" without ever having to elaborate on what you actually believed or what you would do for the country.

All of which probably has some bearing on why, more than a quarter century after Hart disappeared from political life, both our elected leaders and our political media have fallen so far in the esteem of voters who judge both to be smaller than the country deserves. At the outset of Barak Obama's second term in office, only a quarter of Americans said they trusted government to do the right thing all or even most of the time, according to Pew Research polling. (That number later dropped after a series of self-manufactured budget crises in Congress.) Meanwhile, between 1997 and 2013, trust in the mass media fell almost ten points. Four decades after the legend of Woodward and Bernstein came into being, only 28 percent of Americans were willing to say that journalists contributed a lot to society's well-being—a showing that lagged behind almost every other professional group.

Thank heaven for lawyers.

It wasn't simply a kind of default distrust, though, that animated—or perhaps de-animated—our political coverage. It was the new culture of celebrity, too. It's hard to know what Neil Postman, who died in 2003, would have said about Twitter and Facebook and BuzzFeed; perhaps he would have cheered the end of the broadcast era and the rise of citizen voices, even if they transmitted in tiny bites. But it's clear enough that he was right about the eroding boundaries between public service and entertainment. The new obsession with character that began with Hart's collapse sprang mostly from our post-Watergate fear of what lurked in the psyches of needy men. But it also provided an excuse to delve into family lives and ancient histories, to transform politicians into tabloid personalities and their campaigns into performance art. By the time Clinton played saxophone on *The Arsenio Hall Show,* presidential politics had come to resemble nothing so much as a high school talent show.

And if celebrity overwhelmed any discussion of intellect and experience among politicians, the same was true for much of the media. The punditry business that began in the 1980s, with veteran reporters like Jack Germond and Eleanor Clift, exploded in the era of twenty-four-hour news, igniting a desperate scramble to find entertainers who could pass themselves off as political experts. Three decades after *The McLaughlin Group* and *Crossfire* first shouted their way into our collective consciousness, cable channels like Fox and MSNBC featured a never-ending parade of panels populated by "strategists" and "analysts" whose only actual qualifications were a certain facility with language and an almost clinical need to be recognized by strangers. That such professional pundits knew little about political history or practice didn't seem to matter much, nor was there a consequence for being astoundingly wrong in their swami-like predictions. Their role, above all, was to seem wry and knowing and to hold an audience, transforming most political TV news into just the kind of theater that Postman had anticipated.

Adapting to this new environment, some of the era's most important politicians managed to thrive without a discernible worldview, or even despite one. Take, for instance, the case of John McCain when he ran as a Republican insurgent in the 2000 primaries. McCain didn't have the money or star power wielded by the party's front-runner, George W. Bush, and nothing in his record as a congressman and senator set him apart substantively from his fellow conservatives. What McCain had, as a former prisoner of war in Vietnam, was a personal story well suited to the cinema (and in fact, it would later become a made-for-TV movie). And what he and his consultants understood, brilliantly, was that the orchestration of political campaigns, which had been steadily building since the Hart scandal thirteen years earlier, had starved the reporters on the trail of any contact with candidates that felt even remotely genuine. The assembled media were desperate not just to be entertained and to have an entertaining story to tell, but also to feel like they were actually on the inside of something.

Life aboard McCain's campaign bus, which he called the "Straight Talk Express," unfolded like a political reality show in the age before reality programming became commonplace. Flanked by a small cadre of aides but otherwise uncensored, McCain dazzled a rotating but ever growing cast of national reporters (and their adventure-seeking editors), riffing spontaneously on all manner of topics as the bus toured New Hampshire or South Carolina, apparently enjoying himself immensely. As a reporter, you could hardly get away from the candidate; the strategy was to overwhelm you with access, to outlast all skepticism with proximity and sheer endurance. At campaign rallies and unscripted town hall meetings, McCain, like some Catskills comedian, unfailingly made a point of ribbing his media contingent as Communist sympathizers. We were all in on the joke. We understood that it was all being staged for us, and it was vastly entertaining.

Perhaps McCain really did see himself as an evolving politician, an independent-minded Republican who would challenge the weathered orthodoxies of both parties. I certainly believed that at the time. But McCain's burgeoning reputation as a reformer in the Bull Moose tradition had little to do with any actual governing agenda, and almost everything to do with theatrics. As his consultants would later admit, McCain's gambit was conscious and born of desperation; they knew they would never get the media to follow their candidate if they didn't create some kind of spectacle and celebrity persona, and they succeeded. McCain earned sudden fame as a truth teller, despite the fact that none of it added up to any coherent idea of how he would actually govern.

It was a very different story eight years later, when I sat with McCain for an hour during a stopover in Tampa, trying to make sense of his views on foreign policy. By then, he was no longer the renegade with the Borscht Belt routine, but rather, at long last, the presumed nominee of his party. Gone was the entertaining McCain who called you a "little jerk" and couldn't wait to regale you with stories of his visits to Teddy Roosevelt's boyhood home. Unsmiling and guarded, McCain immediately launched into a long, irritated, and well-rehearsed defense of his views on Iraq and foreign intervention generally, before I could even ask a question on the subject. He concluded by telling me, oddly, that it was "always good to be with you," as if he were a guest on a cable TV show rather than sitting across the table from a reporter he had known for years.

In fact, interviewing McCain then wasn't much different from interviewing Kerry. By that time, both *The New York Times* and *The Washington Post* had run stories that effectively accused McCain of sleeping with a lobbyist, and he had come to regard his former allies in the media as enemies bent on his personal destruction. McCain had once thought, perhaps, that his persona as a war hero and maverick Republican would protect him from intimations of scandal, but the reverse turned out to be true. The more compelling a cultural figure you became, the more inevitable your disgrace. The arc of tabloid journalism—now deeply ingrained in even the most elite reaches of the industry—demanded nothing less.

McCain's most consequential nod to the politics of celebrity, however, was yet to come. A few months after our meeting in Tampa, he chose Sarah Palin, the obscure governor of Alaska, as his running mate. Whatever one thought of her politics, it's fair to say nothing on the forty-four-year-old Palin's résumé qualified her to serve as a president-in-waiting. A former pageant queen, she had cycled through five underwhelming colleges before managing to graduate, and she had been a controversial small-town mayor before her unlikely ascension to the governorship—a job she had held, at that point, for less than two years. Her few, tentative TV interviews as a member of the ticket, for which she was heavily prepped, did nothing to counteract the impression that Palin knew less about foreign policy, in particular, than most casual readers of the newspaper.

What Palin brought to the ticket was stagecraft and stardom. Her candidacy was captivating in the way that *American Idol* or *The Biggest Loser* kept you lingering on the channel even as you fingered the remote control and told yourself you were going to watch something more redeeming. She was just like the rest us, or at least like people we knew—insecure and ambitious and beset by family problems, but also beautiful and impassioned—and somehow the spotlight had found her, and every moment she stood in its glow teetered dangerously between greatness and humiliation. It was as if, rather than having chosen an actual running mate, McCain had tried to reinvigorate his flagging campaign by holding a televised contest for the role, and Palin had made it through all the challenges and battle rounds in which you were locked away in a room full of tarantulas or whatever it was, and here she was, learning her lines in front of us. What Postman called the "supra-ideology" of entertainment—that's what Palin's candidacy was all about, and McCain's embarrassed aides would later admit as much.

By then, of course, Palin was more of a superstar than McCain had ever been, and she embodied a new phenomenon in national politics—power as a path to celebrity, rather than the other way around. Once, at the dawn of the satellite age and for a long time after, entertainers like Sonny Bono and Fred Grandy ("Gopher" from *The Love Boat*) had leveraged their Hollywood cachet into political careers. Now, though, a politician was increasingly likely to seek office as a catapult to broader, more lucrative fame—as a TV host or professional speaker, the subject of tabloid covers and Hollywood treatments. You didn't have to win an election to achieve this kind of celebrity, or even campaign. You simply had to be telegenic and provocative. A little shamelessness didn't hurt.

After 2008, Palin made noises now and then about running for president, ensuring she would resurface in newscasts and on front pages. But she resigned the governorship before even finishing out her term (sidestepping multiple ethics investigations), and probably she never seriously contemplated running for office again, with all its inherent limitations. Instead, by 2010, Palin had parlayed her political act into an actual reality show on the network TLC, titled *Sarah Palin's Alaska,* in which her family life became frontier drama. (According to the show's Wikipedia page, the synopsis of a typical episode went like this: "Sarah and family take a road trip to Homer, Alaska. There they meet a Halibut fishing family, who invite Sarah and oldest daughter Bristol deep sea fishing, allowing the two to bond.") The show was canceled after one season, but Palin wasn't going anywhere. She was as famous as an American could get, and rich beyond her imagining.

In some ways, the man who defeated McCain and Palin in 2008 seemed to represent a rejection, finally, of all the personal drama and triviality that had dominated politics since 1987. Barack Obama didn't have Bill Clinton's neediness or George W. Bush's famous family. No intimations of scandal or stories of personal redemption attached themselves to him. "No Drama Obama," as his campaign aides referred to him, ran cool and cerebral; watching him campaign, you could almost come away with the sense that he was indifferent to whether voters really liked him or not. In short, Obama felt like a twenty-first-century version of Hart before the implosion—a harbinger of generational transition taking on his own party's rusted establishment, more interested in finding the way forward than in exploring his own psyche and entertaining the masses. It was possible, in the inaugural winter of 2009, after the collapse of the American economy, to think that a page had been turned, that we had amused ourselves nearly to death but then had somehow been reborn.

And yet, Obama's core appeal, the basic viability of his candidacy, was almost entirely grounded in the culture of entertainment. As a job applicant, Obama's résumé was only marginally more impressive than Palin's; yes, he'd been to Ivy League schools and had taught constitutional law, but he was also a freshman senator who, not three years before he announced his candidacy, had been serving without distinction in the Illinois legislature. Obama's campaign was a story, rather than an argument—the kind of uplifting drama about American life, about racial equality and social mobility, that routinely took home Oscars from the Academy. "No Drama Obama" was a misnomer; the candidate was in fact the leading man in a very real drama, an international celebrity who could draw millions of Germans to the Brandenburg Gate just to catch a glimpse, and who would soon be awarded the Nobel Prize for no other reason than having offered himself up to the world. Obama was brilliant and upright, funny and likable, an adequate if unenthusiastic retail politician. More than any of this, though, he was a well-cast protagonist, conjured from familiar story lines and deliberately marketed to inspire us.

What, exactly, did Obama believe? What vision of governance guided his thinking, and what new argument did he bring to the arena? This was maddeningly hard to know, then and later. His twin mantras were "hope" and "change," the rhetorical equivalent of rainbows and unicorns. There were those who read Obama's books and spent time with him, myself included, who came away thinking he was principally a pragmatist who distrusted the rigid orthodoxies of the last generation. There were others who assumed, mostly because of his race and his background as an activist, that the candidate was in fact a doctrinaire liberal. In office, Obama made a practice of disappointing both groups, veering between Clintonian centrism at some points and rollicking populism at others. He reacted ably to nearly cataclysmic events, but his grasp on the machinery of government often seemed tenuous, and with the exception of his party's long-sought health care law (the details of which he mostly left to Congress), he did little to change the long-term economic or global trajectory of the country.

The truth was that Obama had had neither the time nor the burning inclination to work out his ideas or master the intricacies of governing before ascending to the Oval Office, and we in the media hadn't been very interested in that side of him, anyway. From the start, he was treated more as a pop culture persona than a thought leader. He was a projection on a screen, larger than life but lacking the necessary dimension to propose the kind of bold reassessments that Hart had championed a quarter century earlier.

Of course, it wasn't as if the Republicans desperate to unseat Obama had found some serious thinker on their side to run against him. Leading up to the 2012 election, most of the Washington Republicans I talked to, who were trying to hold off a wave of Palin-inspired, Tea Party extremism that threatened to overrun the party, thought their strongest candidate was someone like Indiana's popular governor, Mitch Daniels. A free-market-loving conservative who had served as budget director in the Bush administration, Daniels was a plainspoken intellectual who argued passionately for a generational shift in the country's thinking about policy. Specifically, he wanted to reform entitlement programs and the tax code for a new century, and he called for a more tolerant and inclusive Republican Party—even when speaking to its more conservative factions. He was, arguably, the most impressive politician in Republican politics, and one of the very few who had the potential to unite besieged moderates and enraged conservatives.

But Daniels had other issues to consider in the age of tabloid politics. The saga of his marriage was the kind of thing you might read in a *Modern Love* column; his wife had left him at one point for a doctor and moved away, only to return to Daniels and their four daughters years later. By all accounts, they had rebuilt a solid family life, and for anyone who spent much time reflecting on the complexities of the human heart, there was actually something inspiring about it all. But Daniels's wife was said to dread the inevitable forensic study of her personal journey that would accompany a presidential campaign, and Daniels finally said, with characteristic bluntness and evident sadness, that his family had effectively vetoed the idea of his running.

No amount of lobbying from Washington could change his mind, and Daniels ultimately settled for the presidency of Purdue. Like a lot of other thoughtful men with imperfect pasts who had considered the presidency in the years since Hart's downfall, Daniels had probably concluded that the process would reduce the totality of his career and personal life to a single embarrassing episode that he and his family would be forced to relive, over and over again, even if he won. Even if he were willing to endure that for the chance of making history, his wife and daughters apparently were not.

Instead, after flirting with a succession of less than serious alternatives, Republican primary voters finally accepted the reality that their leadership had managed to swallow some months earlier—that their party's candidate would be Mitt Romney, the former Massachusetts governor. It would have been hard to make up a candidate who better typified what presidential politics—and, really, national politics as a whole—had now become than Romney, a wealthy businessman who outwardly looked the part of a president but who exuded a vast inner reservoir of nothingness. Too dull and earnest to be in any way vulnerable on the character issue, far too cautious to offer any ideas that might be objectionable to any of his own constituencies (or, really, anything that could fairly be called an idea at all), Romney was more a figurehead than an actual candidate—an actor hired to deliver someone else's message, like the guy in the airline video who tells you to watch your flight attendant so you know how to float on your seat cushion.

Romney offered fewer lengthy interviews in his campaign than any candidate in memory, and even fewer genuine insights into his political worldview. Like most national journalists who wrote about the contest, and probably even some who rode his bus and followed his campaign closely, I never got within twenty feet of the man. Reporters and columnists, who were by now used to the character routine, happily expounded on some embarrassing facts about Romney and what they might tell us about his true nature: he had once driven with a sick dog strapped in a cage on the top of his car, and he had apparently acted the bully during an ugly episode in high school. But in the end, probably no revelation about Romney doomed his candidacy as much as the total absence of revelation that characterized it. His website was full of platitudes and vague positions, but when it came to any sense of the underlying convictions that would define his presidency, he was simply the least known and least knowable nominee in modern history—the logical end, perhaps, to what Hart's downfall and the ensuing era of destructive coverage had wrought.

The famous Dubliner, which bills itself as "America's premier Irish pub," opened on Capitol Hill in 1974, the same year that Gary Hart drove his two-door family Oldsmobile clear across the country and took his seat in the Senate just a few blocks away. On a balmy September night almost four decades later, Hart and I sat at a back table in the Dubliner, talking over what had happened in the intervening years.

Hart had just come from the airport and looked dapper in a suit and tie. He was in town for a meeting of a task force on strategy he was chairing for Kerry, who had recently been named Obama's secretary of state, and in the morning he would meet privately with Kerry to discuss the chaos in Syria, among other issues. This was one of two such panels over which Hart, at seventy-seven, now quietly and ably presided, the other being an advisory board on national security for the new defense secretary, Chuck Hagel. He had accepted that such a role was as close to elder statesmanship as he was going to get in this, the final act of his public career, and it was not without usefulness or intellectual challenge.

I reminded Hart of what he had said back in 1987, during the cathartic rant that formally ended his campaign and infuriated his critics in the press—that a system bent on destroying people's integrity would ultimately destroy itself, that politics would become just another sport staged for our entertainment. I wondered if he thought his prediction had come to pass.

Hart shrugged sadly. Whatever other emotions he may have felt when he looked back over the years, he had long since given up on the prospect of vindication. When he thought back on it now, he said, the two words that became most prevalent in the political media after 1987 were "scrutiny" and "scandal." Scrutiny, he said, became an excuse for going through your telephone logs from a hotel you'd stayed in, or checking which movies you'd rented, back in the days when people did such things. And scandal as a concept became omnipresent and overused—a deplorable word.

"A scandal, to me, is a child living in poverty," Hart said quietly. "An elderly person without medicine. Unemployed workers. Those are scandals." This was the kind of rhetoric one sometimes heard from syrupy politicians these days, but there was no performance in the way Hart said it. "People's sex lives or their personal lives are scandals only in the sense of tabloid journalism, but not in the sense of ethics," he said. "They're not bribery. They're not some under-the-table exchange of money, buying votes. Those, I suppose, would be real political scandals. At least that's what they were called throughout most of American history."

I asked Hart if he had been right to suggest, back in 1987, that if we continued in the direction we were going, we would end up with the leaders we deserved. He paused for a long moment.

"I'll let the record speak for itself," he said finally. "The Congress and the Senate today is not the one I joined in 1975." He tossed out the names of some of his colleagues back then: Mansfield, Muskie, Mathias, Jackson, Javits, Case. "I just don't think the caliber and quality of members of Congress, generally, is what it was in those days."

We talked about the issues that Hart thought would—or at least should—be central in the 2016 campaign: groping the way toward a new fiscal policy, redefining America's role as a global power, setting a course toward energy independence. These were, of course, the same issues that Hart had evangelized and thought deeply about back in the 1980s and had been talking about ever since, and yet little about them had fundamentally changed or been settled. One of the core problems, as Hart saw it, is that even the best and boldest political leaders no longer believe they can make complex ideas understood through a media obsessed with personalities and scandals. And if you couldn't utilize the machinery of persuasion, then it was hard to do anything but talk to the people who already agreed with you.

"The genius of democracy, in my mind, is the ability of an individual to sense the temper and the mood of an electorate and to respond to it and to help shape it," Hart told me. "And once that's gone, once a leader loses confidence in his ability to shape and mold, in a positive sense, public opinion and attitudes, there is no leadership."

Occasionally during this conversation, the last in a series of formal and informal interviews over several years, Hart stole a quick glance toward the bar. Hart's son, John, had chosen the Dubliner for us to meet because in a few minutes a handful of Hart alumni would be meeting at the pub for a reunion of sorts, over several rounds of Hart's favorite whiskey, Jameson.

This was the kind of thing Hart relished. His impact as a politician may have been lost through the years, but as a spotter of talent and an inspiration to the brightest minds of the boomer vanguard, probably no public figure alive could claim to rival Hart's legacy. It was almost certainly Hart's most lasting achievement, and the one in which he took the most pride—the list of young, idealistic Democrats he had mentored during those heady years as a national figure who had gone on to distinguished careers not only in politics, but as purveyors of social change.

Martin O'Malley, who as a law student had driven Hart through the South and Plains on that last, funereal stretch as a candidate in 1988 (and who would soon slip into the Dubliner, virtually unnoticed, after debating Texas governor Rick Perry on *Crossfire* in a studio down the block), was now Maryland's governor. Billy Shore, one of the more universally admired men in Washington, had founded and grown Share Our Strength, the nation's premier anti-hunger organization and a model for social entrepreneurship. John Emerson, in addition to serving in the Clinton White House, had become a venture capitalist and major Democratic fundraiser, and as Hart and I sat at the Dubliner, he was assuming his new post as ambassador to Germany. Jeanne Shaheen, who as a grassroots organizer had helped orchestrate Hart's stunning victory in New Hampshire in 1984, was now that state's senior senator and former governor. Doug Wilson, who had been Hart's principal foreign policy aide, had just left his second senior stint at the Defense Department, this time as assistant secretary for public affairs.

Another Hart aide from back in the day, Alan Khazei, cofounded City Year, which became the inspiration for Clinton's AmeriCorps program. The late Eli Segal, who had run Hart's fundraising operation in 1987, had been the first CEO of AmeriCorps' parent program, the Corporation for National and Community Service. Sue Casey, the trusted advisor who spirited Donna Rice out of Washington, later served on the Denver City Council and ran for mayor. Kevin Sweeney, Hart's press secretary in 1987, became a leading consultant in the field of corporate responsibility. Kathy Bushkin Calvin, who was Hart's press secretary in 1984, now served as president of the United Nations Foundation. And on went the list, which Hart could proudly recite.

Not all of these Hart alums kept in touch with the boss (although a substantial number still called and emailed regularly). Not all had managed to get beyond the resentment they felt at his having acted recklessly and squandered their faith, just as he had never fully gotten beyond his own feelings of intense regret. But to an astonishing degree, most of these former aides, who were now nearing their own retirements, still thought of themselves principally as "Hart people" and would describe themselves that way for the rest of their lives.

One question remained unanswered as we sat at the Dubliner, a piece of unfinished business that lingered in the space between us, as it had now through years of uncomfortably personal conversations about the events of 1987. Hart had pointed out to me many times that his was the only political sex scandal in which "both parties"— that was how he referred to himself and Donna Rice—had denied, then and ever after, the existence of "a relationship." But he did not define what he meant by that, nor did he ever come close to confiding in me about what had actually gone on in that townhouse, and whether Rice had, in fact, spent the night or left through the back door as they both maintained. He did not, in other words, volunteer any more intimate details of the episode than he had for the previous decades, and I stopped short of asking for them.

Even so, I was aware that a reader might have curiosity about this part of the story. Often during this time, when I would tell a friend or a fellow writer about my project on Hart, he or she would immediately grin and ask some variation on what seemed to be the obvious question: "So did he finally come clean? Are you going to get the *real* story?" Even for those who were involved in the events that led to Hart's banishment, the absence of an abject confession— Hart's refusal to "tell his story" in the redemptive way of modern culture—remained a source of frustration.

When I had lunch with Tom Fiedler in 2013, I asked him what he would say to Hart, after all the intervening years, if he had a chance to talk with him now. I expected him to say something about wanting Hart to know he had only been doing his job, or that he bore no ill will. But instead, Fiedler told me: "What I wish I could say to him, and what I wish I could trust if he answered, is what is it he feels we didn't get right, and what did we get right? I suppose I always would want just the truth. And if we didn't get the truth or a close approximation of it, what did we get wrong?"

My own interest in the details had less to do with anything lurid than with the historical implications of what Hart did or didn't do. What if Hart hadn't actually spent the night entwined with Rice? What if, as some of his closest aides still privately believed, he had fooled around with her a few times but hadn't actually consummated the affair? (If Bill Clinton taught us anything, it was that politicians, like the rest of America, tend to define sex with various degrees of technicality.) If that were the case, then the course of our political history would have been forever changed because of a widely held assumption that wasn't even true. It would mean that the rules of political coverage had been overturned not because Hart had carried on some wild affair, but because he was too damn stubborn to set the record straight.

When she spoke to me, Donna Rice certainly implied that she had lied at the time when she claimed nothing untoward had happened. It was an impossible situation, Rice told me, and she had said what she thought she was expected to say. But even twenty-six years later, she declined to be any more specific than that. When I asked her why she continued to shield Hart, long after anyone but me really cared, she sighed.

"I guess it's hard to explain," Rice told me. "Just imagine that your whole life is out of control. Everything completely out of control. And the only thing you have any control over are your own choices going forward. You've made a decision that you want to take the high road, that you want to be seen as a person of integrity and character, in spite of the perception that has formed about you in the media and the public's mind. And so every choice that I made was toward one that would not play into that image."

In other words, it wasn't only Hart's reputation that Rice continued to try, with her silence, to salvage from the wreckage of history. It was also her own.

I was conflicted all along about whether to broach this subject with Hart, or whether to just to let it be. I hadn't wanted to trip that particular emotional wire during our days of conversation on the front porch of the cabin or in the study, and certainly not while Lee was around. I didn't look forward to enduring a lecture about how we journalists were all the same, and I feared that Hart would shut down and stop talking altogether. And so I waited, just as E. J. Dionne had done all those years ago, until all the other questions were asked. And by the time I arrived at the Dubliner, already partway through writing the book and intending for this to be our last interview, I was still trying to decide whether I had a responsibility to fully interrogate Hart about the sordid missing details of his story.

I can't say he didn't give me an opening, either, when he repeated his line, yet again and without my asking, about both parties denying there had been a relationship. I could have told him then that Donna Rice made clear she had obscured the truth. I could hear myself telling him that he had one last opportunity to get right with history, and he needed to take advantage of it.

As we sat there at the dimly lit table in back, though, it occurred to me that I was about to follow the same path, for the same reasons, as all the older journalists who had helped lead our politics into the vacuous black hole it had become. I would be reduced to saying, essentially, that the story of Hart's affair was already "out there," that it needed at long last to be verified or disputed. I would tell him that I didn't want to ask about such things—I had, in fact, spent my entire career avoiding them—but my readers expected me to ask and deserved to know. It would be my turn to argue that I really didn't have a choice but to go where the story led.

But of course, I did have a choice. We all did, and we always had. This was exactly the point I had been stumbling toward all along. And so, as our talk wound down and Hart's old aides began to drift into the pub, I closed my notebook and considered for a long moment this man across the table from me, still with the tailored suit and perfectly knotted tie of a statesman, still clutching his satchel of agenda items pertaining to the nation's business.

For twenty-six years, he had maintained an unwavering silence about the seamy events of that week, and the myriad reasons for this weren't really that hard to deduce, if you knew him at all. He stayed silent partly out of pride and arrogance—a refusal to acknowledge that he had been less than entirely truthful, even with himself. But he stayed silent, too, because he had already played a role in destroying the reputation of a young woman he barely knew, and he didn't think it his prerogative to drag her through it again. Because the truth would only cause more pain to the devoted wife he had loved, in some deep and spiritual way, since they were teenagers, and the children whose admiration he cherished and had never lost. Because he harbored a fierce conviction that private affairs had no place in the public arena, and he was going to hold fast to that conviction until his dying breath, no matter how anachronistic it seemed to others.

There's a way to describe a man who holds that tightly to principle, whatever the cost. The word is character.

I've chosen to cite the sources for my material in the text of the book itself, rather than annotating them separately. At the core of the book are more than twenty hours of conversation with Gary Hart, as well as dozens of interviews with aides, reporters, and other participants in the events of 1987 and afterward. Oral histories, though, can be misleading; years have a way of dulling some memories and cementing some myths. So wherever possible I've confirmed accounts with more than one source or with news accounts from the time. Where the recollections of sources conflict in ways that can't really be reconciled, I've tried to be transparent in pointing that out.

I relied heavily on several books from the period, most notably Richard Ben Cramer's *What It Takes* and Paul Taylor's *See How They Run,* both of which offered excellent accounts. Along with these and the additional books I've cited throughout these pages, a handful of others informed my thinking in ways more general or tangential, and they deserve some mention, too. These include: *The Neoliberals* by Randall Rothenberg (on the rethinking of Democratic orthodoxy undertaken by Hart and his contemporaries); *Boyd* by Robert Coram (on the father of military reform); and *Star* by Peter Biskind (on the life and times of Warren Beatty).

Neil Postman's *Amusing Ourselves to Death* served as a kind of North Star for my evaluation of media and social trends in the

1980s. It's a brilliant, enduring work, and anyone who cares about the state of our public discourse should read it.

As I've learned, sometimes painfully, over the years, no work of reportage is flawless. Where sources have inadvertently led me astray, or where I may have mischaracterized or overlooked the accounts of others, I alone am responsible.

ACKNOWLEDGMENTS

I am deeply indebted to Gary and Lee Hart, without whose immense courage and kindness this book could not have been written. Senator Hart is as sincere, patriotic, and thoughtful a man as I have encountered in American politics, and I hope this book causes others to reevaluate his legacy. He deserves that.

Many of those who worked for Hart or wrote about him in the 1980s took time to share their thoughts and memories. A few deserve special mention. Doug Wilson was the one who first encouraged me to think differently about Hart's undoing when we met back in 2002, and he has been a constant source of encouragement ever since. Billy Shore answered countless queries with the same patience and consideration that endeared him to an earlier generation of campaign reporters. Bill Dixon and Kevin Sweeney shared their invaluable personal archives with me, and Kevin very kindly critiqued some early chapters for accuracy's sake.

Many people went out of their way to track down long-lost primary sources or other leads for me, among them Andrea Owen of ABC News, Max Culhane (formerly of ABC), Valerie Komor and Monika Mathur of the Associated Press, Betsy Fischer of NBC News, Joshua Glasser, Neal McAliley, Tyler Bridges, the helpful folks at Carson Entertainment Group, and the outstanding staff of the Library of

Congress. I am grateful, too, to Keith Wessel and Andrea Modica for so graciously making their beautiful photographs available.

I could not have finished writing without the critical and timely support of the Woodrow Wilson International Center for Scholars in Washington, under the leadership of Jane Harman, Robert Litwak, and Michael Van Dusen. The Wilson Center is a beacon of intellectual integrity in a city riven by ideological extremes, and I am honored to count myself among its extended family. The Hoover Institution at Stanford generously hosted me for a week during the earliest phase of my research, as well.

Several terrific researchers contributed mightily to this book. The historian and writer Jack Bohrer offered excellent material and thoughts on the history of presidents and their personal lives. Brock Groesbeck, my research assistant at the Wilson Center, insisted he knew nothing of politics, but if that's true, he's an awfully fast learner. Janet Spikes in the Wilson Center's library dazzled me with her database wizardry. Kitty Bennett of *The New York Times* made time to assist me in tracking down elusive sources. And my friend Lucy Shackelford, the very best in the business, expertly scoured the manuscript for factual errors.

Two of the most gifted nonfiction writers in America today, Paul Tough and Neil Swidey, read finished drafts of the manuscript and helped me improve it. So did Joan Cramer, who honored me with her incisive notes and avid support at a time when she had far more pressing concerns. Richard Ehrenberg very patiently walked me through the section on electronic newsgathering. Several deep thinkers who lived through the events of 1987 let me bounce ideas off them early in the process, including David Kennedy, Evan Thomas, Mike McCurry, Gina Glantz, Robert Reich, and Anita Dunn.

I am in awe of Jonathan Segal, my sharp and sure-handed editor at Alfred A. Knopf. Jonathan rightly made me earn his trust by pressing me to refine my vision for the book, and then he stood by it fiercely and made it better at every turn. I'm grateful, too, to the legendary Sonny Mehta, as well as to Meghan Houser, Paul Bogaards, Erinn Hartman, Sara Eagle, Anne-Lise Spitzer, Loriel Olivier, Kim

Thornton, Peter Mendelsund, and the rest of the all-star team at Knopf, which really is everything a book publisher ought to be.

I never would have pursued this project, or not for long anyway, without the unwavering conviction of my agent, Sarah Chalfant, at the Wylie Agency. She is a friend, an ally, and a fellow believer in the power of words. That Andrew Wylie weighed in with encouragement meant a lot, too; when Andrew tells you to go write a book already, you write one, and you don't ask why.

As it turned out, I completed this book during the last of my eleven years at *The New York Times Magazine,* a publication of which I will always be enormously proud. I owe a huge debt to the fabulous editors and researchers who were my partners over the years, among them Paul Tough, Gerry Marzorati, Joel Lovell, Ilena Silverman, Vera Titunik, Alex Star, Chris Suellentrop, Kathy Ryan, Aaron Retica, Ann Clarke, Sarah Smith, William Lin, Renee Michael, and Charles Wilson. I also benefited from the support and wisdom of such incredible fellow writers as Jonathan Mahler, Michael Sokolove, Sara Corbett, Peter Baker, and Adam Nagourney. Hugo Lindgren and Jill Abramson granted me time to write the book without a moment's complaint. Megan Liberman brilliantly and indefatigably edited my online columns for both the magazine and the newspaper, and then offered me the irresistible chance to begin a whole new adventure with her at *Yahoo News,* which is trying to reimagine political coverage for a new generation.

Thinking back on my career to this point reminded me of how grateful I am to the editors who have given me extraordinary opportunities along the way: Matt Storin, Ann McDaniel, Adam Moss, Bill Keller, and especially my friend and mentor Gerry Marzorati. They are giants of the craft, and I hope I have justified their faith.

It would be impossible to mention all the friends and relatives who sustained this project, starting with my mother, Rhea Bai, and my sisters, Dina and Caroline. None gave more of themselves, or have given more to my writing over the years, than Jon Cowan, who is both a fearless thinker and a naturally gifted editor. Our great friends Debra Rosenberg and David Lipscomb read drafts and offered wise suggestions, and Ilana and Jonathan Drimmer tormented me until I came up with a title they liked. My screenwriting partner Jay Carson inspired me with his unflagging enthusiasm, and Gina Cooper kept me going with homemade jam and wine. John and Ali Lapp and David Durman responded within seconds to my pleas for 1980s cultural references. Mary Grace Gatmaitan walled off my writing space from invading Pokemons and princesses, as she has for the last eight years.

Finally, and above all, there is the amazing Ellen Uchimiya, whose passion infuses every page of this book, including some that she bravely insisted I rip up and rewrite. If our beautiful children, Ichiro and Allegra, inherit half of Ellen's curiosity, compassion, and blazing intellect, they'll do just fine. That they've inherited her easy laughter is enough for me.

Page numbers in *italics* refer to illustrations.

258 | Index